Communication and Concurrency

Prentice Hall International Series in Computer Science

C. A. R. Hoare, Series Editor

BACKHOUSE, R. C., *Program Construction and Verification*
BACKHOUSE, R. C., *Syntax of Programming Languages: Theory and practice*
DE BAKKER, J. W., *Mathematical Theory of Program Correctness*
BIRD, R., and WADLER, P., *Introduction to Functional Programming*
BJÖRNER, D., and JONES, C. B., *Formal Specification and Software Development*
BORNAT, R., *Programming from First Principles*
BUSTARD, D., ELDER, J., and WELSH, J., *Concurrent Program Structures*
CLARK, K. L., and McCABE, F. G., *micro-Prolog: Programming in logic*
CROOKES, D., *Introduction to Programming in Prolog*
DROMEY, R. G., *How to Solve it by Computer*
DUNCAN, F., *Microprocessor Programming and Software Development*
ELDER, J., *Construction of Data Processing Software*
ELLIOTT, R. J., and HOARE, C. A. R., *Scientific Applications of Multiprocessors*
GOLDSCHLAGER, L., and LISTER, A., *Computer Science: A modern introduction (2nd edn)*
GORDON, M. J. C., *Programming Language Theory and its Implementation*
HAYES, I. (ed.), *Specification Case Studies*
HEHNER, E. C. R., *The Logic of Programming*
HENDERSON, P., *Functional Programming: Application and implementation*
HOARE, C. A. R., *Communicating Sequential Processes*
HOARE, C. A. R., and JONES, C. B. (ed.), *Essays in Computing Science*
HOARE, C. A. R., and SHEPHERDSON, J. C. (eds.), *Mathematical Logic and Programming Languages*
HUGHES, J. G., *Database Technology: A software engineering approach*
INMOS LTD, *occam Programming Manual*
INMOS LTD, *occam 2 Reference Manual*
JACKSON, M. A., *System Development*
JOHNSTON, H., *Learning to Program*
JONES, C. B., *Software Development: A rigorous approach (OOP)*
JONES, C. B., *Systematic Software Development using VDM*
JONES, G., *Programming in occam*
JONES, G., and GOLDSMITH, M., *Programming in occam 2*
JOSEPH, M., PRASAD, V. R., and NATARAJAN, N., *A Multiprocessor Operating System*
LEW, A., *Computer Science: A mathematical introduction*
MACCALLUM, I., *Pascal for the Apple*
MACCALLUM, I., *UCSD Pascal for the IBM PC*
MARTIN, J. J., *Data Types and Data Structures*
MEYER, B., *Object-oriented Software Construction*
MILNER, R., *Communication and Concurrency*
PEYTON JONES, S. L., *The Implementation of Functional Programming Languages*
POMBERGER, G., *Software Engineering and Modula-2*
REYNOLDS, J. C., *The Craft of Programming*
RYDEHEARD, D. E., and BURSTALL, R. M., *Computational Category Theory*
SLOMAN, M., and KRAMER, J., *Distributed Systems and Computer Networks*
SPIVEY, J. M., *The Z Notation: A reference manual*
TENNENT, R. D., *Principles of Programming Languages*
WATT, D. A., WICHMANN, B. A., and FINDLAY, W., *ADA: Language and methodology*
WELSH, J., and ELDER, J., *Introduction to Modula-2*
WELSH, J., and ELDER, J., *Introduction to Pascal (3rd edn)*
WELSH, J., ELDER, J., and BUSTARD, D., *Sequential Program Structures*
WELSH, J., and HAY, A., *A Model Implementation of Standard Pascal*
WELSH, J., and McKEAG, M., *Structured System Programming*
WIKSTRÖM, Å., *Functional Programming using Standard ML*

Communication and Concurrency

ROBIN MILNER
Department of Computer Science,
University of Edinburgh

PRENTICE HALL
New York   London   Toronto   Sydney   Tokyo

First published 1989 by
Prentice Hall International (UK) Ltd
66 Wood Lane End, Hemel Hempstead
Hertfordshire, HP2 4RG
A division of
Simon & Schuster International Group

Printed and bound in Great Britain by
BPCC Wheatons Ltd, Exeter

British Library Cataloguing in Publication Data

Milner, R.
    Communication and concurrency
    1. Computer systems. Operating systems.
    Concurrent programming
    I. Title
    005.4'2

    ISBN 0-13-114984-9
    ISBN 0-13-115007-3 Pbk

2 3 4 5 93 92 91 90 89

to
Lucy

Contents

Foreword

Concurrency remains one of the major challenges facing Computer Science, both in theory and in practice. The wide variation in structure and architecture of concurrent machines is now as great as in the early days of sequential machines, implemented with valves, drums, and delay lines. Equally wide is the variation of programming methods and languages for such machines. Such variations give rise to confusion and fear of innovation.

Fortunately, progress in theoretical Computer Science brings understanding in place of confusion, and confidence in place of fear. A good theory reveals the essential unities in computing practice, and also classifies the important variations. Such a theory was propounded by Robin Milner ten years ago in his Calculus of Communicating Systems. The theory has inspired a school of researchers throughout the world, who have contributed to its refinement, development and application.

This book contains the latest thoughts of the original author of the theory. It gives guidance for practical application, as well as a basis for further theoretical advance. Its message is not confined to the study of communication and concurrency; its inspiration spreads to the general study of machines, architectures, programming methods and languages. I recommend the book as a model exposition of the fruitful interplay of theory and practice in Computer Science.

C. A. R. Hoare

Preface

This book offers a theory of communicating systems, for people who would like to understand them in terms of a few primitive ideas. It builds a general mathematical model, which is also ready to be applied; the aim is to give the reader practice in representing real systems by the *terms* or *expressions* of the model, and skill in manipulating these terms in order to analyse the behaviour of the systems.

How does such a theory become established? It is a different thing from a physical theory, at least superficially; it does not stand or fall by experiment in the conventional scientific sense. But there is a kind of experimental yardstick with which to measure it. People will use it only if it enlightens their design and analysis of systems; therefore the experiment is to determine the extent to which it is *useful*, the extent to which the design process and analytic methods are indeed improved by the theory. The experimental element is present because the degree of this usefulness is hard – I suspect impossible – to predict from the mathematical nature of the theory. Of course, there is a hard core of any theory which can only be assessed mathematically (and hence non-experimentally). This is also the case in physics; but, just as in physics the *truth* of a theory rests upon experiment, so in computer science there is something which one may call the *pertinence* of a theory which must be judged by experiment.

This book is an experiment, or more accurately it incites experiment, in the above sense of the word. If readers will apply it to their own problems in designing concurrent systems, or use it to clarify their conceptual grasp of existing systems (man-made or otherwise), then we can learn from their experience more about the pertinent concepts for concurrency and communication and how they should be managed.

The work in the book arose from an earlier experiment. In 1972, in the Artificial Intelligence Laboratory at Stanford, I tried to apply semantic ideas – known from work on sequential programming – to a concurrent programming language and I found them insufficient. One

1

of the problems was quite simple and specific, and is worth recounting. A natural way to understand a sequential program is as a mathematical function over memory states; if you know the function (corresponding to a particular program) and you know the start state, then you can deduce the finishing state. But this way of looking at the problem tacitly assumes that the program concerned has sole control of the memory; the memory is subservient to it. The story is completely different if other programs may interfere and change the values stored in memory while the program is running. It turns out then that the 'functional' theory is no longer pertinent; in fact, two programs which have the same semantic function (assuming no interference) can exhibit widely different behaviour when subjected to the same interference. It is worth giving the simplest possible example. No one would deny that the following two fragments of computer program have exactly the same effect, in the absence of interference:

$$(1)\ X:=1 \qquad\qquad (2)\ X:=0;\ \ X:=X+1$$

But suppose there is an interfering demon (another program, perhaps) which will at some unpredictable moment perform $X:=1$; then the total effect of fragment (1) plus demon is different from that of fragment (2) plus demon. In the first case the resulting value for X can only be 1; in the second case it can be either 1 or 2. In the presence of concurrency or interference the memory is no longer under the control of a single program, but instead it interacts with programs. From being a slave, the memory has become an independent agent; he who serves two masters, serves none.

This small experiment, and others, led me to look for a semantic theory in which *interaction* or *communication* is the central idea. For a number of years I worked in this direction, trying to achieve a smooth mathematical treatment. Around 1977 I learned that Tony Hoare had chosen the same primitive notion – the idea of indivisible interaction – for a strikingly different reason: from this single programming primitive one can derive many others, such as semaphores and monitors, which had previously been taken as primitive constructions themselves. This convergence from different viewpoints was cogent evidence that the notion was a pivotal one. Further evidence was provided by the quick and widespread appreciation of Hoare's *Communicating Sequential Processes*, published in the *Communications of the ACM* in 1978; it describes a programming language (CSP) beautifully designed around the primitive of indivisible interaction.

Meanwhile I found that a notion called *observation equivalence* of processes, whose behaviour is described by transition rules, has pleasant algebraic characteristics; moreover, it expresses the equivalence of processes whose *external* communications follow the same pattern but whose *internal* behaviour may differ widely. This abstraction from internal differences is essential for any tractable theory of processes. The theory of *observation equivalence* was recorded in *A Calculus of Communicating Systems*, published by Springer-Verlag in 1980. The calculus was called CCS. Since then the theory has developed in several directions, but the calculus of this book is essentially unchanged except in one vital ingredient. Shortly after the Springer-Verlag publication, David Park addressed a serious shortcoming in my formulation of observation equivalence. The equivalence needed a very slight correction, but much more significantly I had missed a notion and a proof technique which, thanks to Park's discovery, now form a cornerstone of the theory. The notion is *bisimulation*, a kind of invariant holding between a pair of dynamic systems, and the technique is to prove two systems equivalent by establishing such an invariant, much as one can prove correctness of a single sequential program by finding an invariant property.

This idea has even had repercussions on the foundations of mathematics. Peter Aczel has found a striking analogy between the notion of *non-terminating processes*, where we can take a successor of a successor of ... a process state ad infinitum, and the notion of *non-well-founded sets* where we can take a member of a member of ... a set ad infinitum. This parallel, expounded in his recent book, suggests that the theory of processes may be as fundamental as the (well-founded!) set theory which most of us were taught at school.

Special tribute should be paid to the work of Carl Petri and his followers; Petri's Net theory was the first general theory of concurrency, and dates from the early 1960s. Net theory is a generalisation of the theory of automata, to allow for the occurrence of several actions (state-transitions) independently. At the time of developing CCS I became aware of one aspect which was not treated prominently in Net theory, namely the *structural* properties of systems composed from many interacting parts; one of my main objectives was therefore to treat this structural aspect carefully. As the theory in this book has grown, many insights (particularly to do with behaviour rather than structure) have been found to be present earlier in Net theory; I hope also that new light is thrown upon them by viewing them algebraically.

One particular difference from Net theory should be mentioned. Net theorists pay particularly close attention to *causality* among actions; the present theory is by contrast observational – some would call it exten-

sional – and does not deal with causality because it is not observable, at
least in the way we conceive observation in this book. Some regret this
neglect; at the same time the extensional approach leads to a tractable
algebraic theory – which has yet to be found if causation is to be treated.
I believe that no single theory will serve all purposes.

I would prefer to call the theory of this book 'process calculus', rather
than continue to call it CCS. The latter term connotes too much a programming language, implying a formalism which cannot be extended.
For programming languages there are good reasons to resist extension,
but for theories these reasons do not apply (nor any other reasons that I
know). The Dutch researchers J.A.Bergstra and J.W.Klop use the term
'process algebra' for a closely related approach. The calculus of this
book is indeed largely algebraic, but I make no claim that everything
can be done by algebra, and so I prefer the more generous term 'calculus'
– which may include the use of logic and other mathematical disciplines.
Indeed there has recently been a strong advance in the application of
logics, mainly temporal or tense logic, to concurrent systems. It is perhaps equally true that not everything can be done by logic; thus one
of the outstanding challenges in concurrency is to find the right mar-
riage between logical and behavioural approaches. In fact it is one of
the outstanding challenges in computer science generally, because the
whole subject is concerned with the relationship between assertion and
action – or, if you like, between the specification of systems and their
performance.

Outline of the book

Chapter 1 introduces the notation of communicating systems in an informal way, by means of examples. Chapter 2 then makes this notation
precise; each syntactic construction is given an operational meaning,
and the notions of derivation and derivation tree are explained.

In Chapter 3 several equational laws are introduced, their justification being deferred to later chapters; these laws are illustrated in
proving properties of very simple systems. Chapter 4 begins the algebraic theory; the fundamental definition of *strong bisimulation* is given,
and this leads to a notion of equality over the calculus, called *strong
equivalence* or *strong bisimilarity*. Some of the laws of Chapter 3 are
then proved. In Chapter 5 bisimulation is relaxed to allow some – but
not all – of the internal behaviour of a system to be ignored; this leads
to the notion of *observation equivalence*, or *weak bisimilarity*. Some
of the properties of this notion are used (with their justification post-

poned) in proofs about non-trivial systems; the most realistic of these is a distributed scheduling system.

Chapter 6 deals with still more case-studies, distinguishing particular kinds of system such as those which change their structure with time; the main case-study is the verification of a communications protocol. In Chapter 7 the basic algebraic theory is completed; observation equivalence is slightly refined to yield the main notion of equality over the calculus, called *weak* or *observation congruence*, and all the laws and properties used in previous chapters are justified. The complete axiom systems of this chapter are not only of theoretical interest, but should also interest people who wish to build software tools to aid design and verification.

In Chapter 8 it is shown that an imperative concurrent programming language can be derived from the calculus; a detailed discussion is given of how to model variables and procedures of the language. Chapter 9 explores extensions of the process calculus, including a discussion of different means of defining new operators, and of alternative calculi – particularly a calculus for synchronous concurrency. At the end of Chapter 9 is a short treatment of two other equivalence relations, which are of practical significance.

In Chapter 10 the relationship between algebraic expression and logical specification is studied, using a logic in which the notion of bisimilarity can be characterised. It is also shown how a logic can be derived to accompany the programming language discussed in Chapter 8. In Chapter 11 the concepts of determinacy and confluence are introduced and analysed, and it is shown that a subcalculus exists in which all definable agents are confluent. Systems defined in this calculus are shown to be particularly easy to analyse.

No reference to publications is made in the main text, but Chapter 12 contains a short section for each earlier chapter, identifying relevant sources and related work.

Concurrency is a delightfully rich and varied subject; I have tried to make the best of this variety and richness by presenting examples, techniques and theories within the same whole, allowing readers to combine the practical and theoretical elements according to their particular tastes and abilities.

How to use the book

Each new element in the calculus is discussed informally, before it is given a precise definition. The mathematics used – some algebra, some logic – can be found before the final year in good computer science degree courses. The practically-inclined reader can for the most part concentrate upon modelling realistic systems and practising the analytical techniques which are developed. He can largely ignore the proofs of theorems, particularly in Chapters 4 and 7, and devote most effort to the wealth of examples in Chapters 1, 2, 3, 5, 6 and 8. The more theoretically-inclined reader can give greater emphasis to the mathematical details; it is possible to follow the basic theory in detail through Chapters 2, 3, 4, 5 and 7, ignoring all but the simple examples. Thereafter, Chapters 9, 10 and 11 may be tackled more or less independently of each other; they all contain both further theory and further examples. These three chapters should also be a source of ideas for future research.

I do not believe that it is wise to try to teach the whole book in a single course. In my experience, a fairly intense eighteen-lecture course for final year undergraduates can be built from the first (more applied) thread suggested above, covering rather more than half the book but restricting detailed proofs mainly to the specific examples. A course for graduates, who should have a greater concern for the theory, can follow the second (more theoretical) thread suggested above, and can choose parts of Chapters 9–11 as time and inclination allows.

There are over a hundred exercises distributed through the text. Sometimes they are important to fill in part of the development, while at other times they are just for practising the techniques; it should be clear from the context which purpose is served by each exercise. Solutions to the exercises will be made available.

Conventions

Definitions are numbered consecutively throughout each chapter; so are exercises; so are examples. Propositions, lemmas and corollaries are numbered in a single sequence in each chapter. Proposition 7 of Chapter 4 will be referred to, within Chapter 4, just as Proposition 7, and its third part will be referred to as Proposition 7(3); elsewhere the proposition will be called Proposition 4.7, and its third part Proposition 4.7(3).

The basic combinators of the calculus, and some which are important but not basic, are given names which start with a capital letter, for example 'Prefix', 'Summation', and 'Composition'; this is done to avoid possible confusion with the more general meanings of these terms.

The notational conventions are almost all defined when first used, and are summarised in the Glossary.

Acknowledgements

I would like to express my appreciation of the incisive understanding which Tony Hoare has brought to the concepts of communication and concurrency over the last twenty years, and my thanks to him for the stimulus and encouragement which he has given me in making my own contribution. I am especially grateful to David Park for his discovery of the right way to treat observation equivalence mathematically; it has greatly increased my incentive to write this book, since the ideas now seem to me compellingly natural. I owe much to Gordon Plotkin for his general insights into semantics and semantic method.

I am also indebted to many people with whom I have worked on this subject with great pleasure for many years: Gerardo Costa, Matthew Hennessy, Kim Larsen, George Milne, Kevin Mitchell, Rocco de Nicola, Mogens Nielsen, Joachim Parrow, K.V.S.Prasad, Michael Sanderson, Mike Shields, Bernhard Steffen, Colin Stirling, David Walker.

A draft of the book was read by Mike Gordon, Cliff Jones, Joachim Parrow, Bernhard Steffen and David Walker, and I am most grateful for the care which they devoted to it. They plunged to a level of detail quite beyond what I could reasonably expect, found many inaccuracies, and gave me many constructive ideas on presentation.

I would like to thank Caroline Guthrie for adding a human touch with her drawing of the jobshop in Chapter 1; also thanks to Dorothy McKie and Margaret Melvin for their valuable help in typing the first draft.

I dedicate the book to my wife Lucy, because without her support it would not have come about.

Glossary

Below are the notations used in this book for important entities and constructions, together with (in the right-hand column) the number of the section in which each notation is defined or first appears.

ENTITIES

Entity set	Entity name	Type of entity	
$\mathcal{A}$	$a, b, \ldots$	names	2.2
$\overline{\mathcal{A}}$	$\overline{a}, \overline{b}, \ldots$	co-names	2.2
$\mathcal{L}$	ℓ	labels	2.2
Act	$\alpha, \beta, \ldots$	actions	2.2
Act^*	$r, s, \ldots$	action sequences	2.2
	K, L	sorts	2.4
	f, g	relabelling functions	2.4
$\mathcal{X}$	$X, Y, \ldots$	agent variables	2.4
$\mathcal{K}$	$A, B, \ldots$	agent Constants	2.4
	I, J	indexing sets	2.4
$\mathcal{P}$	$P, Q, \ldots$	agents	2.4
$\mathcal{E}$	$E, F, \ldots$	agent expressions	2.4
$\mathcal{E}^+$	$E, F, \ldots$	value-passing agent expressions	2.8
V	u, v	values	2.8
	$x, y, \ldots$	value variables	2.8
	e	value expressions	2.8
	b	boolean expressions	2.8
	$\mathcal{S}$	bisimulations	4.2
$\mathcal{PL}$	F, G	formulae of process logic	10.2
$\mathcal{O}$	κ, λ	ordinal numbers	10.4

Set constructions

$\emptyset$	empty set	2.4
$\{z : \Phi\}$	set of z such that Φ	2.4
$\tilde{z}$	indexed set $\{z_i : i \in I\}$ (I understood)	2.4
$\langle v_1, \ldots, v_k \rangle$	sequence of values	1.2
ε	empty sequence; same as $\langle\rangle$	1.2
$f \restriction D$	function f restricted to domain D	3.4
$g \circ f$	function composition; $(g \circ f)(z) = g(f(z))$	3.4
f^{-1}	inverse function; $f^{-1}(L) = \{f(\ell) : \ell \in L\}$	3.4
Id_D	identity function or relation over set D	3.3
R^*	transitive reflexive closure of relation	3.2
R^{-1}	converse relation	4.2
$R_1 R_2$	composition of relations	4.2

Action constructions

τ	silent or perfect action	2.2
$\bar{\ell}$	label complement	2.2
$\hat{s}$	action sequence s with τ removed	5.1
r/s	excess of r over s	11.3
1	unit action	9.3
$\alpha \times \beta$	Product of actions	9.3

Basic agent constructions

$\alpha.E$	Prefix	1.3
$\mathbf{0}$	inactive agent	2.4
$E + F$	Summation	1.3
$\sum_{i \in I} E_i$	Summation over indexing set	2.4
$E \mid F$	Composition	1.3
$\prod_{i \in I} E_i$	Composition over indexing set	5.5
$E \backslash L$	Restriction	1.3
$E[f]$	Relabelling	1.3
$\{\tilde{E}/\tilde{X}\}$	simultaneous substitution	2.4
$\mathbf{fix}(\tilde{X} = \tilde{E})$	Recursion	2.9

Value-passing agent constructions

$a(x).E$	Prefix (input of values)	2.8
$\bar{a}(e).E$	Prefix (output of values)	2.8
if b **then** E	Conditional	2.8
$A(\tilde{x}) \overset{\text{def}}{=} E$	parametric agent definition	2.8
$\widehat{E}$	translation to basic calculus	2.8

Agent equivalence relations

$E \equiv F$	syntactic identity	2.4
$E \sim F$	strong equivalence	4.2
$E \approx F$	observation (or weak) equivalence	5.1
$E = F$	equality, or observation congruence	7.2
$E \sim_1 F$	strong trace equivalence	10.4
$E \approx_1 F$	weak trace equivalence	9.4
$E \sim_f F$	strong failures equivalence	10.4
$E \approx_f F$	failures equivalence	9.4
$E \sim_\kappa F$	approximations to $\sim$	10.4
$E \approx_\kappa F$	approximations to $\approx$	10.5

Further agent constructions

$E ^\frown F$	linking	3.3
$E \mid_L F$	Restricted Composition	11.4
E/L	Hiding	5.5
$E \;_K\|_L F$	Conjunction (of agents)	9.2
$E\,;F$	Sequential Composition	9.2

Synchronous agent constructions

$\alpha{:}E$	synchronous Prefix	9.3
$E \times F$	Product (of agents)	9.3
∂E	delay	9.3
$\mathbf{1}$	idle agent	9.3
ΔE	asynchronisation	9.3

Basic logical constructions

$\langle s \rangle F$	possibility	10.2
$\neg F$	negation	10.2
$\bigwedge_{i \in I} F_i$	conjunction	10.2
$P \models F$	satisfaction	10.2

Derived logical constructions

true	truth	10.2
false	falsity	10.2
$[s]F$	necessity	10.2
$\langle\langle s \rangle\rangle F$	weak possibility	10.2
$[\![s]\!]F$	weak necessity	10.2
$\bigvee_{i \in I} F_i$	disjunction	10.2

1

Modelling Communication

Communication and concurrency are complementary notions, both essential in understanding complex dynamic systems. On the one hand such a system has diversity, being composed of several parts each acting concurrently with, and independently of, other parts; on the other hand a complex system has unity (or else we should not call it a system), achieved through communication among its parts.

Underlying both these notions is the assumption that each of the several parts of such a system has its own identity, which persists through time; we shall call these parts *agents*. Indeed, without the assumption that the parts of a system have identity as agents we would hardly be able to discriminate among the events of the system's behaviour. For if we wish to identify a particular event we have little choice but to identify the agents which participate in it; this amounts to determining *where*, i.e. at which part or parts, the event occurs. It is hard to understand the behaviour of a computing chip without thinking of its gates and transistors, and hard to understand the behaviour of a company without thinking of its employees and managers.

The more complex an organism is, the greater is the need to think of it as a network of agents. We think of a company as a network of departments, and of a department as a network of people. But the level to which we proceed in decomposition depends upon our present interest, not upon the entities; we do not treat a person as a network of parts while we are interested in companies, though this treatment is essential for an anatomist. Therefore, in a theory which we wish to apply at different levels, we should make no distinction of kind between systems and their components, nor between systems with and systems without substructure. This leads us to use the term *agent* very broadly, to mean any system whose behaviour consists of discrete actions; an agent which for one purpose we take to be atomic may, for other purposes, be decomposed into sub-agents acting concurrently and interacting.

Indeed, when we consider the *actions* of an agent we are quickly led back to the point of our opening sentence. Each action of an agent is either an interaction with its neighbouring agents, and then it is a *communication*, or it occurs independently of them and then it may occur *concurrently* with their actions. But there is a further twist: often these independent actions of an agent are themselves nothing but communications among the components of that agent. An example of this is the state-change which occurs in a computer when its program executes the assignment of a value to a variable; this action is just an interaction (or, in other words, communication) between two of the computer's subagents, the central processor and the memory. It is even plausible to imagine that *all* independent actions are internal communications.

Whether or not we go to this extreme, it is rather natural to begin our analysis of systems by considering communication; it seems to be the more accessible of the two complementary notions. But before embarking we wish to add one further reason for emphasising communication. An essential part of a theory of complex systems is a precise and tractable notion of *behaviour*. What matters when we install a microprocessor in a system is not its physical attributes like weight, smell and colour, nor even its internal constitution, but simply the way in which it will interact with the rest of the system. So it is reasonable to define the behaviour of a system to be nothing more or less than its entire capability of communication. We can put this another way: the behaviour of a system is exactly what is observable, and to observe a system is exactly to communicate with it. This will lead to our central idea of *observation equivalence* between agents.

In this chapter we shall first examine some different media for communication; we argue that they can all be reduced to the primitive notion of *handshake communication* between agents, and that agents need not and should not be divided into two classes, the performers (active) and the media (passive). We then go on to discuss some examples of compound communicating systems. In the course of the discussion we shall introduce all five of the basic ways of constructing expressions for agents in our calculus, namely Prefix, Summation, Composition, Restriction and Relabelling. In terms of our examples we shall also indicate several equations which should hold among agent expressions. The chapter is largely informal, and the examples are designed to prepare for the more rigorous treatment which begins in Chapter 2.

1.1   Communication media

Let us try to analyse the transmission of information from one agent to another. In computing systems there are various methods of implementing transmission, and we would like to isolate what they have in common; we hope that this will help us to choose the correct basic elements in a mathematical model of communication.

We may start with the natural idea that three entities are involved in transmission; two agents, the *Sender* and *Receiver*, and an entity called the MEDIUM where items of information reside while in transit.

A second natural idea is that items are transmitted in the form of messages. Each message (containing a single item) corresponds to a single act of sending; a message is therefore sent exactly once. Also, it is usually understood that each act of receiving involves a distinct message; so each message is received at most once. Let us stay a little while with the idea of message, and crudely classify media according to the discipline under which sending and receiving occur. We shall call our first medium an ETHER:

The ETHER discipline is as follows:

- The *Sender* may always send a message.
- The *Receiver* may always receive a message, provided the medium is not empty.
- The order of receiving messages may differ from the order of sending messages.

Thus, an ether is just that which contains an unordered set of messages and enables them to move from source to destination. Of course, a perfect ether is never implemented, but it may be approximated by a BOUNDED ETHER:

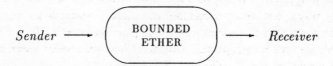

The BOUNDED ETHER discipline is:

- The *Sender* may always send a message, provided the medium is not full.
- (as for ETHER) The *Receiver* may always receive a message, provided the medium is not empty.
- (as for ETHER) The order of receiving messages may differ from the order of sending messages.

A different natural constraint is to preserve message sequence by using a BUFFER as medium:

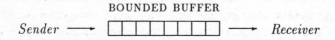

The BUFFER discipline is:

- (as for ETHER) The *Sender* may always send a message.
- (as for ETHER) The *Receiver* may always receive a message, provided the medium is not empty.
- The order of receiving messages is equal to the order of sending messages.

Finally, we may apply both the boundedness constraint and the order constraint by using a BOUNDED BUFFER:

BOUNDED BUFFER

Sender ⟶ ☐☐☐☐☐☐☐ ⟶ *Receiver*

The BOUNDED BUFFER discipline is:

- (as for BOUNDED ETHER) The *Sender* may always send a message, provided the medium is not full.
- (as for ETHER) The *Receiver* may always receive a message, provided the medium is not empty.
- (as for BUFFER) The order of receiving messages is equal to the order of sending messages.

This simple classification of message media can of course be refined in many ways, but we have fulfilled our only purpose in giving it – that is, to demonstrate the great variety of possible media. It is clear that the medium and its properties will need just as careful treatment in a general model as the *Sender* and *Receiver* agents.

Before looking at how to treat these various entities comparably, it is well to see that media are not always properly considered to contain messages. That is, our second natural idea may be natural but is not essential. For consider the case in which the medium is a SHARED MEMORY consisting of a collection of registers, to which the *Sender* may write and from which the *Receiver* may read:

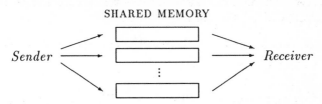

The SHARED MEMORY discipline is:

- The *Sender* may always write an item to a register.
- The *Receiver* may always read an item from a register.
- Writing and reading may occur in any order.

This discipline is hard to line up with the previous ones, because the previous disciplines were described in terms of the idea of *message*, which is inappropriate in describing the shared memory; here an item which is *sent* (written) once may be *received* (read) many times, so messages have no identity. Of course a buffer, for example, is often implemented in terms of a shared memory.

Let us now see what is basic to all these forms of transmission. One ingredient is strongly suggested by all our diagrams, which is why we have taken the trouble to draw them: each arrow in each diagram is a vehicle for a single action, indivisible in time, consisting of the passage of an item of information between two entities. Thus, having first considered two kinds of entity – agents like *Sender* and *Receiver* on the one hand, and various media on the other – we are led to treat them as similar in one most important aspect: they all participate in these single indivisible acts of communication.

There is a second reason to assimilate media to active agents. Perhaps we first considered *Sender* and *Receiver* to be active agents, or performers, while we thought of media (as the name implies) as being passive entities – mere vehicles or tools for performance. We have now admitted that, even when passive, media are performers at least in the sense that they participate in acts of communication. But we must admit more than this. When we accept that one medium may be implemented in terms of another, as we suggested above for the buffer, then we also have to admit that media may not be fully passive; for such an implementation may well involve agents which are active (e.g. in the buffer implementation they move data around or at least increment and decrement counters). By refusing to admit channels as entities distinct from agents we hope to keep the primitive notions of our theory as few as possible. More than this, we avoid early commitment to a sharp distinction between 'active' and 'passive' agents.

The upshot is that we are led to take as basic just one kind of agent, or performer, and that such agents participate in indivisible acts of communication, experienced simultaneously by both participants. These acts, which we may call *handshakes*, are what occur along the arrows of our diagrams:

$$Sender \longrightarrow Receiver$$

An arrow in these diagrams never represents a channel, in the sense that a channel has capacity; rather, it represents an adjacency or contiguity of two agents, allowing them to interact (or handshake).

In what follows, we shall develop a calculus in which arbitrary configurations of agents may be expressed. Often we shall use a diagram like the following:

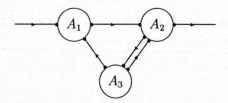

It represents a composite agent consisting of three component agents which may interact with each other, and also with the environment, by handshakes. One interpretation of the diagram could be that A_1, A_2 are 'active' agents, while A_3 is a register which may be read by A_1 or A_2, but only written to by A_2. But many other interpretations are possible, and will not necessarily distinguish 'active' from 'passive' components. It is striking that, in terms of such a diagram, the communications in which a system participates fall into three classes: those between the system and its environment, those between two components (e.g. A_1 and A_2) of the system, and those within a single component.

1.2   Simple examples

In this section we shall introduce our symbolism carefully but informally, through the medium of simple examples. The symbolism – not only its meaning – is important, because we wish to model events and communications concretely at first, as the manipulation of symbolic expressions. Later we develop a more abstract view from this concrete foundation.

Consider first an agent C, a cell which may hold a single data item:

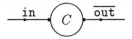

The diagram shows that the cell has two *ports* (the small blobs), but does not define the cell's behaviour. We shall suppose that, when empty, C may accept an item or value at the left-hand port, labelled in; when holding a value, it may deliver it at the right-hand port, labelled $\overline{\text{out}}$. From now on, output ports (or more accurately, their labels) will be distinguished from input ports (labels) by an overbar. We write the behaviour of C as follows:

$$C \ \stackrel{\text{def}}{=} \ \text{in}(x).C'(x)$$
$$C'(x) \ \stackrel{\text{def}}{=} \ \overline{\text{out}}(x).C$$

We shall deal with this language formally later, but a few remarks will be enough to show what is meant here:

- Agent names like C or C' can take parameters. In this case C' takes one but C takes none.
- The Prefix 'in(x).' stands for a handshake in which a value is received at port in and becomes the value of the variable x.
- in(x).$C'(x)$ is an agent expression; its behaviour is to perform the described handshake and then proceed according to the definition of C'.
- $\overline{\text{out}}(x).C$ is an agent expression; its behaviour is to output the value of x at port $\overline{\text{out}}$ and then proceed according to the definition of C.

We must distinguish two ways in which a variable is given 'scope':

(1) The first way is by its occurrence in an *input* Prefix like '$\text{in}(x)$.', and then its scope is the agent expression (determined if necessary by parentheses) which begins with the prefix. We say that, in the expression $\text{in}(x).C'(x)$, the variable x is *bound* by the prefix.

(2) The second way is by its occurrence as a formal parameter on the left-hand side of a defining equation, as in the equation $C'(x) \stackrel{\text{def}}{=} \overline{\text{out}}(x).C$, and then its scope is the whole equation. We say that, in this equation, x is *bound* by its occurrence on the left.

Note that a variable never has scope larger than a single equation; so the x's in our two defining equations are 'different' – that is, the second equation could be equivalently written as $C'(y) \stackrel{\text{def}}{=} \overline{\text{out}}(y).C$. Note also that an *output* Prefix, like '$\overline{\text{out}}(x)$.', does not define the scope of the variable x. We say that x is *free*, or *not bound*, in the expression $\overline{\text{out}}(x).C$.

The auxiliary definition of $C'(x)$ is only a convenience; the behaviour of C can equally be defined by the single equation

$$C \stackrel{\text{def}}{=} \text{in}(x).\overline{\text{out}}(x).C$$

Exercise 1 Without reading further, consider the equation

$$A \stackrel{\text{def}}{=} \text{in}(x).\text{in}(y).\overline{\text{out}}(x).\overline{\text{out}}(y).A$$

How does the behaviour of A differ from that of C? Write it instead as a pair of equations, or as four equations.   ∎

The answer to the first part is that – according to the understanding we have developed so far – A will alternately input *two* values and output *two* values, while C will alternately input and output a single value. For the second part, we may write

$$
\begin{aligned}
A &\stackrel{\text{def}}{=} \text{in}(x).A_1(x) \\
A_1(x) &\stackrel{\text{def}}{=} \text{in}(y).A_2(x,y) \\
A_2(x,y) &\stackrel{\text{def}}{=} \overline{\text{out}}(x).A_3(y) \\
A_3(y) &\stackrel{\text{def}}{=} \overline{\text{out}}(y).A
\end{aligned}
$$

(From now on we shall not give the answers to exercises.)

We may loosely think of agent expressions like C and $C'(x)$ as standing for the different possible *states* of an agent; in general there will be many states which an agent may traverse. Rather than distinguishing

between two concepts – agent and state – we find it convenient to identify them, so that both *agent* and *state* will always be understood to
mean an agent in some state.

Now C is accurately described as a bounded buffer of capacity one.
We should like to see what happens if we join two or more copies of C
together. We shall draw two copies joined together as follows:

and we shall represent the result by the agent expression $C^\frown C$. Later,
we shall see how to define the binary combinator $\frown$, so that $A_1 \frown A_2$
represents the agent formed by linking the $\overline{\text{out}}$ port of A_1 to the in
port of A_2 allowing handshakes to occur via the link. We shall use the
term *combinator* to mean an operator which builds agent expressions.
Many such combinators exist, and we shall be able to prove important
facts about them, in particular, that $\frown$ is associative. This means that
a linkage of n copies of C

can be unambiguously defined as

$$C^{(n)} \quad \overset{\text{def}}{=} \quad \overbrace{C^\frown C^\frown \ldots \frown C}^{n\ times}$$

(Do not confuse the superscribed (n) with a value parameter.) Note
that $C^{(n)}$ still only has two external ports, labelled in and $\overline{\text{out}}$; all
other ports have been internalised.

How does $C^{(n)}$ behave? It is not too difficult to see that it behaves
like a bounded buffer of capacity n, as far as can be observed at the
two external ports. But we should like to be able to state and prove
this fact mathematically, and to do so we must find an independent
way of defining the behaviour $Buff_n$ of a buffer of capacity n, without
assuming that it is built from n copies of C, or in any other particular
way. That is, we want to define $Buff_n$ as a specification, and then
prove that $Buff_n = C^{(n)}$. The equality symbol '=' here means 'same
behaviour', and we shall define it when we have studied behaviour.

Now the specification $Buff_n$ is easy to write down, using our freedom to parameterise agent names. In fact we define $Buff_n(s)$, where the parameter s may be any sequence $\langle v_1, \ldots, v_k \rangle$ of k values, $0 \leq k \leq n$, as follows:

$$Buff_n\langle\rangle \stackrel{\text{def}}{=} \text{in}(x).Buff_n\langle x \rangle$$

$$Buff_n\langle v_1, \ldots, v_n \rangle \stackrel{\text{def}}{=} \overline{\text{out}}(v_n).Buff_n\langle v_1, \ldots, v_{n-1} \rangle$$

$$Buff_n\langle v_1, \ldots, v_k \rangle \stackrel{\text{def}}{=} \text{in}(x).Buff_n\langle x, v_1, \ldots, v_k \rangle$$
$$+ \overline{\text{out}}(v_k).Buff_n\langle v_1, \ldots, v_{k-1} \rangle \qquad (0 < k < n)$$

(We have omitted parentheses around the parameters of $Buff_n$ here; we shall often omit such parentheses when no confusion arises.) Then what we expect to prove is that $Buff_n\langle\rangle = C^{(n)}$.

Note, in passing, the scopes of the variables in the third equation; the scope of each v_i is the *whole* equation, while the scope of x is just the first term on the right-hand side. The variables x and v_i both stand for the same kind of value; here we have tried to make the equations a little easier to read by using x for a variable bound by an input prefix, and v_i otherwise.

In this definition we have used a new basic combinator '+', Summation. The agent $P + Q$ behaves either like P or like Q; as soon as one performs its first action the other is discarded. Often the environment will only permit one of these alternatives; for example, at a particular moment the environment of the buffer may only offer to receive output from it, not to supply input to it. But if both alternatives are permitted, then $P + Q$ is non-deterministic; that is, it may behave like P on one occasion and like Q on another.

The binary operator + combines two agent expressions as alternatives, while '.' prefixes an action to a single agent expression. Later we shall find out how to define the sequential composition of two behaviours; in our basic calculus '.' will be the *only* method of sequencing. To avoid too many parentheses, we give '.' greater binding power than +.

We can also write the specification more succinctly as follows, if we write ε for the empty sequence, ':' for sequence concatenation and $|s|$

for the length of a sequence s:

$$Buff_n(\varepsilon) \stackrel{\text{def}}{=} in(x).Buff_n\langle x \rangle$$

$$Buff_n(s:v) \stackrel{\text{def}}{=} \overline{out}(v).Buff_n(s) \qquad (|s| = n - 1)$$

$$Buff_n(s:v) \stackrel{\text{def}}{=} in(x).Buff_n(x:s:v) + \overline{out}(v).Buff_n(s) \quad (|s| < n - 1)$$

This example has shown us that we can express an agent at different levels of abstraction – either directly (as in the case of C or $Buff_n$) in terms of its interactions with the environment, or indirectly in terms of its composition from smaller agents (as in the case of $C^{(n)}$). Of course we have to defer the details of proof until we have given formal definitions – both for our combinators and for the meaning of equality between agents.

We shall now amplify our example a little. Suppose that we wish the receipt of each value to be acknowledged to the sender, by a separate communication. Then, analogous to the one-cell buffer C, we wish to define an agent D whose interface looks as follows:

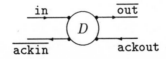

Let us first deal with the case in which D will acknowledge receipt of an input value only after it has delivered the value as output and also received acknowledgment for it. This is what we would require if the agent which supplies input values to D wishes to interpret D's acknowledgment as meaning that the value has arrived at its final destination. In this case, we define

$$D \stackrel{\text{def}}{=} in(x).\overline{out}(x).ackout.\overline{ackin}.D$$

Note that there are no value parameters in the actions $ackout$, $\overline{ackin}$; these actions represent pure synchronisation between agents.

In this case also, we can define a linking combinator $\frown$; it now links the two right-hand ports of the first agent to the two left-hand ports of the second. Thus the combination of n copies of D:

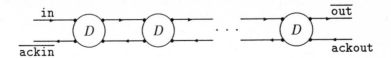

will be defined by

$$D^{(n)} \stackrel{\text{def}}{=} \overbrace{D^\frown D^\frown \ldots ^\frown D}^{n \text{ times}}$$

It only takes a little thought to see that $D^{(n)}$, far from behaving like a buffer with capacity n, actually behaves exactly like a single copy of D. The acknowledgment discipline has prevented $D^{(n)}$ from receiving a second value until the first has passed through and out. In fact, the proof that $D^{(n)} = D$ will be easy, because all that is needed is to prove $D^\frown D = D$.

The behaviour is very different if we replace D by D', which acknowledges its input as soon as it is received:

$$D' \stackrel{\text{def}}{=} \text{in}(x).\overline{\text{ackin}}.\overline{\text{out}}(x).\text{ackout}.D'$$

Intuitively, the double action $\text{in}(x).\overline{\text{ackin}}$, and likewise $\overline{\text{out}}(x).\text{ackout}$, has very similar effect to the corresponding single action in C. We therefore expect to be able to prove, just as for C, that $Buff'_n(\varepsilon) = D'^{(n)}$, where the specification $Buff'_n$ differs only slightly from $Buff_n$; it requires the addition of acknowledgment actions.

Exercise 2   Define $Buff'_n$, in the same style as $Buff_n$, but with acknowledgment actions added so that $Buff'_n(\varepsilon) = D'^{(n)}$ will hold.   ■

Exercise 3   Here is a two-way buffer:

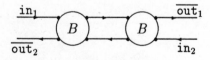

$$B \stackrel{\text{def}}{=} \text{in}_1(x).\overline{\text{out}}_1(x).B + \text{in}_2(x).\overline{\text{out}}_2(x).B$$

It can transmit any number of messages in either direction, repeatedly. Now consider two copies of B linked together:

Call this system $B^{(2)}$. Then

(1) Explain how $B^{(2)}$ can repeatedly transmit any number of messages in either direction.

(2) Explain also how $B^{(2)}$ can fail to do this; in other words, show that it is unreliable.

(3) Amend the definition of B, without adding any ports, so that $B^{(2)}$ will function reliably as a two-way buffer, always ready to transmit a message in either direction.   ∎

Now let us consider a different kind of system: a vending machine. Here (with thanks to Tony Hoare) is a picture of a machine for selling chocolates:

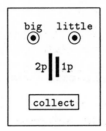

We suppose that a big chocolate costs 2p, a little one costs 1p, and only these coins can be used. One natural way to define the vending machine, V, is in terms of its interaction with the environment at its five ports (2p, 1p, big, little and collect), as follows:

$$V \overset{\text{def}}{=} \text{2p.big.collect.}V + \text{1p.little.collect.}V$$

This means, for example, that to buy a big chocolate you must put in a 2p coin, press the button marked 'big', and collect your chocolate from the tray. Note already some interesting points:

• There are no parameters involved in any of these actions.
• The machine's behaviour is quite restrictive; it will not let you pay for a big chocolate with two 1p coins, or put in more money before you've collected your purchase.

Exercise 4   Modify V so after that inserting 1p you can either buy a little chocolate or insert 1p more and buy a big one.   ∎

Exercise 5   Further modify V so that after inserting 2p you can buy either one big chocolate or two little ones.   ∎

But there is still much more freedom we can give to the machine:

Exercise 6   Design a user-friendly vending machine, called W, which can communicate at any of its five ports at any time, subject to the following constraints (assuming it never runs out of chocolates):

- *W* does not make a loss or a profit.
- *W* cannot hold a credit of more than 4p (this may stop you putting in a coin).
- *W*'s tray cannot hold more than one uncollected chocolate (this may lock the `big` and `little` buttons).

Hint: There are more than five states.   ■

Now let us return to actions which carry parameters. If an input action carries a parameter then this must be a variable, but the parameter of an output action can be any expression, using whatever functions over values we like. For example, here is an agent which acts like a buffer except that it multiplies every value by two:

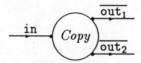

$$Twice \stackrel{\text{def}}{=} in(x).\overline{out}(2 \times x).Twice$$

Exercise 7

(1) Define an agent *Copy*:

$$\xrightarrow{\text{in}} \left(\begin{array}{c} Copy \end{array}\right) \begin{array}{c} \xrightarrow{\overline{\text{out}}_1} \\ \xrightarrow{\overline{\text{out}}_2} \end{array}$$

which inputs a value and outputs it at two ports, repeatedly.

(2) Define an agent *Sum*:

$$\begin{array}{c} \xrightarrow{\text{in}_1} \\ \xrightarrow{\text{in}_2} \end{array} \left(\begin{array}{c} Sum \end{array}\right) \xrightarrow{\overline{\text{out}}}$$

which inputs two numbers and then outputs their sum, repeatedly. Define *Diff* and *Prod* (for difference and product) similarly.

(3) Draw the diagram of a system, built from these agents, which repeatedly inputs a pair of numbers (at two different ports) and outputs the difference of their squares. Are you sure that your

system cannot deadlock – that is, are you sure that it never reaches a state in which no further action is possible?

(4) Modify your system if necessary (perhaps adding new components) so that a new pair of numbers cannot be input until the result from the previous pair has been output.   ∎

In the next section we shall see how to write down expressions which stand for compound systems, such as the one in the foregoing exercise.

1.3   A larger example: the jobshop

For a more elaborate example, we shall show how to model a simple production line. In this example we take care to introduce all the basic combinators of our calculus, rather than (as in Section 1.2) to use combinators like ⌒ which will turn out to be definable in terms of the basic ones.

We suppose that two people are sharing the use of two tools – a hammer and a mallet – to manufacture objects from simple components. Each *object* is made by driving a peg into a block. We call a pair consisting of a peg and a block a *job*; the jobs arrive sequentially on a conveyor belt, and completed objects depart on a conveyor belt.

The jobshop

The jobshop could involve any number of people, whom we shall call *jobbers*, sharing more or fewer tools. These – jobbers and tools – will be the agents of our system, and the way we model the system will not depend upon their number. In contrast, the jobs and objects are the data (values) which enter and leave the system.

The jobshop system, with two jobbers and a hammer and a mallet, may be illustrated as follows:

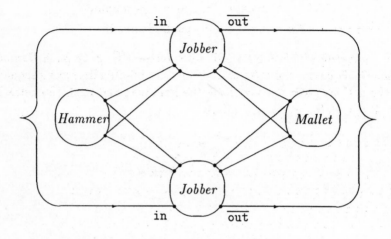

Before describing the agents, note something new about this diagram; a port is sometimes linked to more than one other port. This represents, for example, the possibility that the two jobbers may compete in their bids to use the hammer, and is a potential source of non-determinism in the system's behaviour. The jobbers may also compete to take the next job from the inward conveyor belt, whose port is not shown. In fact we are omitting the belts from our system, so the ports labelled in and $\overline{\text{out}}$ are external, while the ports by which the jobbers acquire or release the tools are internal (indicated by the absence of port labels). Diagrams like the above are, for the present, just aids to understanding; in Section 3.4 we shall see that they too are exact mathematical objects even without their interpretation in terms of behaviour. We shall call them *flow graphs*. The interpretation of a flow graph can be seen as a homomorphism from an algebra of flow graphs to an algebra of behaviours, but such mathematical devices need not yet concern us.

First, we describe the *Hammer*. We regard it as a resource which may just be acquired or released:

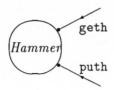

$$Hammer \stackrel{\text{def}}{=} geth.Busyhammer$$
$$Busyhammer \stackrel{\text{def}}{=} puth.Hammer$$

An equivalent definition would be $Hammer \stackrel{\text{def}}{=} geth.puth.Hammer$. Thus the behaviour of a *Hammer* is just an infinite alternating sequence of the actions geth (for acquiring the hammer) and puth (for releasing it). For a *Mallet* we have similarly

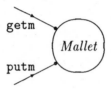

$$Mallet \stackrel{\text{def}}{=} getm.Busymallet$$
$$Busymallet \stackrel{\text{def}}{=} putm.Mallet$$

It is clear that the behaviour of a *Mallet* is exactly the same as that of a *Hammer*, if we replace geth, puth by getm, putm; we shall see later how to present them as instances of one and the same agent.

This is a good moment to introduce the notion of *sort*. A *sort* is just a set of labels. We say that an agent P *has sort* L, and write $P : L$, if all the actions which P may perform at any time in the future have labels in L (i.e. occur at ports whose labels are in L). Clearly if $P : L$ and $L \subseteq L'$ then $P : L'$. We normally determine the smallest L we can such that $P : L$, and then we expect the flow graph for P to contain as port-labels exactly the members of L. Thus we have

$$
\begin{aligned}
Hammer &: \{geth, puth\} \\
Mallet &: \{getm, putm\} \\
Jobshop &: \{in, \overline{out}\}
\end{aligned}
$$

Note particularly that the jobshop flow graph has many ports, but only four are labelled – two labelled in and two labelled $\overline{out}$.

We now turn to describing the *Jobber*. To make the example more specific, we shall assume that the nature of the job influences his or her

actions in a particular way. (Hereafter we shall refer to the *Jobber* as
'he', for brevity.) We suppose that he may use two predicates *easy* and
hard over jobs, to determine whether a job is easy or hard or neither.
He will do easy jobs with his hands, hard jobs with the *Hammer*, and
other jobs with either *Hammer* or *Mallet* (nondeterministically, if both
are free). We also use a function *done* from jobs to objects, representing
the assembly of a job into an object.

It is convenient, though not necessary, to express the *Jobber*'s behaviour in terms of several states, representing stages in his activity:

Start(*job*)	he has received the job
Usehammer(*job*)	he uses the *Hammer* for the job
Usemallet(*job*)	he uses the *Mallet* for the job
Usetool(*job*)	he uses a tool for the job
Finish(*job*)	he has completed the job

The *Jobber* has sort $\{\texttt{in}, \overline{\texttt{out}}, \overline{\texttt{geth}}, \overline{\texttt{puth}}, \overline{\texttt{getm}}, \overline{\texttt{putm}}\}$ and may be illustrated as follows:

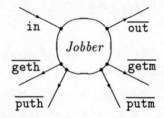

The *Jobber*'s description (or program, if you like) is as follows:

$$Jobber \stackrel{\text{def}}{=} \texttt{in}(job).Start(job)$$

$$Start(job) \stackrel{\text{def}}{=} \textbf{if } easy(job) \textbf{ then } Finish(job)$$
$$\textbf{else if } hard(job) \textbf{ then } Usehammer(job)$$
$$\textbf{else } Usetool(job)$$

$$Usetool(job) \stackrel{\text{def}}{=} Usehammer(job) + Usemallet(job)$$

$$Usehammer(job) \stackrel{\text{def}}{=} \overline{\texttt{geth}}.\overline{\texttt{puth}}.Finish(job)$$

$$Usemallet(job) \stackrel{\text{def}}{=} \overline{\texttt{getm}}.\overline{\texttt{putm}}.Finish(job)$$

$$Finish(job) \stackrel{\text{def}}{=} \overline{\texttt{out}}(done(job)).Jobber$$

Just as with our previous agent descriptions, the names for auxiliary
states may be eliminated by substituting right-hand sides for their corresponding left-hand sides; essentially we have given a recursive definition
of the agent *Jobber*. The style is reminiscent of functional programming;

in particular, the conditional expressions have their usual meaning. But there are important differences. First, the Prefixes $\overline{\text{geth}}$ etc. represent potential interaction with other agents which is absent from functional programming. Second, the Summation of agents (+) represents alternative courses of action, which may be determined by the abilities of other agents to interact; in this case, the first action of *Usetool(job)* may be determined by which of the *Hammer* and *Mallet* is free. Third, we must distinguish between *value expressions* like *easy(job)* and *done(job)*, which may occur either as condition in a conditional or as parameter to an action (e.g. $\overline{\text{out}}$) or to an agent (e.g. *Finish*), and *agent expressions* like *Finish(job)*.

In order to compose our jobshop system from its components we shall introduce three further agent combinators which, together with Prefix and Summation, make up the full complement of basic combinators in our calculus. Let us proceed in stages, first considering the subsystem consisting of a *Jobber* and a *Hammer*.

The *Jobber–Hammer* subsystem will be represented as

$$Jobber \mid Hammer$$

using the binary combinator |, called Composition. Intuitively, the agent $P \mid Q$ is a system in which P and Q may proceed independently but may also interact through complementary ports (e.g. geth, $\overline{\text{geth}}$ in our example). *Jobber | Hammer* can be illustrated as follows:

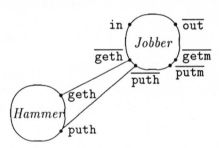

(From now on we shall omit arrows from unconnected ports, and arrow heads on arcs.) The rule in forming such flow graphs is just to join all pairs of complementary ports. The sort of *Jobber | Hammer* is the union of the sorts of *Jobber* and of *Hammer*; more generally, if $P : L$ and $Q : M$ then $P \mid Q : L \cup M$. This tells us that no ports are internalised by Composition; all ports are still open for further linkage. Thus, the subsystem consisting of two *Jobbers* sharing a *Hammer* may be written

$$(Jobber \mid Hammer) \mid Jobber$$

and its flow graph is

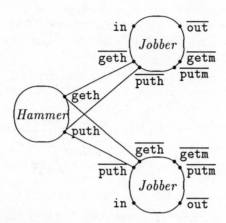

We now meet an important technical point. It is easy to see that, as far as forming flow graphs is concerned, Composition is both commutative and associative; the same flow graph also serves for *Jobber* | (*Hammer* | *Jobber*) and (*Jobber* | *Jobber*) | *Hammer*. This follows from our informal description of flow graph Composition, as the joining of pairs of complementary ports. (Note that the flow graph for *Jobber* | *Jobber* will have no linked ports, because there are no pairs of complementary ports between two *Jobber*s.) When we come to defining the behavioural meaning of Composition, we shall have to ensure that it possesses these important properties.

Clearly, further *Jobber*s could be added to this subsystem, to share the same *Hammer*; there is no limit to the number of agents to which a particular port may be connected. But we also need the ability to *internalise* a port so that no further agents may be connected to it; that is, it becomes unavailable for external communication. To internalise the ports geth and $\overline{\text{geth}}$ so that further sharing of the *Hammer* is prohibited, for example, we must apply a further combinator called Restriction. Restriction takes a parameter which is a set L of port-labels, and is a unary operator on agents which we write as $\backslash L$ in postfixed position. Thus to internalise the ports geth, puth and their complements we form the system

$$(Jobber \mid Jobber \mid Hammer) \backslash \{\text{geth}, \text{puth}\}$$

which may be illustrated as follows:

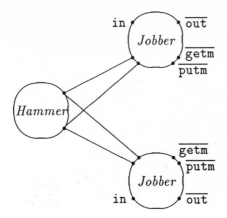

Note that the Restriction $\backslash L$ internalises both the ports L and their complements; it therefore decreases the sort of an agent by the port labels L and their complements.

It is now clear that our complete system *Jobshop*, whose flow graph appeared at the beginning of this subsection, can be defined by

$$Jobshop \overset{\text{def}}{=} (Jobber \mid Jobber \mid Hammer \mid Mallet)\backslash L$$
$$\text{where } L = \{\texttt{geth}, \texttt{puth}, \texttt{getm}, \texttt{putm}\}$$

In this definition we have omitted parentheses in the Composition of the four agents, since Composition is associative; it is also commutative, so the order of the components is also immaterial. Thus there are several ways of composing a given system from subsystems – or, in other words, several ways of decomposing a composite system into subsystems. This freedom of decomposition extends further, for (as our development has already hinted) there is no reason why all Restrictions should be applied outermost; another equivalent expression for *Jobshop* is

$$((Jobber \mid Jobber \mid Hammer)\backslash\{\texttt{geth}, \texttt{puth}\} \mid Mallet)\backslash\{\texttt{getm}, \texttt{putm}\}$$

and there are many others. It can now be seen that our combinators are developing into an algebra in which there are certain laws of equivalence; it will be an important task later to state and prove these laws when we have defined the behavioural meaning of the combinators.

Exercise 8   How many other different expressions can you find for *Jobshop*, by using Composition and Restriction in different ways? Do not count differences which only arise by using the associativity or commutativity of Composition.

Hint: There are more than five but less than ten.   ∎

Before asking questions about the behaviour of *Jobshop*, we wish to introduce our fifth and last combinator, which has not been needed hitherto but will be essential for later work. Here, it serves to allow the *Hammer* and *Mallet* to be presented as instances of one and the same agent, as we promised earlier.

If ℓ stands for an arbitrary label, then $\overline{\ell}$ stands for its complement. Thus for example $\overline{\overline{\texttt{geth}}} = \texttt{geth}$. Now we say that a function f from labels to labels is a *relabelling function* if it respects complements; that is, whenever $f(\ell) = \ell'$ then $f(\overline{\ell}) = \overline{\ell'}$. For each relabelling function f, the Relabelling combinator $[f]$, postfixed to an agent, has the effect of relabelling the ports of the agent as dictated by f. We shall often write $\ell'_1/\ell_1, \ldots, \ell'_n/\ell_n$ for the relabelling function f for which $f(\ell_i) = \ell'_i$ and $f(\overline{\ell}_i) = \overline{\ell'}_i$, for $i = 1, \ldots, n$, and otherwise $f(\ell) = \ell$.

Now let us define a simple *semaphore* as follows:

$$Sem \stackrel{\text{def}}{=} \texttt{get.put.}Sem$$

(**get** and **put** correspond to the P and V operations on a semaphore as originally used by Dijkstra). Clearly a semaphore is just a resource which may be acquired and released alternately, and we can define the *Hammer* and *Mallet* by

$$Hammer \stackrel{\text{def}}{=} Sem[\texttt{geth/get}, \texttt{puth/put}]$$
$$Mallet \stackrel{\text{def}}{=} Sem[\texttt{getm/get}, \texttt{putm/put}]$$

We have now introduced all five basic combinators of our calculus; they are as follows:

Combinator	Examples
Prefix	$\texttt{in}(x).P \quad \overline{\texttt{geth}}.Q$
Summation	$P + Q$
Composition	$P \mid Q$
Restriction	$P \backslash \{\ell_1, \ldots, \ell_n\}$
Relabelling	$P[\ell'_1/\ell_1, \ldots, \ell'_n/\ell_n]$

1.4   Equality of agents

We have already hinted that many agent expressions will be equivalent, i.e. they will denote the same behaviour, in a sense which we shall have to make precise later. For example, we gave various equivalent expressions for *Jobshop* in terms of its components, and earlier we indicated that a construction of a buffer with capacity n should be behaviourally equivalent to its specification.

As another simple example, let us define an n-ary semaphore ($n \geq$ 1), which admits any sequence of gets and puts in which the number of gets minus the number of puts lies in the range 0 to n inclusive.

$$Sem_n(0) \stackrel{\text{def}}{=} \text{get}.Sem_n(1)$$
$$Sem_n(k) \stackrel{\text{def}}{=} \text{get}.Sem_n(k+1) + \text{put}.Sem_n(k-1) \qquad (0 < k < n)$$
$$Sem_n(n) \stackrel{\text{def}}{=} \text{put}.Sem_n(n-1)$$

Compared with the definition of $Buff_n$ above, Sem_n behaves like a buffer of capacity n in which all items are identical. But since the items are all identical, their order is insignificant, and this allows us to 'realise' Sem_n as a construction in a completely different way from $Buff_n$, namely as the Composition (in parallel) of n simple semaphores:

$$Sem^{(n)} \stackrel{\text{def}}{=} \overbrace{Sem \mid Sem \mid \ldots \mid Sem}^{n \text{ times}}$$

which may be illustrated

get $\lhd Sem \rhd$ put

get $\lhd Sem \rhd$ put

$\vdots$

get $\lhd Sem \rhd$ put

Intuitively, each get on $Sem^{(n)}$ acquires any one of the component simple semaphores which is free. So we expect to be able to prove the equation

$$Sem_n(0) = Sem^{(n)}$$

and indeed the proof of this equation will be very easy.

This example prepares us for a specification of our *Jobshop* system. It is fairly easy to see that the *Jobshop* behaves nearly, but not quite, like a buffer of capacity two – with the refinement that each job turns into an object as it passes through. It is not quite like a buffer, because a job can overtake another which is already in the system.

Let us define a *Strongjobber* to be, in effect, a very strong *Jobber*; he can do every job with his hands and therefore needs no tools:

$$Strongjobber \stackrel{\text{def}}{=} in(job).\overline{out}(done(job)).Strongjobber$$

Now we claim that a *Jobshop*, i.e. two *Jobbers* working side-by-side with the help of a hammer and a mallet, is exactly equivalent to two *Strongjobbers* working side-by-side. That is, we claim that

$$Jobshop = Strongjobber \mid Strongjobber$$

Thus the simple system *Strongjobber* | *Strongjobber*, which is very easy to understand, serves as a specification which is satisfied by the *Jobshop*. The proof of this theorem is not as simple as the previous one, but can be given in two or three pages; see Section 5.6.

We have now seen two examples – a buffer and a jobshop – in which a system can be proved correct by proving an equation between a concrete system and its abstract specification. Although this approach was natural in both cases, we do not wish to imply that an equation is always the right way to express the fact that a system meets its specification. In Chapter 10 we shall develop a logic in which it is natural to express a *partial* specification: a property which should be satisfied by a system but which does not fully determine its behaviour. We shall also indicate there how our agents may be proved to satisfy such partial specifications.

Exercise 9 Adjust the *Jobber* equations so that he puts down the tool in use (if any) only *after* outputting the completed object.

Suppose now that jobs and objects can be distinguished from one another – for example by a serial number stamped on the block. Then there is a subtle distinction between the original and the adjusted systems, which can be detected without looking inside the systems, but only by examining their external behaviour. Can you find the distinction?

If there were two *Hammers* instead of a *Hammer* and a *Mallet*, would the distinction remain?   ∎

Exercise 10 Write down an expression, using Composition and other combinators, for the agent of Exercise 7(3) which repeatedly computes the difference of squares of a pair of numbers. Try to express the modified system, in part (4) of the exercise, so that it has the system of part (3) as a component. How would you describe, in general terms, the modifying role played by the other components?   ∎

2

Basic Definitions

In this chapter we shall begin by discussing the foundation of the calculus, the notion of *labelled transition*. Special care is taken in introducing the treatment of internal actions – those actions of a system which cannot be observed. This discussion leads to a formal presentation of the basic language and of its transition rules. The notion of *sort*, discussed briefly in Chapter 1, is treated in more detail. The full value-passing calculus, as used in the examples of Chapter 1, is then explained in terms of the basic calculus. Finally, Section 9 gives an alternative (more mathematical) treatment of recursion, and Section 10 defines and illustrates the proof technique of *transition induction*, which will be used sometimes in later theoretical development, but not in applications. These last two sections can safely be omitted on first reading, particularly by those who are only concerned with the applications.

2.1 Synchronisation

In Chapter 1 we introduced our calculus informally, using applications which were not too abstract and were therefore able to serve as a vehicle for introducing a new symbolism. We prepared for these examples by modelling an atomic communication as a handshake, an indivisible action in which a data value is simultaneously emitted by one party and received by the other. It may therefore appear that the notion of data value is essential to the notion of communication.

On the other hand, we saw a use more than once in these applications for a communication in which no data value was transmitted; we found it natural both for acknowledging a transmission (`ackin`, Section 1.2) and for picking up a hammer (`geth`, Section 1.3). There is no directionality in such communications, since no value passes in either direction; it is therefore appropriate to call them synchronisations.

At first sight synchronisations alone do not seem to be enough, if we wish to describe systems whose future behaviour depends upon information received. For one might argue that the proper way to express this dependence is by a conditional expression, whose condition contains variables which stand for input values; therefore such a variable must occur earlier as a parameter in an input prefix, which represents value-passing communication.

This first impression is probably justified, if we are concerned with describing systems in the most convenient way in practice. However, we shall later see that it is a false impression in a theoretical sense: it turns out in our calculus that synchronisation and Summation, working together, give the power to express the communication of values of any kind! This claim, which we shall fully justify in Section 2.8, gives us a large advantage. It means that for the purposes of precise definition and theoretical development we may restrict ourselves to a basic calculus of pure synchronisations, in which value variables and expressions are entirely absent. Once this is done, we can give a precise meaning to a larger calculus – using value variables, value expressions and conditionals – by translating it into the basic calculus.

2.2   Action and transition

We shall now examine actions more closely. We shall henceforward assume an infinite set $\mathcal{A}$ of *names*, and use $a, b, c, \ldots$ to range over $\mathcal{A}$. Examples of names are geth, ackin etc., used in the examples of Chapter 1. In further examples we shall sometimes use teletype font in this way, for certain particular names; but in many examples we shall just use the generic names $a, b, \ldots$. We denote by $\overline{\mathcal{A}}$ the set of *co-names* like $\overline{\text{geth}}$, $\overline{\text{ackin}}$; $\overline{a}, \overline{b}, \overline{c}, \ldots$ will range over $\overline{\mathcal{A}}$. Then we set $\mathcal{L} = \mathcal{A} \cup \overline{\mathcal{A}}$; $\mathcal{L}$ is the set of *labels* (which label ports) and we shall use ℓ, ℓ' to range over $\mathcal{L}$. We extend complementation to the whole of $\mathcal{L}$, so that $\overline{\overline{a}} = a$.

The set $\mathcal{L}$ comprises almost all, but not quite all, of the actions which agents can perform; we shall meet one more special action shortly. In our basic calculus, we shall not allow labels to carry value parameters; thus for example we disallow $\text{in}(job)$ and $\overline{\text{out}}(done(job))$. But we shall see how to recover these convenient forms in Section 2.8.

Since we declared that agents are to be identified with states, and since a transition from state to state is accomplished by an action, it is reasonable to write such a transition as

$$P \xrightarrow{\ell} Q$$

For example, corresponding to the definition of the *Hammer* in Section

1.3 we have the transitions

$$Hammer \xrightarrow{\text{geth}} Busyhammer$$

$$Busyhammer \xrightarrow{\text{puth}} Hammer$$

and indeed these transitions define the behaviour of a *Hammer* just as precisely as the equational definition of Section 1.3. In fact we may say that the transitions define the meaning of the Prefix combinators 'geth.' and 'puth.', and our goal in this chapter is to define the meaning of all our combinators in terms of transitions. We shall do this formally in Section 2.4; for the present we continue to discuss examples.

To define what Composition means, we shall need to determine what transitions are possible for a composite agent $P|Q$, in terms of the transitions possible for P and Q separately. Let us take an example, and suppose that A and B are given as follows, where a, b, c are distinct names:

$$A \overset{\text{def}}{=} a.A' \qquad\qquad B \overset{\text{def}}{=} c.B'$$

$$A' \overset{\text{def}}{=} \bar{c}.A \qquad\qquad B' \overset{\text{def}}{=} \bar{b}.B$$

Now consider the composite agent $A|B$:

Our first transition rule will dictate that if A can do an action alone, then it can also do the action in the context $A|B$, leaving B undisturbed (and similarly for B, leaving A undisturbed). Thus:

Since $A \xrightarrow{a} A'$,   we infer $A|B \xrightarrow{a} A'|B$

Also, even though the $\bar{c}$ port of A is linked to the c port of B, our rule dictates:

Since $A' \xrightarrow{\bar{c}} A$,   we infer $A'|B \xrightarrow{\bar{c}} A|B$

This does *not* represent a communication between A' and B; instead it represents the possibility that A' may communicate with a third agent – not yet supplied – through its $\bar{c}$ port, still leaving B undisturbed (later we shall see how Restriction on c prevents this possibility).

So how shall we represent the handshake communication which should be inferred from the actions $A' \xrightarrow{\bar{c}} A$ and $B \xrightarrow{c} B'$? Recalling that a handshake communication consists of simultaneous actions by both parties, we expect another transition rule, which in this particular case should dictate:

$$\text{Since } A' \xrightarrow{\bar{c}} A \text{ and } B \xrightarrow{c} B', \text{ we infer } A'|B \xrightarrow{?} A|B'$$

This embodies the idea that A and B change state simultaneously – the Composition being preserved – but what do we write in place of '?' ?

The answer to this question is one of the most important decisions in the design of our calculus. We take the view that '?' represents a *completed* or *perfect* action by the composite agent $A'|B$, and moreover that – since this action is internal to that composite agent – the *same* perfect action arises from *any* pair $(b, \bar{b})$ of complementary actions by the components of a composite agent. We therefore find it sufficient to introduce a single perfect action, which we shall denote by τ, to represent all such handshakes. This is why we said that $\mathcal{L}$ comprises not quite all of the actions which agents can perform; in fact τ is the only extra action we need. Henceforward we shall let $Act = \mathcal{L} \cup \{\tau\}$, the set of all possible actions, and let α, β range over Act. (The action τ has no complement.) Thus, in our example, we shall deduce from our second rule:

$$\text{Since } A' \xrightarrow{\bar{c}} A \text{ and } B \xrightarrow{c} B', \text{ we infer } A'|B \xrightarrow{\tau} A|B'$$

Let us anticipate a little, to show why τ will play such an important role in the calculus. Our aim in analysing the behaviour of composite systems is to ignore, as far as possible, their internal (perfect) actions; for τ (having no complement) does not represent a potential communication, and is therefore not directly observable. We wish to regard two systems as equivalent if they exhibit the same (in some sense) pattern of *external* actions. This amounts to abstracting from such a system just that external aspect of its behaviour which is relevant when it occurs as a component of a still larger system. It will often turn out, for example, that a sequence

$$P \xrightarrow{\tau} P_1 \xrightarrow{\tau} \cdots \xrightarrow{\tau} P_n$$

of internal actions is equivalent to a single internal action

$$P \xrightarrow{\tau} P_n$$

and this may allow considerable simplification, via appropriate algebraic equations, of the expression for the agent P.

Returning to our example, let us discuss the effect of imposing the

Restriction $\backslash c$ upon $A|B$. (We abbreviate the singleton Restriction $\backslash\{c\}$ to $\backslash c$.) The flow graph for $(A|B)\backslash c$ is

where the port-labels c and $\bar{c}$ have been dropped, to signify that the restricted composite agent $(A|B)\backslash c$ may not perform c or $\bar{c}$ actions, though – crucially – it *may* perform a τ action which results from $(c,\bar{c})$ communication between its components. In fact the general rule for Restriction will be stated as follows:

If $P \xrightarrow{\alpha} P'$, then infer $P\backslash L \xrightarrow{\alpha} P'\backslash L$ provided that $\alpha, \bar{\alpha} \notin L$

We are now in a position to state all the transitions which may occur in the system $(A|B)\backslash c$, and it is convenient to arrange them in a tree – an infinite tree in this case – which we shall call a *transition tree* or *derivation tree*:

$$
\begin{array}{c}
(A|B)\backslash c \\
\downarrow a \\
(A'|B)\backslash c \\
\downarrow \tau \\
(A|B')\backslash c \\
\end{array}
$$

$$
\begin{array}{cc}
\bar{b} \swarrow & \searrow a \\
(A|B)\backslash c & (A'|B')\backslash c \\
a \downarrow & \downarrow \bar{b} \\
(A'|B)\backslash c & (A'|B)\backslash c \\
\vdots & \vdots \\
\end{array}
$$

We can see that the tree repeats itself. In fact we can summarise the action-behaviour of the system by folding it up into a *transition graph*:

From this we can see that $(A|B)\backslash c$ is behaviourally equal to C_1, where we define the agents $C_0, \ldots, C_3$ by

$$C_0 \overset{\text{def}}{=} \overline{b}.C_1 + a.C_2$$
$$C_1 \overset{\text{def}}{=} a.C_3$$
$$C_2 \overset{\text{def}}{=} \overline{b}.C_3$$
$$C_3 \overset{\text{def}}{=} \tau.C_0$$

Alternatively, we may say that

$$(A|B)\backslash c = a.\tau.C, \text{ where } C \overset{\text{def}}{=} a.\overline{b}.\tau.C + \overline{b}.a.\tau.C$$

This argumentation is not yet properly supported by precise definitions; we have only described the meaning of the combinators informally, and have not said what we mean by behavioural equality. For one thing, our claim that $(A|B)\backslash c = C_1$ will only be justified if the behavioural meaning of an agent is determined by its derivation tree, ignoring the syntactic nature of the expressions at the nodes of the tree. But our example illustrates something which is often useful – namely, to equate the behaviour of some composite system to a behaviour defined without use of the Composition combinator '|' or the Restriction combinator which often accompanies it.

One further remark is in order before we leave this example. When we have defined behavioural equality we shall be able to prove an important equational law, $\alpha.\tau.P = \alpha.P$, which allows many occurrences of τ to be eliminated. We hinted earlier that we wished to abstract away from details of internal communication, and this law is one means by which we shall perform this abstraction. With its help, we can now finally deduce that

$$(A|B)\backslash c = a.D, \text{ where } D \overset{\text{def}}{=} a.\overline{b}.D + \overline{b}.a.D$$

2.3 The pre-emptive power of internal action

Let us now turn to other properties of the τ action, which will show us that – contrary to what the reader may now suppose – it cannot always be 'dropped'. Consider a simple recursively defined agent

$$A \overset{\text{def}}{=} a.A + \tau.b.A$$

whose transition graph looks as follows:

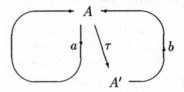

If we were allowed to 'drop' τ – that is, if the equation $\tau.P = P$ were always valid – we would have to admit that $A = B$, where $B \overset{\text{def}}{=} a.B + b.B$:

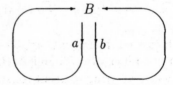

However, assuming that $a \neq b$, we have strong intuitive grounds for *not* admitting $A = B$! For B is an agent which may perform either of the actions a and b, whatever state it reaches (in fact it can only ever reach the single state B). A, on the other hand, may reach (via τ) a state A' in which the action b is possible, while a is impossible. Since τ is an internal action of A – the result of communication between two of its components if we were to analyse its composition – its occurrence is autonomous in the sense that it needs no external participation; thus A is uncontrollable, or nondeterministic, while B is perfectly controllable and deterministic.

   If we believe that this intuition captures a property which is (perhaps undesirably) present in real communicating systems, then we must admit that the equation $\tau.P = P$ is invalid in general. We also have to admit that we cannot conclude that two agents are behaviourally equal merely from the fact that they can perform the same sequences of external actions (as A and B can in the example). Thus we are forced to abandon – or at least to refine – much of classical automata theory, since in that theory two machines are normally taken to be equivalent if and only if they can perform the same action sequences.

In the discussion so far we have informally prepared the way for a precise definition of our calculus, in terms of state transitions. In the course of it, we have seen how important it will be to get a good treatment of the internal nature of communication between the components of a system.

2.4   The basic language

In this section we describe the syntax of our basic calculus, with examples. In Section 2.2 we introduced the *names* $\mathcal{A}$, the *co-names* $\overline{\mathcal{A}}$, and the *labels* $\mathcal{L} = \mathcal{A} \cup \overline{\mathcal{A}}$. Recall that $a, b, c, \ldots$ range over $\mathcal{A}$ and $\overline{a}, \overline{b}, \overline{c}, \ldots$ over $\overline{\mathcal{A}}$; also that ℓ, ℓ' range over $\mathcal{L}$. We also introduced the *silent* or *perfect* action τ, and defined $Act = \mathcal{L} \cup \{\tau\}$ to be the set of *actions*; α, β range over Act.

We shall use K, L to stand for subsets of $\mathcal{L}$, and we shall use $\overline{L}$ for the set of complements of labels in L. A *relabelling function* f is a function from $\mathcal{L}$ to $\mathcal{L}$ such that $f(\overline{\ell}) = \overline{f(\ell)}$; we also extend f to Act by decreeing that $f(\tau) = \tau$.

Further, we introduce a set $\mathcal{X}$ of *agent variables*, and a set $\mathcal{K}$ of *agent constants*; we let $X, Y, \ldots$ range over $\mathcal{X}$, and $A, B, \ldots$ over $\mathcal{K}$. We shall capitalise 'Constant' when referring to agent constants, as we do for our combinators, since it is convenient to think of each agent constant as a nullary combinator.

We shall sometimes use I or J to stand for an indexing set; then we write $\{E_i \ : \ i \in I\}$ for a family of expressions indexed by I.

We shall now define $\mathcal{E}$, the set of *agent expressions*, and let $E, F, \ldots$ range over $\mathcal{E}$. $\mathcal{E}$ is the smallest set which includes $\mathcal{X}$ and $\mathcal{K}$ and contains the following expressions, where E, E_i are already in $\mathcal{E}$:

(1) $\alpha.E$, a *Prefix* ($\alpha \in Act$)
(2) $\sum_{i \in I} E_i$, a *Summation* (I an indexing set)
(3) $E_1 | E_2$, a *Composition*
(4) $E \backslash L$, a *Restriction* ($L \subseteq \mathcal{L}$)
(5) $E[f]$, a *Relabelling* (f a relabelling function)

Of these expressions, we only need to explain (2) more fully. It is the sum of all expressions E_i as i ranges over I, and can also be written $\sum\{E_i \ : \ i \in I\}$, or abbreviated to $\sum_i E_i$ when I is understood. In place of (2) we might have expected just a binary Summation $E_1 + E_2$; indeed, this is how we shall write a Summation when $I = \{1, 2\}$. We shall most often use binary Summations, but for theoretical reasons we shall sometimes need to use an infinite sum – i.e. the case in which I is infinite. (In particular, we shall need infinite Summation in Section 8 when we treat the full value-passing calculus.) Another special case is when $I = \emptyset$, the empty set; this gives us (as we shall see) the inactive agent, capable of no action whatever. This is so important that we give it the special name $\mathbf{0}$; that is, we define $\mathbf{0} \stackrel{\text{def}}{=} \sum_{i \in \emptyset} E_i$.

To avoid too many parentheses we adopt the convention that the combinators have decreasing binding power, in the following order: Restriction and Relabelling (tightest binding), Prefix, Composition, Summation. Thus for example,

$$R + a.P \mid b.Q\backslash L \qquad \text{means} \qquad R + ((a.P) \mid (b.(Q\backslash L)))$$

We shall often abbreviate the singleton Restriction $E\backslash\{\ell\}$ to $E\backslash\ell$.

We write $Vars(E)$ for the set of variables occurring free in E. We say that an agent expression E is an *agent* if it contains no free variables. (At present this means that it contains no variables at all, but later we shall deal with an alternative form of expressions in which bound variables may occur.) We denote the set of agents by $\mathcal{P}$, and we shall let $P, Q, \ldots$ range over agents.

A Constant is an agent whose meaning is given by a defining equation, as for $A, B, C_0, C_1, \ldots$ in Section 2.2. In fact we assume that for *every* Constant A there is a defining equation of the form

$$A \stackrel{\text{def}}{=} P$$

Consider for example the two defining equations $A \stackrel{\text{def}}{=} a.A'$ and $A' \stackrel{\text{def}}{=} \overline{c}.A$ from Section 2.2; they illustrate that Constants can be defined in terms of each other – in other words, by mutual recursion. This definitional mechanism is the only way that agents with infinite behaviour can be defined, in the calculus as we have presented it.

There is an alternative treatment of recursion which allows us to do without Constants altogether. We present it in Section 2.9; it is more convenient for certain theoretical developments, but less easy to apply than our treatment using Constants.

We sometimes find it convenient to abbreviate the indexed family $\{E_i : i \in I\}$ of expressions by $\tilde{E}$, when I is understood. For example, a Summation $\sum\{E_i : i \in I\}$ can be written $\sum \tilde{E}$.

We shall often need to substitute expressions for variables. Let $\{X_i : i \in I\}$ or $\tilde{X}$ be an indexed family of variables, all distinct; then we write $\{E_i/X_i : i \in I\}$ or $\{\tilde{E}/\tilde{X}\}$ for the operation which simultaneously replaces all free occurrences of X_i by E_i for all $i \in I$. We shall postfix this operation to the expression in which the substitution is to be made.

We shall always use $E_1 \equiv E_2$ to mean that the expressions E_1 and E_2 are *syntactically identical*. A large part of our work in later chapters will concern *equivalence relations* over $\mathcal{E}$; in particular, we shall define *equality*, $E_1 = E_2$, which holds between widely differing expressions.

There is a glossary provided at the beginning of this book, where the user will find a useful summary of the notations and conventions introduced in this section and elsewhere.

2.5   Transitional semantics

In giving meaning to our basic language, we shall use the general notion of a *labelled transition system*

$$(S, T, \{\xrightarrow{t} \; : \; t \in T\})$$

which consists of a set S of *states*, a set T of *transition labels*, and a *transition relation* $\xrightarrow{t} \; \subseteq \; S \times S$ for each $t \in T$.

In our transition system we shall take S to be $\mathcal{E}$, the agent expressions, and T to be *Act*, the actions; our semantics for $\mathcal{E}$ consists in the definition of each transition relation $\xrightarrow{\alpha}$ over $\mathcal{E}$. This definition will follow the structure of expressions; as we hinted in Section 2.2, we wish to define the transitions of each composite agent in terms of the transitions of its component agent or agents. For example, in Section 2.2 we indicated that from $A \xrightarrow{\alpha} A'$ we wish to infer $A|B \xrightarrow{\alpha} A'|B$; the general rule which permits this inference will be

From $E \xrightarrow{\alpha} E'$ infer $E|F \xrightarrow{\alpha} E'|F$

and we shall write it in the form

$$\frac{E \xrightarrow{\alpha} E'}{E|F \xrightarrow{\alpha} E'|F}$$

There will be one or more transition rules associated with each combinator, and one associated with Constants. Each rule will have a *conclusion* and zero or more *hypotheses*. In a rule associated with a combinator, the conclusion will be a transition of an agent expression consisting of the combinator applied to one or more components, and the hypotheses will be transitions of some of the components. The set of rules associated with each combinator can be understood as giving the meaning of that combinator; the rule for Constants asserts that each Constant has the same transitions as its defining expression.

We now give the complete set of transition rules; the names **Act,**

Sum, Com, Res, Rel and **Con** indicate that the rules are associated respectively with Prefix, Summation, Composition, Restriction, Relabelling and with Constants.

$$\text{Act} \quad \frac{}{\alpha.E \xrightarrow{\alpha} E} \qquad\qquad\qquad \text{Sum}_j \quad \frac{E_j \xrightarrow{\alpha} E_j'}{\sum_{i \in I} E_i \xrightarrow{\alpha} E_j'} \; (j \in I)$$

$$\text{Com}_1 \quad \frac{E \xrightarrow{\alpha} E'}{E|F \xrightarrow{\alpha} E'|F} \qquad\qquad \text{Com}_2 \quad \frac{F \xrightarrow{\alpha} F'}{E|F \xrightarrow{\alpha} E|F'}$$

$$\text{Com}_3 \quad \frac{E \xrightarrow{\ell} E' \quad F \xrightarrow{\bar{\ell}} F'}{E|F \xrightarrow{\tau} E'|F'}$$

$$\text{Res} \quad \frac{E \xrightarrow{\alpha} E'}{E \backslash L \xrightarrow{\alpha} E' \backslash L} \; (\alpha, \bar{\alpha} \notin L) \qquad \text{Rel} \quad \frac{E \xrightarrow{\alpha} E'}{E[f] \xrightarrow{f(\alpha)} E'[f]}$$

$$\text{Con} \quad \frac{P \xrightarrow{\alpha} P'}{A \xrightarrow{\alpha} P'} \; (A \overset{\text{def}}{=} P)$$

The rule for Summation can be read as follows: if any one summand E_j of the sum $\sum_{i \in I}$ has an action, then the whole sum also has that action. *Finite* Summation, which is enough for many practical purposes, can be presented in a more convenient form. If $I = \{1,2\}$ then we obtain two rules for $E_1 + E_2$, by setting $j = 1, 2$:

$$\frac{E_1 \xrightarrow{\alpha} E_1'}{E_1 + E_2 \xrightarrow{\alpha} E_1'} \qquad \frac{E_2 \xrightarrow{\alpha} E_2'}{E_1 + E_2 \xrightarrow{\alpha} E_2'}$$

Also, recall that $\mathbf{0} \overset{\text{def}}{=} \sum_{i \in \emptyset} E_i$; since $I = \emptyset$ in this case, there are *no* rules for $\mathbf{0}$, and this reflects the fact that $\mathbf{0}$ has no transitions.

We said that our set of rules is complete; by this we mean that there are no transitions except those which can be inferred by the rules. We can now set out the justification for a transition of any agent expression in the form of an inference diagram, in which we annotate each inference with the name of the rule which justifies it. For example, the justification of the transition

$$((a.E + b.0) \mid \bar{a}.F) \backslash a \xrightarrow{\tau} (E|F) \backslash a$$

is given as follows:

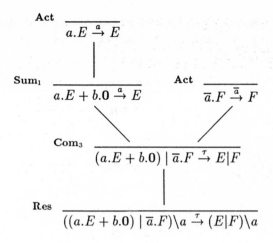

Act $\dfrac{}{a.E \xrightarrow{a} E}$

Sum$_1$ $\dfrac{}{a.E + b.0 \xrightarrow{a} E}$ **Act** $\dfrac{}{\overline{a}.F \xrightarrow{\overline{a}} F}$

Com$_3$ $\dfrac{}{(a.E + b.0) \mid \overline{a}.F \xrightarrow{\tau} E\mid F}$

Res $\dfrac{}{((a.E + b.0) \mid \overline{a}.F)\backslash a \xrightarrow{\tau} (E\mid F)\backslash a}$

Exercise 1   Assuming that $a \neq b$, draw the inference diagrams for each of the transitions

$$(a.E + b.0) \mid \overline{a}.F \xrightarrow{a} E \mid \overline{a}.F$$

$$(a.E + b.0) \mid \overline{a}.F \xrightarrow{\overline{a}} (a.E + b.0) \mid F$$

$$(a.E + b.0) \mid \overline{a}.F \xrightarrow{b} 0 \mid \overline{a}.F$$

$$((a.E + b.0) \mid \overline{a}.F)\backslash a \xrightarrow{b} (0 \mid \overline{a}.F)\backslash a$$

(They are all simpler than the one we have given.)   ∎

In fact, we have now given the only two transitions which are possible for $((a.E+b.0) \mid \overline{a}.F)\backslash a$; you can check this by trying to find all possible inference diagrams (including the one given above) of the form

$$\vdots$$
$$\dfrac{}{((a.E + b.0) \mid \overline{a}.F)\backslash a \xrightarrow{?} ?}$$

The last step can only be by **Res**, and we therefore proceed to

$$\vdots$$
$$\dfrac{}{(a.E + b.0) \mid \overline{a}.F \xrightarrow{\alpha} G}$$

Res $\dfrac{}{((a.E + b.0) \mid \overline{a}.F)\backslash a \xrightarrow{\alpha} G\backslash a}$

where α and G are still unknown, but α cannot be a or $\overline{a}$ because of the side-condition on **Res**. Thus the first two transitions of Exercise 1 cannot be used, but the third can be used – and so can the transition

$$(a.E + b.0) \mid \overline{a}.F \xrightarrow{\tau} E \mid F$$

which led to our first inference diagram. By this example we have shown how Composition and Restriction work together to represent internal communication via the labels $(a, \overline{a})$.

As another example, consider how to infer the action

$$(A \mid B) \backslash c \xrightarrow{a} (A' \mid B) \backslash c$$

with the definitions of A and B given in Section 2.2. The inference is

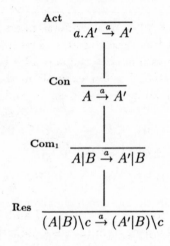

Exercise 2 Using the same definitions, give the inference diagram for

$$(A' \mid B) \backslash c \xrightarrow{\tau} (A \mid B') \backslash c \qquad\qquad \blacksquare$$

We hasten to assure the reader that this lengthy generation of inference diagrams is never needed in practice! But the inference of transitions is fundamental to our calculus, so we have dwelt upon it at some length.

2.6 Derivatives and derivation trees

Whenever $E \xrightarrow{\alpha} E'$, we call the pair (α, E') an *immediate* derivative of E, we call α an *action* of E, and we call E' an α-*derivative* of E.

Analogously, whenever $E \xrightarrow{\alpha_1} \cdots \xrightarrow{\alpha_n} E'$, we call $(\alpha_1 \cdots \alpha_n, E')$ a *derivative* of E, we call $\alpha_1 \cdots \alpha_n$ an *action-sequence* of E, and we call E' an $\alpha_1 \cdots \alpha_n$-*derivative* (or sometimes just a *derivative*) of E. In the case

$n = 0$, we have that ε is an action-sequence of E, and E is a derivative of itself.

It is convenient to collect the derivatives of an expression E into the *derivation tree* of E; this has the general form

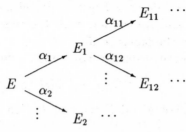

where for each expression at a non-terminal node all its immediate derivatives are represented by outgoing arcs. The tree may be infinite; we call it *total* if the expressions at terminal nodes have no immediate derivatives, otherwise *partial*. For our example in the previous section we have the following partial derivation tree:

$$((a.E + b.0) \mid \overline{a}.F)\backslash a \quad \overset{\tau}{\nearrow} \quad (E|F)\backslash a$$
$$\underset{b}{\searrow} \quad (0 \mid \overline{a}.F)\backslash a$$

It is partial because we need to know what E and F are in order to complete it. But you should be able to check that the lower terminal node $(0 \mid \overline{a}.F)\backslash a$ has *no* derivatives, whatever F is; try to complete the inference diagram

$$\frac{\vdots}{(0 \mid \overline{a}.F)\backslash a \overset{?}{\rightarrow}?}$$

and you will fail, because of the Restriction $\backslash a$.

We gave an example of a derivation tree in Section 2.2, and there we indicated that the meaning of an agent should be a property of its derivation tree disregarding the expressions which lie at the nodes. Thus our transitional semantics is only a prelude to the important topic of behavioural equivalence of agents, which we shall pursue in the next chapter.

We are considering the derivations of arbitrary agent expressions, which may contain agent variables $X, Y, \ldots$. For such an expression, $a.X + b.Y$ say, its derivation tree

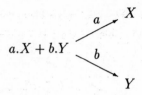

is total but indeterminate, since the variables are uninstantiated. Any instantiation of these variables will allow us to develop the tree further.

On the other hand, an *agent* – that is, an agent expression without variables – has the important property that all its immediate derivatives are also agents. We shall omit the proof of this, although it is not too hard. What it means is that the derivation tree of an agent can always be completed – it never generates a node which is indeterminate because of a variable. And in view of our earlier remark that the meaning of an agent should be a property of its derivation tree (disregarding the agents at the nodes), this tree tells us all we need to know about an agent.

With this in mind, let us prepare for the next chapter by giving a foretaste of behavioural equivalence, which we shall study there. Consider the partial derivation tree of an agent P consisting just of its immediate derivatives:

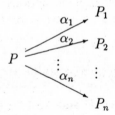

Now consider the agent $P' \overset{\text{def}}{=} \sum\{\alpha_i.P_i \ : \ 1 \leq i \leq n\}$. The rules for Prefix and Summation show that P' has essentially the same partial derivation tree as P:

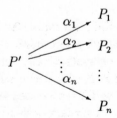

In fact, P' clearly has essentially the same *total* derivation tree as P. From what we have said earlier, we wish to conclude from this that P and P' are equivalent; this is in spite of the fact that P and P' may be

very different expressions. But our equivalence must be more generous
than this; for example, if P' has instead the partial derivation tree

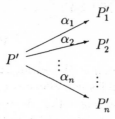

and each P'_i is *equivalent*, but not *identical*, to P_i, then we shall still
want P and P' to be equivalent – because again they will have essentially
the same total derivation trees.

These remarks indicate that the notion of equivalence will need careful definition. The reward will be a very powerful algebra of agents.

2.7   Sorts

We can now make precise the notion of sort, which was illustrated in
Chapter 1.

Definition 1   For any $L \subseteq \mathcal{L}$, if the actions of P and all its derivatives
lie in $L \cup \{\tau\}$ then we say P *has sort* L, or L *is a sort of* P, and write
$P : L$.   ∎

Now the following useful property can be very simply proved:

Proposition 1   For every E and L, L is a sort of E if and only if,
whenever $E \xrightarrow{\alpha} E'$, then

(1) $\alpha \in L \cup \{\tau\}$
(2) L is a sort of E' ∎

Clearly every agent has a minimum sort – the intersection of all its sorts
– but this is not always easy to determine. (The reason is that, even
though a label ℓ may occur syntactically in P, the analysis required
to determine whether or not P ever performs the action ℓ can be very
complex; in fact, theorists will be interested to learn that this question
is not decidable.) However, there is a perfectly natural way to assign a
sort $\mathcal{L}(E)$ to each agent expression E (even containing variables) on the
basis of its syntax. First, we assume that to each variable X is assigned
a sort $\mathcal{L}(X)$, and to each Constant A is assigned a sort $\mathcal{L}(A)$.

Definition 2 Given the sorts $\mathcal{L}(A)$ and $\mathcal{L}(X)$ of Constants and variables, the *syntactic sort* (which we sometimes just call *the sort*) $\mathcal{L}(E)$ of each agent expression E is defined as follows:

$$
\begin{aligned}
\mathcal{L}(\ell.E) &= \{\ell\} \cup \mathcal{L}(E) \\
\mathcal{L}(\tau.E) &= \mathcal{L}(E) \\
\mathcal{L}(\textstyle\sum_i E_i) &= \bigcup_i \mathcal{L}(E_i) \\
\mathcal{L}(E|F) &= \mathcal{L}(E) \cup \mathcal{L}(F) \\
\mathcal{L}(E\backslash L) &= \mathcal{L}(E) - (L \cup \overline{L}) \\
\mathcal{L}(E[f]) &= \{f(\ell) : \ell \in \mathcal{L}(E)\}
\end{aligned}
$$

Further, for any defining equation $A \stackrel{\text{def}}{=} P$ the inclusion

$$\mathcal{L}(P) \subseteq \mathcal{L}(A)$$

must hold. ∎

The final condition means that we must assign a sufficiently generous sort to every Constant; for example, if we wish to define

$$A \stackrel{\text{def}}{=} a.b.A$$

then it is forbidden to assign the sort $\{a\}$ to A, since then the right-hand side will be assigned the larger sort $\{a, b\}$ by our rules. But it is allowed to assign the sort $\{a, b, c\}$ to A, since then our rules will give the right-hand side the same sort.

Of course we have to show that $\mathcal{L}(E)$, as defined, is indeed a sort of E, i.e. that $E : \mathcal{L}(E)$. First we need a proposition whose proof we defer to Section 10.

Proposition 2 Let $E \stackrel{\alpha}{\to} E'$. Then

(1) $\alpha \in \mathcal{L}(E) \cup \{\tau\}$
(2) $\mathcal{L}(E') \subseteq \mathcal{L}(E)$ ∎

From this we immediately get what we want:

Corollary 3 $E : \mathcal{L}(E)$

Proof Let α be an action of some derivative F of E. By iterating Proposition 2(2) we immediately have $\mathcal{L}(F) \subseteq \mathcal{L}(E)$. But from Proposition 2(1) we also have $\alpha \in \mathcal{L}(F) \cup \{\tau\}$, and hence $\alpha \in \mathcal{L}(E) \cup \{\tau\}$ as required.   ■

Very often, calculating $\mathcal{L}(E)$ involves little more than collecting up the labels which occur 'free' in E – i.e. not 'bound' by a Restriction $\backslash L$. Thus, if

$$P \equiv ((a.0 + b.0) \mid (\overline{b}.0 + c.0))\backslash b$$

then we easily and intuitively compute

$$\mathcal{L}(P) = \{a, c\}$$

But in cases where Constants (with their defining equations), Restriction and Relabelling are interwoven the calculation can be delicate, and it is important to be able to resort to the explicit rules of Definition 1.

Besides the above properties – in particular the use of syntactic sorts – there is another reason for the importance of sorts. We shall discover that certain equational laws depend upon the sorts of the expressions concerned. An example is

$$(E\mid F)\backslash b \;\; = \;\; (E\backslash b) \mid F$$
$$\text{provided that } b, \overline{b} \notin \mathcal{L}(F)$$

Intuitively, this says that if the Restriction $\backslash b$ is irrelevant for F, then we can move it inside the Composition $E\mid F$ without change of behaviour.

2.8   The value-passing calculus

At the beginning of this chapter we promised to show how the full calculus with value-passing, which we illustrated in Chapter 1, can be reduced to the basic calculus which we have described formally in the present chapter.

Many of our examples in this book will be done in the full calculus – they would be tedious otherwise – so it is important to define this calculus precisely. We shall also define precisely here its translation into the basic calculus, and this will enable us, in later chapters, to derive laws for the full calculus which we shall need in proving properties of our examples.

For simplicity, we shall assume that all values belong to some fixed value set V, though of course in applications we shall use values of different types – e.g. integers, jobs (see Chapter 1), sequences of values etc. We shall begin by showing how some of the examples in Chapter 1 can be reduced to the basic calculus; thereafter the general translation will be easier to grasp. Take our very first example, the buffer cell:

$$C \stackrel{\text{def}}{=} \text{in}(x).C'(x)$$
$$C'(x) \stackrel{\text{def}}{=} \overline{\text{out}}(x).C$$

Consider first the parameterised Constant C'. It will become a *family* of Constants C'_v, one for each value $v \in V$. Similarly the parameterised negative Prefix '$\overline{\text{out}}(x)$.' becomes a family of Prefixes '$\overline{\text{out}_v}$.', one for each value v. Thus the single defining equation for C' becomes a family of defining equations

$$C'_v \stackrel{\text{def}}{=} \overline{\text{out}_v}.C \qquad (v \in V)$$

Now consider the Prefix '$\text{in}(x)$.'. To reflect the fact that it can accept *any* input value, because it binds the variable x, we translate it to '$\sum_{v \in V} \text{in}_v$.'; in this way the use of a bound variable x is replaced by Summation. Thus the defining equation for C becomes

$$C \stackrel{\text{def}}{=} \sum_{v \in V} \text{in}_v.C'_v$$

Next, let us take the first two equations in Section 1.3 defining the *Jobber*:

$$Jobber \stackrel{\text{def}}{=} \text{in}(job).Start(job)$$
$$Start(job) \stackrel{\text{def}}{=} \text{if } easy(job) \text{ then } Finish(job)$$
$$\text{else if } hard(job) \text{ then } Usehammer(job)$$
$$\text{else } Usetool(job)$$

Since *Start* takes a parameter, like C', we expect the second equation to be reduced to a family of equations, one for each $job \in V$. But in this case the form of the right-hand side of each equation depends upon the nature of the job, as determined by the predicates *easy* and *hard*. The translation is as follows:

$$Jobber \stackrel{\text{def}}{=} \sum_{job \in V} \text{in}_{job}.Start_{job}$$

$$Start_{job} \stackrel{\text{def}}{=} \begin{cases} Finish_{job} & (\text{ if } easy(job) \text{)} \\ Usehammer_{job} & (\text{ if } \neg easy(job) \wedge hard(job) \text{)} \\ Usetool_{job} & (\text{ if } \neg easy(job) \wedge \neg hard(job) \text{)} \end{cases}$$

Thus the boolean expressions *internal* to an agent expression have become *external* conditions describing the members of an indexed family, in this case a family of defining equations.

Proceeding to the general translation, let us first give the set $\mathcal{E}^+$ of agent expressions of the full calculus. We assume that to each agent Constant $A \in \mathcal{K}$ is assigned an *arity*, a non-negative integer representing the number of parameters which it takes. Also we assume value expressions e and boolean expressions b, built from value variables $x, y, \ldots$ together with value constants v and any operator symbols we wish. Then $\mathcal{E}^+$ is the smallest set containing every agent variable $X \in \mathcal{X}$, every parameterised Constant $A(e_1, \ldots, e_n)$ (for $A \in \mathcal{K}$ with arity n), and also the following expressions, where E, E_i are already in $\mathcal{E}^+$:

(1) $a(x).E$, $\overline{a}(e).E$, $\tau.E$, *Prefixes* $(a \in \mathcal{A})$
(2) $\sum_{i \in I} E_i$, a *Summation* (I an indexing set)
(3) $E_1 | E_2$, a *Composition*
(4) $E \backslash L$, a *Restriction* $(L \subseteq \mathcal{L})$
(5) $E[f]$, a *Relabelling* (f a relabelling function)
(6) **if** b **then** E , a *Conditional*

Furthermore, each Constant A with arity n has a defining equation

$$A(x_1, \ldots, x_n) \stackrel{\text{def}}{=} E$$

where the right-hand side E may contain no agent variables, and no free value variables except $x_1, \ldots, x_n$ (which must be distinct).

The one-armed conditional expression in (6) is enough, because the two-armed conditional **if** b **then** E **else** E' can be defined as

$$(\text{if } b \text{ then } E) + (\text{if } \neg b \text{ then } E')$$

Also, for simplicity we have assumed that every action name a takes a value parameter (those which do not will require no translation).

In translating $\mathcal{E}^+$ to $\mathcal{E}$, we confine our attention to agent expressions which contain no free value variables $x, y, \ldots$. (If $E \in \mathcal{E}^+$ contains x free, then it can be considered as a family of expressions $E\{v/x\}$, one for each value constant v.) Our translation of $\mathcal{E}^+$ into $\mathcal{E}$ rests upon the idea that to each label ℓ in the full calculus corresponds a set $\{\ell_v : v \in V\}$ of labels in the basic calculus. Thus we think of a single port labelled ℓ as a *set* of ports labelled ℓ_v, one for each value $v \in V$.

The translation will be given recursively on the structure of expressions. In stating it, we shall only need to consider value expressions e and boolean expressions b which contain no value variables. This is because the translation of an input Prefix '$a(x)$.' will replace x by a Summation over all values $v \in V$, as we have already illustrated, thus eliminating all occurrences of the bound variable x. We are therefore also free to consider each value expression e as identical with the fixed value v to which it evaluates, and each boolean expression b as identical with one of the boolean values $\{true, false\}$.

For each expression $F \in \mathcal{E}^+$ without free value variables, its translated form $\widehat{F} \in \mathcal{E}$ is given as follows:

F	$\widehat{F}$
X	X
$a(x).E$	$\sum_{v \in V} a_v.E\widehat{\{v/x\}}$
$\overline{a}(e).E$	$\overline{a}_e.\widehat{E}$
$\tau.E$	$\tau.\widehat{E}$
$\sum_{i \in I} E_i$	$\sum_{i \in I} \widehat{E_i}$
$E_1 \mid E_2$	$\widehat{E_1} \mid \widehat{E_2}$
$E \backslash L$	$\widehat{E} \backslash \{\ell_v : \ell \in L,\ v \in V\}$
$E[f]$	$\widehat{E}[\widehat{f}]$, where $\widehat{f}(\ell_v) = f(\ell)_v$
if b then E	$\begin{cases} \widehat{E} & \text{if } b = true \\ 0 & \text{otherwise} \end{cases}$
$A(e_1, \ldots, e_n)$	$A_{e_1, \ldots, e_n}$

Furthermore, the single defining equation $A(\tilde{x}) \overset{\text{def}}{=} E$ of a Constant, where $\tilde{x} = x_1, \ldots, x_n$, is translated into the indexed set of defining equations

$$\{A_{\tilde{v}} \overset{\text{def}}{=} E\widehat{\{\tilde{v}/\tilde{x}\}} : \tilde{v} \in V^n\}$$

As an example, suppose that V is the set of natural numbers, and consider the agent

$$F \equiv \text{in}(x).(\text{if } x < 5 \text{ then } \overline{\text{out}}(x).0)$$

Then the translation is

$$\widehat{F} \equiv \sum_{v \in V} E_v$$

where the expressions $E_0, E_1, \ldots$ (one for each natural number) are given schematically by

$$E_v \equiv \begin{cases} \overline{\text{out}_v}.0 & \text{if } v < 5 \\ 0 & \text{otherwise} \end{cases}$$

We shall later move freely between the forms of the full calculus and their basic equivalents.

2.9   Recursion expressions

In applications, like those in Chapter 1, we certainly wish to use Constants and defining equations freely. But for theoretical purposes it is sometimes convenient to have a calculus which need not be extended by *recursive* definitions, but in which new Constants can be treated just as abbreviations for existing expressions.

Now there is *no* expression for which the Constant A defined by

$$A \overset{\text{def}}{=} a.A$$

is an abbreviation, because the only way in which we have been able to express recursion is by means of defining equations. We shall now introduce recursion expressions: in this simple case the appropriate expression will be

$$\mathbf{fix}(X = a.X)$$

which may be pronounced 'the agent X such that $X \overset{\text{def}}{=} a.X$'. In this so-called **fix** expression, X is a bound variable and can be renamed without any semantic effect. By this means we have separated recursion from the definition facility. Of course we are perfectly at liberty to define

$$A \overset{\text{def}}{=} \mathbf{fix}(X = a.X)$$

and this *non-recursive* definition has exactly the effect of our original *recursive* definition.

In general then, to be precise, we add a sixth kind of expression to those listed in Section 2.4, namely

(6) $\mathbf{fix}_j(\{X_i = E_i \ : \ i \in I\})$, a Recursion (I an indexing set, and $j \in I$)

What this means, informally, is the jth component of the family of agents defined recursively by $X_i \overset{\text{def}}{=} E_i$, $i \in I$. We can write it more briefly as $\mathbf{fix}_j(\tilde{X} = \tilde{E})$. In the case of a *single* equation we write just $\mathbf{fix}(X = E)$.

To go with this new form we need a new inference rule. For the simple case of a single equation it takes the form

$$\text{Rec} \quad \frac{E\{\mathbf{fix}(X = E)/X\} \overset{\alpha}{\rightarrow} E'}{\mathbf{fix}(X = E) \overset{\alpha}{\rightarrow} E'}$$

This says, informally, that any action which may be inferred for the **fix** expression 'unwound' once (by substituting itself for its bound variable) may be inferred for the **fix** expression itself. It can be shown fairly easily that this gives the **fix** expression exactly the same behaviour as if X had been a Constant and we applied our **Con** rule to the defining equation

$$X = E$$

For the full form of the rule, we shall use $\widetilde{\mathbf{fix}}(\tilde{X} = \tilde{E})$ to mean the family of components $\{\mathbf{fix}_j(\tilde{X} = \tilde{E}) : j \in I\}$. Then the full rule is as follows:

$$\mathbf{Rec}_j \quad \frac{E_j\{\widetilde{\mathbf{fix}}(\tilde{X} = \tilde{E})/\tilde{X}\} \xrightarrow{\alpha} E'}{\mathbf{fix}_j(\tilde{X} = \tilde{E}) \xrightarrow{\alpha} E'}$$

People wishing mainly to apply the calculus will rightly recoil from this rule, and will be happy to know that almost all the theory in thi⸱ ᵒok ignores the **fix** form.

2.10   Transition induction

Several times in developing our theory we shall need to prove a property of transitions $E \xrightarrow{\alpha} E'$. Now – as we saw in Section 5 – every transition is justified by an inference diagram, which is a finite tree whose root is the transition itself. Therefore it is appropriate to prove properties of transitions by induction on the depth of inference diagrams; we shall call this *proof by transition induction*.

This section can be safely skipped by those who are not concerned with proofs of general results. It is devoted to a proof of Proposition 2 by transition induction.

Proposition 2 (restated)   Let $E \xrightarrow{\alpha} E'$. Then

(1) $\alpha \in \mathcal{L}(E) \cup \{\tau\}$
(2) $\mathcal{L}(E') \subseteq \mathcal{L}(E)$

Proof   By transition induction on the inference of $E \xrightarrow{\alpha} E'$. We consider the different ways in which last step of the inference is done:

Case 1   By **Act**, with $E \equiv \alpha.E'$. Then by Definition 2 we have $\mathcal{L}(E) = \{\alpha\} \cup \mathcal{L}(E')$ if $\alpha \neq \tau$, and $\mathcal{L}(E) = \mathcal{L}(E')$ if $\alpha = \tau$. The result follows easily.

Case 2   By **Sum**$_j$, with $E \equiv \sum_i E_i$, and – by a shorter inference – $E_j \xrightarrow{\alpha} E'$. Then, by induction, $\alpha \in \mathcal{L}(E_j) \cup \{\tau\}$ and $\mathcal{L}(E') \subseteq \mathcal{L}(E_j)$, and the result follows since, by Definition 2, $\mathcal{L}(E_j) \subseteq \mathcal{L}(\sum_i E_i)$.

Case 3   By **Com**$_1$, with $E \equiv E_1|E_2$, $E' \equiv E_1'|E_2$ and – by a shorter inference – $E_1 \xrightarrow{\alpha} E_1'$. Then by induction $\alpha \in \mathcal{L}(E_1) \cup \{\tau\}$ and $\mathcal{L}(E_1') \subseteq \mathcal{L}(E_1)$, and the result follows analogously to Case 2.

Case 4   By **Com**$_2$; similar.

Case 5   By **Com**$_3$; similar, but with two induction hypotheses.

Case 6   By **Res**, with $E \equiv E_1\backslash L$, $E' \equiv E_1'\backslash L$, $\alpha \notin L \cup \overline{L}$ and – by a shorter inference – $E_1 \xrightarrow{\alpha} E_1'$. Then by induction $\alpha \in \mathcal{L}(E_1) \cup \{\tau\}$

and $\mathcal{L}(E_1') \subseteq \mathcal{L}(E_1)$. But Definition 2 defines $\mathcal{L}(E) = \mathcal{L}(E_1) - (L \cup \overline{L})$ and $\mathcal{L}(E') = \mathcal{L}(E_1') - (L \cup \overline{L})$; the result follows easily.

Case 7   By **Rel**; similar.

Case 8   By **Con**, with $E \equiv A$, and – by a shorter inference – $P \xrightarrow{\alpha} E'$, where $A \stackrel{\text{def}}{=} P$. So by induction $\alpha \in \mathcal{L}(P) \cup \{\tau\}$ and $\mathcal{L}(E') \subseteq \mathcal{L}(P)$, and the result follows because of the condition in Definition 2 that $\mathcal{L}(P) \subseteq \mathcal{L}(A)$.   ∎

Having seen this fairly simple example of the method, the reader should be well prepared to follow the more complex proofs by transition induction in later chapters, for example Proposition 4.12 and Lemma 4.13.

3

Equational Laws and Their Application

The purpose of this chapter is to become familiar with the calculus through application to a graded sequence of examples, paying particular attention to the use of equations. We touched on this topic briefly in Sections 2.2 and 2.3.

The equational laws of the calculus fall naturally into three groups, and our presentation takes advantage of this grouping. After defining the classification in Section 1, we deal with one group of laws in each of the remaining three sections. Each group represents one aspect of the behavioural equality of agents, and these aspects are brought to attention by the examples which illustrate each group.

In later chapters the equality of agents will be defined in terms of their derivations, and all the equational laws which we use will be formally derived. It seems better to get used to using the laws before tackling their formal derivation. For one thing, each law is quite easy to justify by appealing to intuitive understanding of transition graphs or flow graphs; in addition to this, the formal treatment of equality (and its relationship with the transition relations) requires more mathematics than its application does. But we would not encourage anyone, however practically minded, to ignore the formal treatment; it is only by understanding *why* the laws hold that one grasps the nature of processes.

3.1   Classification of combinators and laws

Though there are many equational laws, we shall find that they fall into groups with a very distinct character. This classification is possible because the combinators of the calculus fall neatly into two categories.

The first category consists of Composition, Restriction and Relabelling, which may be called the *static combinators*. The rules of action for these combinators are all of the form

$$\frac{E_{i_1} \overset{\alpha_1}{\to} E'_{i_1} \quad \dots \quad E_{i_m} \overset{\alpha_m}{\to} E'_{i_m}}{comb(E_1, \dots, E_n) \overset{\alpha}{\to} comb(E'_1, \dots, E'_n)}$$

where $\{i_1, \dots, i_m\}$ is a subset of $\{1, \dots, n\}$, and E'_i is identical with E_i unless $i \in \{i_1, \dots, i_m\}$. The significant point is that the combinator *comb* is present after the action as well as before, and moreover the only components which have changed are those whose actions have contributed to the action of the compound agent. It follows that any construction $\mathcal{C}[E_1, \dots, E_n]$ built from these combinators will persist through action. That is why Composition, Restriction and Relabelling can be regarded as operations upon flow graphs; the structure that they represent is undisturbed by action, and is therefore *static* structure. It specifies how the components are linked, which parts of their interfaces are hidden or internal, and how the ports are labelled.

The second category consists of the *dynamic combinators*: Prefix, Summation and Constants. In each rule for these combinators, an occurrence of the combinator is present before the action and absent afterwards; thus these combinators lack the persistent or static quality of the others. (You may feel that it is unnatural to think of Constants as combinators. In fact they are *nullary* combinators – they are constructions without parameters; in Chapter 9 we shall find that they can be generalised to constructions with any number of parameters. The Recursion combinator, which in Section 2.9 was shown to be an alternative to the use of Constants, should also be classified as dynamic.)

We thus gain a three-way classification of equational laws, which we shall use in our presentation:

- The *static laws*, involving only the static combinators. These laws can be regarded as an algebra of flow graphs.
- The *dynamic laws*, involving only the dynamic combinators. These laws can be regarded as an algebra of transition graphs.
- The laws which relate one group to the other. As far as the present chapter is concerned, these laws may all be collected into a single one known as the *expansion law*; it gives all the actions of any static combination of agents $P_1, \dots, P_n$ in terms of the actions of $P_1, \dots, P_n$ themselves.

In the ensuing sections we introduce laws under these three headings, with discussion and examples. For clarity of presentation we only give enough laws to allow an interesting sequence of examples, without trying to be exhaustive.

3.2   The dynamic laws

The first set of laws concerns Summation alone:

Proposition 1: monoid laws

(1) $P + Q = Q + P$
(2) $P + (Q + R) = (P + Q) + R$
(3) $P + P = P$
(4) $P + 0 = P$ ∎

We cannot do many interesting proofs with only these laws, but we can at least justify them informally. The best way to do this is to note that if we write any of the laws as $E_1 = E_2$, then E_1 and E_2 in each case have exactly the same derivatives; that is,

$$E_1 \xrightarrow{\alpha} E' \text{ iff } E_2 \xrightarrow{\alpha} E'$$

This is strong enough to ensure that the laws are valid under *any* definition of equality based upon the structure of derivation trees, disregarding the expressions which lie at the nodes, and we stated in Section 2.2 that our definition will be of this kind.

The second set of laws concerns Prefix, and focuses on the meaning of the silent action τ:

Proposition 2: τ laws

(1) $\alpha.\tau.P = \alpha.P$
(2) $P + \tau.P = \tau.P$
(3) $\alpha.(P + \tau.Q) + \alpha.Q = \alpha.(P + \tau.Q)$ ∎

These laws look a little strange at first, and some discussion in terms of derivation trees is in order. Let us draw the derivation trees of both sides of Proposition 2(3), denoting the left- and right-hand sides by E_1 and E_2:

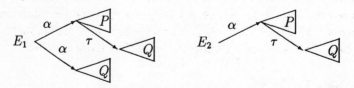

Now E_1 and E_2 do not have exactly the same α-derivatives, since

$$E_1 \xrightarrow{\alpha} Q \text{ but not } E_2 \xrightarrow{\alpha} Q$$

But we may argue that Q is, in a more generous sense, an α-derivative of E_2, since $E_2 \xrightarrow{\alpha} P + \tau.Q$, and this may be followed by the *silent* action $P + \tau.Q \xrightarrow{\tau} Q$. This argument motivates the definition of a new transition relation, which we shall use more fully when we come to treat equality formally:

Definition 1 $P \xRightarrow{\alpha} P'$ if $P(\xrightarrow{\tau})^* \xrightarrow{\alpha} (\xrightarrow{\tau})^* P'$.   ∎

In this definition we use $(\xrightarrow{\tau})^*$, the transitive reflexive closure of $\xrightarrow{\tau}$, meaning 'zero or more τ actions'. (Note that, by the definition, $\xRightarrow{\tau}$ means '*one* or more τ actions'.) Now if we write either (2) or (3) of Proposition 2 as $E_1 = E_2$, then for any α

$$E_1 \xRightarrow{\alpha} E' \text{ iff } E_2 \xRightarrow{\alpha} E'$$

as may be checked by drawing the derivation trees. This property is enough to ensure equality, under the definition which will be given in Chapter 7. Something a little looser is needed to justify Proposition 2(1).

We can give some insight into these laws by means of a few examples; first we state a simple corollary of Proposition 2.

Corollary 3 $P + \tau.(P + Q) = \tau.(P + Q)$ ∎

Exercise 1   Prove this; it only takes two or three lines, and needs only Proposition 2(2) with Proposition 1.   ∎

We can understand this result in the following way. On the left-hand side, P represents some action capabilities which are initially available, and are still available (together with further capabilities represented by Q) after the τ action. The corollary says that nothing is lost by deferring the P capabilities until after the τ action, as represented by the right-hand side. Of course, such verbal explanation is highly fragile; this is why we firmly intend to define our notion of equality in terms of the transition rules which embody our operational intuitions about processes; these are the only intuitions which may be trusted.

Here are some more examples, somewhat more specific:

Exercise 2   Prove

(1) $\alpha.(P + \tau.\tau.P) = \alpha.P$

(2) $\tau.(P + \alpha.(Q + \tau.R)) = \tau.(P + \alpha.(Q + \tau.R)) + \alpha.R$ ∎

The second half of this exercise is important, since it is an instance of a general property of equality – namely:

$$\text{Whenever } E \xRightarrow{\alpha} E' \text{ then } E = E + \alpha.E'$$

In other words, whenever E can do an α action accompanied by several τ actions to reach E', it is consistent with equality to assume that it can do the same without any accompanying τ actions. (In the exercise R plays the role of E'.) In fact, after doing the above exercise you may like to tackle the following, though we don't need it for further development:

Exercise 3 Let E be any agent expression built using only variables, **0**, + and Prefixing. Prove for this special case that

$$\text{Whenever } E \xRightarrow{\alpha} E' \text{ then } E = E + \alpha.E'$$

Hint: Use induction on the structure of E. You only need Propositions 1 and 2. ∎

Now, before proceeding to recursion, it is illuminating to pause and to ask why some attractive 'laws' must be rejected.

First, consider the 'law' $\tau.P = P$. If we allowed it, we could deduce $a.P + \tau.b.Q = a.P + b.Q$. But in Section 2.3 we saw that the left-hand agent has, via a τ action, the power to pre-empt the a action, while the right-hand agent does not have this power. Thus if the environment or observer is demanding an a action, the right-hand agent must meet the demand while the left-hand agent may not meet it.

Second, consider the distributive 'law' $\alpha.(P + Q) = \alpha.P + \alpha.Q$. If we allowed it we could deduce $a.(b.P + c.Q) = a.b.P + a.c.Q$. But our transitional semantics allows $b.P$ as an a-derivative of the right-hand agent, and – assuming $b \neq c$ – this derivative is incapable of a c action; on the other hand every (i.e. the *only*) a-derivative of the left-hand agent is capable of a c action. Thus a deadlock may occur for one agent but not for the other, if the environment or observer demands an a action followed by a c action.

The next set of laws is to do with solving recursive equations. It often arises that we have a recursively defined agent $A \stackrel{\text{def}}{=} P$, where A occurs in P; that is, P is of the form $E\{A/X\}$ where the expression E contains the variable X. Clearly, by defining

$$A \stackrel{\text{def}}{=} E\{A/X\}$$

we must intend that A is a solution of the equation $X = E$; that is, we surely expect that $A = E\{A/X\}$, and this is indeed the case. Further, suppose some agent Q, defined by other means, is also a solution of $X = E$; that is, we have been able to prove

$$Q = E\{Q/X\}$$

The question is: under what conditions can we then conclude that $Q = A$? To put it another way, under what conditions is there a *unique* solution to the equation $X = E$? To answer the questions we need two simple ideas.

Let E be any expression. We say that a variable X is *sequential* in E if it only occurs within Prefix or Summation combinators in E; we say that X is *guarded* in E if each occurrence of X is within some subexpression $\ell.F$ of E. For example:

- X is sequential but not guarded in $\tau.X + a.(b.\mathbf{0} \mid c.\mathbf{0})$
- X is guarded in $a.X \mid b.\mathbf{0}$, but not sequential since it occurs inside a Composition.
- X is both guarded and sequential in $\tau.(P_1 + a.(P_2 + \tau.X))$.

The idea of sequentiality is this: Suppose X is sequential in E – for example, $E \equiv \tau.(P_1 + a.(P_2 + \tau.X))$. Then if A is defined by $A \overset{\text{def}}{=} E\{A/X\}$, i.e.

$$A \overset{\text{def}}{=} \tau.(P_1 + a.(P_2 + \tau.A))$$

then A's recursive behaviour, as it unfolds, is derived by the transition rules for the *dynamic* combinators alone, and these combinators represent only sequential – not concurrent – behaviour.

We can now state an important result, the second part of which is the unique solution property which we were looking for.

Proposition 4

(1) If $A \overset{\text{def}}{=} P$, then $A = P$.
(2) Let the expressions E_i $(i \in I)$ contain at most the variables X_i $(i \in I)$ free, and let these variables be guarded and sequential in each E_i. Then

$$\text{If } \tilde{P} = \tilde{E}\{\tilde{P}/\tilde{X}\} \text{ and } \tilde{Q} = \tilde{E}\{\tilde{Q}/\tilde{X}\}, \text{ then } \tilde{P} = \tilde{Q} \qquad \blacksquare$$

(1) needs little comment. (2) is concerned with the uniqueness of solution of the equations $\tilde{X} = \tilde{E}$, i.e. $X_i = E_i$ $(i \in I)$. To see why guardedness is needed, consider the case of a single equation $X = \tau.X$, which violates the condition.

Exercise 4   Prove that both $\tau.0$ and $\tau.a.0$ are solutions of the equation $X = \tau.X$. More generally, show that *any* agent of the form $\tau.P$ is a solution of $X = \tau.X$.   ∎

Exercise 5   Consider the equation

$$X = a.0 + \tau.X$$

Show that any agent of the form $\tau.(\tau.P + a.0)$ is a solution. Now consider the pair of equations

$$X \;=\; a.0 + \tau.Y$$
$$Y \;=\; b.0 + \tau.X$$

Can you find an infinite family of solutions?   ∎

Proposition 4(2) is vitally important, and indeed we have already appealed to it implicitly in Section 2.2. We showed there that for a certain composite agent $(A|B)\backslash c$, we have

- $(A|B)\backslash c = a.(A'|B)\backslash c$
- $(A'|B)\backslash c$ is a solution of $X = a.\overline{b}.X + \overline{b}.a.X$

But the latter equation satisfies the conditions of Proposition 4(2), and so we were justified in concluding that $(A|B)\backslash c = a.D$, where $D \overset{\text{def}}{=} a.\overline{b}.D + \overline{b}.a.D$, since by Proposition 4(1) D is the unique solution of the equation concerned.

  We shall find that many concurrent systems can be shown equal to the solution of a set of guarded sequential equations, in a similar manner.

Exercise 6   Let $A \overset{\text{def}}{=} a.A$ and $B \overset{\text{def}}{=} a.a.B$. Use Proposition 4 to prove that $A = B$ (you will need *both* parts of Proposition 4).   ∎

Exercise 7   Suppose that $P = a.b.P$ and $Q = b.a.Q$. Prove that $P = a.Q$ and $Q = b.P$.   ∎

Exercise 8   Consider the equations

$$X_1 \;=\; a.X_1 + \tau.X_2$$
$$X_2 \;=\; a.X_1 + b.X_2$$

Show that the conditions of Proposition 4(2) are satisfied if X_2 is replaced by its defining expression in the first equation, and that the unique solution for X_1 is $\tau.A$ where $A \stackrel{\text{def}}{=} a.A + b.A$.   ■

The last exercise needs a combination of the τ laws (Proposition 2) with the recursion laws. This is a common phenomenon, and we shall see more realistic examples of it in the next section.

The need for guardedness, to be sure of unique solutions, is clear enough from Exercises 4 and 5, but perhaps the reason for sequentiality is less obvious. The following exercise will be helpful.

Exercise 9   After reading Section 3 below, consider the equation

$$X = (a.X \mid \overline{a}.0)\backslash a$$

Note that X is guarded, but *not* sequential, in the right-hand side. Show that $\tau.P$ solves this equation, for any P such that $a, \overline{a} \notin \mathcal{L}(P)$.   ■

We can see here that – due to communication – X can 'call itself' recursively before any observable action has occurred.

It is possible to weaken the condition of sequentiality and still ensure unique solutions, as Michael Sanderson showed in his PhD thesis, but we shall not pursue the question further in this book.

3.3   The expansion law

Very often a concurrent system is naturally expressed as a restricted Composition, i.e. in the form

$$(P_1 \mid \ldots \mid P_n)\backslash L$$

The first example we defined explicitly was the *Jobshop* of Section 1.3:

$$(Jobber \mid Jobber \mid Hammer \mid Mallet)\backslash\{\texttt{getm}, \texttt{putm}, \texttt{geth}, \texttt{puth}\}$$

We also treated a simple system $(A|B)\backslash c$ in Section 2.2. A slightly more involved example is provided by the linking combinator of Section 1.2. We did not define it there in terms of the basic combinators, but we shall now do so. Its purpose is to take two copies of C, with sort $\{\texttt{in}, \overline{\texttt{out}}\}$:

and chain them together:

For this purpose, we must relabel the ports in the middle, before composing and restricting; therefore the definition of the appropriate linking combinator $\frown$, applied to arbitrary agents P and Q, is

$$P \frown Q \stackrel{\text{def}}{=} (P[\text{mid/out}] \mid Q[\text{mid/in}]) \backslash \text{mid}$$

where mid is a fresh name (i.e. neither mid nor $\overline{\text{mid}}$ is in $\mathcal{L}(P)$ or $\mathcal{L}(Q)$).

In fact this form, a restricted Composition of relabelled components, arises so often that we shall call it a *standard concurrent form* (scf); its general format is

$$(P_1[f_1] \mid \ldots \mid P_n[f_n]) \backslash L$$

Very often the agents P_i will be purely sequential, i.e. defined using Prefix and Summation only. It is worth noticing that the expression for *Jobshop* takes standard concurrent form even if we replace the *Hammer* and *Mallet* respectively by the relabelled semaphores

$$Sem[\text{geth/get}, \text{puth/put}]$$

$$Sem[\text{getm/get}, \text{putm/put}]$$

as justified by Section 1.3.

The expansion law is concerned with the immediate actions of an agent in standard concurrent form, as displayed schematically above. Rather clearly, these actions will be of two kinds. The first kind is due to an action α of a single component, P_i say; then the scf will have an action $f_i(\alpha)$ (provided this action is not in $L \cup L'$), and the derivative will be a new scf

$$(P_1[f_1] \mid \ldots \mid P_i'[f_i] \mid \ldots \mid P_n[f_n]) \backslash L$$

– that is, only the ith component of the expression has changed. The other kind is a τ action, a communication resulting from actions ℓ_1 by P_i and ℓ_2 by P_j ($1 \leq i < j \leq n$), such that $f_i(\ell_1) = \overline{f_j(\ell_2)}$; then the derivative will be a new scf

$$(P_1[f_1] \mid \ldots \mid P_i'[f_i] \mid \ldots \mid P_j'[f_j] \ldots \mid P_n[f_n]) \backslash L$$

in which exactly two components have changed.

With this preliminary explanation, we now state the law formally. The reader may find both Corollary 6 and Example 1, which follow, helpful in understanding the law.

Proposition 5: the expansion law

Let $P \equiv (P_1[f_1] \mid \ldots \mid P_n[f_n]) \setminus L$, with $n \geq 1$. Then

$$P = \sum \Big\{ f_i(\alpha).(P_1[f_1] \mid \ldots \mid P_i'[f_i] \mid \ldots \mid P_n[f_n]) \setminus L \; : $$
$$P_i \xrightarrow{\alpha} P_i', f_i(\alpha) \notin L \cup \overline{L} \Big\}$$
$$+ \sum \Big\{ \tau.(P_1[f_1] \mid \ldots \mid P_i'[f_i] \mid \ldots \mid P_j'[f_j] \mid \ldots \mid P_n[f_n]) \setminus L \; : $$
$$P_i \xrightarrow{\ell_1} P_i' , \; P_j \xrightarrow{\ell_2} P_j' , \; f_i(\ell_1) = \overline{f_j(\ell_2)} , \; i < j \Big\} \qquad \blacksquare$$

A frequent use of expansion is when the relabelling functions f_i are all the identity function Id, and if we take advantage of the law $P[Id] = P$ – one of the static laws introduced in Section 3.4 – then we get a simplified form of the law which is worth stating.

Corollary 6

Let $P \equiv (P_1 \mid \ldots \mid P_n) \setminus L$, with $n \geq 1$. Then

$$P = \sum \Big\{ \alpha.(P_1 \mid \ldots \mid P_i' \mid \ldots \mid P_n) \setminus L \; : \; P_i \xrightarrow{\alpha} P_i', \alpha \notin L \cup \overline{L} \Big\}$$
$$+ \sum \Big\{ \tau.(P_1 \mid \ldots \mid P_i' \mid \ldots \mid P_j' \mid \ldots \mid P_n) \setminus L \; : $$
$$P_i \xrightarrow{\ell} P_i', \; P_j \xrightarrow{\overline{\ell}} P_j', \; i < j \Big\} \qquad \blacksquare$$

Example 1   We first illustrate the expansion law with a small, rather artificial, example. Let a, b, c be distinct names and suppose that

$$P_1 \equiv a.P_1' + b.P_1''$$
$$P_2 \equiv \overline{a}.P_2' + c.P_2''$$
$$P \equiv (P_1 | P_2) \setminus a$$

Then P has two derivatives of the first kind, arising from b by P_1 and c by P_2; it also has one of the second kind arising from communication via a. So we get

$$P = b.(P_1'' | P_2) \setminus a + c.(P_1 | P_2'') \setminus a + \tau.(P_1' | P_2') \setminus a$$

Further, suppose that

$$P_3 \equiv \overline{a}.P_3' + \overline{c}.P_3''$$
$$Q \equiv (P_1 | P_2 | P_3) \setminus \{a, b\}$$

Then, since a and b are restricted, Q will have only two derivatives of the first kind, arising from c by P_2 and $\bar{c}$ by P_3; it will have three derivatives of the second kind, arising from communications via a, a and c respectively. Note that the b action by P_1 cannot contribute to either kind of derivative, since b is restricted and no other agent can contribute a $\bar{b}$ action. The resulting expansion is therefore (writing L for $\{a, b\}$)

$$Q \;=\; c.(P_1|P_2''|P_3)\backslash L + \bar{c}.(P_1|P_2|P_3'')\backslash L +$$
$$\tau.(P_1'|P_2'|P_3)\backslash L + \tau.(P_1'|P_2|P_3')\backslash L + \tau.(P_1|P_2''|P_3'')\backslash L$$

We shall only rarely find that our expansions yield so many terms; this example was chosen just to show the generality of the expansion law. ∎

The case $n = 1$ of the expansion law has special interest; we see that in this case the law specialises to some important laws relating Prefix with Restriction and Relabelling. (These laws also have simple direct proofs.)

Corollary 7

(1) $(\alpha.Q)\backslash L = \begin{cases} 0 & \text{if } \alpha \in L \cup \bar{L} \\ \alpha.Q\backslash L & \text{otherwise} \end{cases}$

(2) $(\alpha.Q)[f] = f(\alpha).Q[f]$

(3) $(Q + R)\backslash L = Q\backslash L + R\backslash L$

(4) $(Q + R)[f] = Q[f] + R[f]$

Proof

(1) We use the expansion law without Relabelling, with $n = 1$ and $P_1 \equiv \alpha.Q$. Clearly the second Summation contains no terms – i.e. it yields $\mathbf{0}$ – since there are no distinct components to communicate. The first Summation yields

$$\sum \left\{ \beta.P_1'\backslash L \;:\; P_1 \xrightarrow{\beta} P_1', \beta \notin L \cup \bar{L} \right\}$$

but $\alpha.Q \xrightarrow{\alpha} Q$ is the only action of P_1, so the Summation yields $\mathbf{0}$ or $\alpha.Q\backslash L$ depending on whether $\alpha \in L \cup \bar{L}$ or not.

(2) In this case we use the law $P\backslash \emptyset = P$, which will be introduced in Proposition 9(1). Then, applying the expansion law in the case $n = 1$, with $P_1 \equiv \alpha.Q$ and $L = \emptyset$, the result follows immediately.

(3) This result again follows from the expansion law by setting $n = 1$ and $f_1 = Id$, together with the fact that $Q + R \xrightarrow{\alpha} P'$ iff $(Q \xrightarrow{\alpha} P'$

or $R \xrightarrow{\alpha} P'$).

(4) Similar, but this time setting $n = 1$ and $L_1 = \emptyset$ in the expansion law.   ∎

Exercise 10 Assuming Corollary 7(2), show how to deduce the general form of the expansion law from its simplified form (Corollary 6).   ∎

Example 2 A second, less artificial, application of the expansion law is provided by the simple example of Section 2.2:

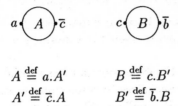

$$A \overset{\text{def}}{=} a.A' \qquad B \overset{\text{def}}{=} c.B'$$
$$A' \overset{\text{def}}{=} \overline{c}.A \qquad B' \overset{\text{def}}{=} \overline{b}.B$$

In that section we argued informally, by working out the derivation tree of $(A|B)\backslash c$, that $(A|B)\backslash c = a.D$ where $D \overset{\text{def}}{=} a.\overline{b}.D + \overline{b}.a.D$. The argument was informal because we assumed, without giving precise definitions, that two processes are equal when their derivation trees are 'sufficiently similar'. But now we can give a rigorous argument. For we can first apply the expansion law (without Relabelling) a few times to deduce

$$\begin{aligned}
(A|B)\backslash c &= a.(A'|B)\backslash c \\
(A'|B)\backslash c &= \tau.(A|B')\backslash c \\
(A|B')\backslash c &= a.(A'|B')\backslash c + \overline{b}.(A|B)\backslash c \\
(A'|B')\backslash c &= \overline{b}.(A'|B)\backslash c
\end{aligned}$$

Then with the help of Proposition 2(1) we show that $(A|B')\backslash c$ satisfies the defining equation of D, and hence by Proposition 4(2) $(A|B')\backslash c = D$; finally $(A|B)\backslash c = a.(A|B')\backslash c$ by Proposition 2(1). We see from this example that applying the expansion law repeatedly is just another way of growing a derivation tree, or of building a complete transition graph.   ∎

Example 3: buffers For our next example, we consider a simplified form of the buffer cell discussed in Section 1.2:

where we assume $a \neq b$. The simplification is to ignore the values input at a and output at $\bar{b}$; that is, we define

$$C \overset{\text{def}}{=} a.C'$$
$$C' \overset{\text{def}}{=} \bar{b}.C$$

We shall need to define the linking combinator $\frown$; then we may form the chain $C^{(n)}$ of n buffer cells, given by

$$C^{(1)} \overset{\text{def}}{=} C$$
$$C^{(n+1)} \overset{\text{def}}{=} C \frown C^{(n)}$$

$C^{(n)}$ may be depicted as follows:

We shall prove that $C^{(n)} = Buff_n(0)$, where $Buff_n(k)$ is defined as follows for $0 \leq k \leq n$:

$$Buff_n(0) \overset{\text{def}}{=} a.Buff_n(1)$$
$$Buff_n(k) \overset{\text{def}}{=} a.Buff_n(k+1) + \bar{b}.Buff_n(k-1) \qquad (0 < k < n)$$
$$Buff_n(n) \overset{\text{def}}{=} \bar{b}.Buff_n(n-1)$$

To start with something simple, let us first prove the result for $n = 2$; we return to the general case as a later example. So we wish to prove that $C \frown C = Buff_2(0)$, where

$$Buff_2(0) \overset{\text{def}}{=} a.Buff_2(1)$$
$$Buff_2(1) \overset{\text{def}}{=} a.Buff_2(2) + \bar{b}.Buff_2(0)$$
$$Buff_2(2) \overset{\text{def}}{=} \bar{b}.Buff_2(1)$$

Notice that the parameter k in $Buff_n(k)$ stands for the number of values presently stored in the buffer; clearly each input at a increases k by 1, and each output at $\bar{b}$ decreases k by 1.

Recalling the start of this section, the linking combinator which will link $\bar{b}$ to a is given by

$$P \frown Q \overset{\text{def}}{=} (P[c/b] \mid Q[c/a]) \backslash c$$

where c is chosen so that $c, \bar{c} \notin \mathcal{L}(P) \cup \mathcal{L}(Q)$. (In forming $C \frown C$, we merely have to choose c distinct from a and b.) Later in Example 6 we shall show that $\frown$ is associative, but we do not need this for the present purpose.

But now we shall see that, to prove $C^\frown C = \textit{Buff}_2(0)$, we have done most of the work in the previous example! For by definition

$$C^\frown C = (C[c/b] \mid C[c/a])\backslash c$$

and using Corollary 7(2) we easily prove

$$
\begin{aligned}
C[c/b] &= a.\bar{c}.C[c/b] \\
C[c/a] &= c.\bar{b}.C[c/a]
\end{aligned}
$$

so by the unique solution property Proposition 4(2), applied to the definitions of A and B in the previous example, we have shown that

$$
\begin{aligned}
C[c/b] &= A \\
C[c/a] &= B
\end{aligned}
$$

and hence

$$C^\frown C = (A \mid B)\backslash c$$

But in the previous example we showed

$$(A\mid B)\backslash c = a.D \quad \text{where} \quad D \stackrel{\text{def}}{=} a.\bar{b}.D + \bar{b}.a.D$$

so, using the first defining equation of $\textit{Buff}_2$, all that remains is to prove that $D = \textit{Buff}_2(1)$. For this, by Proposition 4(2), it will suffice to show that $\textit{Buff}_2(1)$ satisfies the defining equation of D, i.e.

$$\textit{Buff}_2(1) = a.\bar{b}.\textit{Buff}_2(1) + \bar{b}.a.\textit{Buff}_2(1)$$

and this follows immediately from the defining equations of $\textit{Buff}_2$, so we are done.

An important step in this proof is the elimination of internal τ actions, using Proposition 2(1). This corresponds to the fact that the transfer of an item in the buffer from the first to the second cell cannot be observed, being an internal action. To be able to hide – or discard – such actions is vitally important; in larger systems there will be a profusion of internal actions, and they would clutter our working to such an extent that systems would rapidly become unmanageable.

Exercise 11   Using the result above, prove also that

$$C'^\frown C' = \textit{Buff}_2(2) \qquad\qquad\qquad \blacksquare$$

This example has shown how the behavioural properties of a derived combinator, the linking combinator, can be analysed by means of expansion.   ∎

Example 4: cyclers   Consider the *cycler* defined by

$$C \overset{\text{def}}{=} a.C'$$
$$C' \overset{\text{def}}{=} b.C''$$
$$C'' \overset{\text{def}}{=} c.C$$

(C fires its ports in cyclic order.) Assume that $a_1, \ldots, a_n$ and $b_1, \ldots, b_n$ are all distinct. We can form a ring $C^{(n)}$ of n cyclers as follows, where addition of integer subscripts is modulo n:

$$C_i \overset{\text{def}}{=} C[f_i]$$
$$C_i' \overset{\text{def}}{=} C'[f_i]$$
$$C_i'' \overset{\text{def}}{=} C''[f_i]$$
$$\text{where } f_i = (a_i/a, b_{i+1}/b, \overline{b_i}/c)$$
$$C^{(n)} \overset{\text{def}}{=} (C_1 \mid C_2'' \mid \cdots \mid C_n'')\backslash L$$
$$\text{where } L = \{b_1, \cdots, b_n\}$$

Part of $C^{(n)}$ is shown below; we show ports which are ready to fire by ringing them:

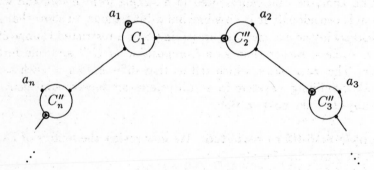

Note that only C_1 is ready to fire at its external port; each of the other cyclers is waiting to be enabled by its predecessor.

Exercise 12   Use the expansion law to show that

$$C^{(n)} = a_1. \cdots . a_n . C^{(n)}$$ ∎

Exercise 13   The system S in the flow graph below consists of five cyclers, each ready to fire first at its ringed port:

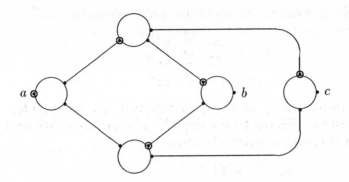

By considering S to be constructed from $C^{(4)}$ – suitably relabelled – and one other cycler, prove that $S = M$, where $M \stackrel{\text{def}}{=} a.(b.c.M + c.b.M)$. ($M$ is a kind of *multiplier*; given an 'input' at a, it produces 'output' at both b and c, in arbitrary order. Many interesting agents can be built from cyclers and the static combinators alone.) ■

The importance of Exercise 13 is that it is often a good idea to consider a complex system as composed of subsystems, whose behaviour may be analysed and represented in a simple form before the whole system is considered. It is possible, but a bit tedious, to show that $S = M$ *directly* in the exercise, i.e. presenting S as a restricted Composition of five cyclers, rather than as a Composition of $C^{(4)}$ and one further cycler. The static laws, which tell us that different ways (such as the above) of building a system from subsystems are indeed equivalent, are the subject of the next section.

Example 5: buffers revisited   We now revisit the buffers of Example 3, to prove that for all $n \geq 1$

$$C^{(n)} = \mathit{Buff}_n(0)$$

which we have hitherto only shown for $n = 2$. We proceed by induction on n. The inductive step, in which we assume the result for $C^{(n)}$ in proving it for $C^{(n+1)} = C^\frown C^{(n)}$, is another example of the analysis of a system in terms of its subsystems.

The intuition of the proof is that $\mathit{Buff}_n(k)$ is equal to

$$\overbrace{C^\frown \cdots {}^\frown C}^{n\,times} {}^\frown \underbrace{C'{}^\frown \cdots {}^\frown C'}_{k\,times}$$

and that when the left-hand cell C is filled (i.e. becomes C') then its contents may percolate to the right, by a sequence of internal actions, yielding $Buff_n(k+1)$. This is the essence of the equation $(*)$ which is the heart of the proof below.

For the base case $n = 1$, note that the defining equations of $Buff_n$ take the form

$$Buff_1(0) = a.Buff_1(1)$$
$$Buff_1(1) = \overline{b}.Buff_1(0)$$

and by comparing the defining equations of C we deduce $C = Buff_1(0)$, from Proposition 4. Now assume $C^{(n)} = Buff_n(0)$, and consider $C^{(n+1)}$. Let us prove that $C^{(n+1)}$ satisfies the equations which define $Buff_{n+1}(0)$. Now

$$C^{(n+1)} = C^\frown C^{(n)} = C^\frown Buff_n(0)$$

by the inductive hypothesis, so it will be enough to prove that the defining equations of $Buff_{n+1}$ (given in Example 3) are satisfied when we replace

$$Buff_{n+1}(k) \quad \text{by} \quad C^\frown Buff_n(k) \qquad (0 \le k \le n)$$
$$Buff_{n+1}(n+1) \quad \text{by} \quad C'^\frown Buff_n(n)$$

So the equations we need to prove are as follows:

$$C^\frown Buff_n(0) = a.(C^\frown Buff_n(1))$$
$$C^\frown Buff_n(k) = a.(C^\frown Buff_n(k+1)) + \overline{b}.(C^\frown Buff_n(k-1))$$
$$(1 \le k < n)$$
$$C^\frown Buff_n(n) = a.(C'^\frown Buff_n(n)) + \overline{b}.(C^\frown Buff_n(n-1))$$
$$C'^\frown Buff_n(n) = \overline{b}.(C^\frown Buff_n(n))$$

First, we compute the left-hand sides using expansion with the definitions of C and $Buff_n$:

$$C^\frown Buff_n(0) = a.(C'^\frown Buff_n(0))$$
$$C^\frown Buff_n(k) = a.(C'^\frown Buff_n(k)) + \overline{b}.(C^\frown Buff_n(k-1))$$
$$(1 \le k \le n)$$
$$C'^\frown Buff_n(n) = \overline{b}.(C'^\frown Buff_n(n-1))$$

Now we can see that the result will follow by Proposition 2(1), $P + \tau.P = \tau.P$, if we can prove

$$C'^\frown Buff_n(k) = \tau.(C^\frown Buff_n(k+1)) \qquad (0 \le k < n) \qquad (*)$$

For this, we proceed by induction on k. For $k = 0$, $(*)$ follows immediately by expansion of $C'^\frown Buff_n(0)$. Now assume $(*)$ for $k < n - 1$, and

consider $k + 1$. By expansion,

$$
\begin{aligned}
C'^\frown Buff_n(k+1) &= \tau.(C^\frown Buff_n(k+2)) + \overline{b}.(C'^\frown Buff_n(k)) \\
&= \tau.(C^\frown Buff_n(k+2)) + \overline{b}.(C^\frown Buff_n(k+1))
\end{aligned}
$$

by the inductive hypothesis for k, with the help of Proposition 2(1). Then $(*)$ will follow (with $k+1$ for k) if we can absorb the second term in the first.

To see that this absorption is possible, we recall Corollary 3, $\tau.(P + Q) + P = \tau.(P + Q)$. To apply this we take P to be $\overline{b}.(C^\frown Buff_n(k+1))$ and require that, for some Q,

$$
C^\frown Buff_n(k+2) = \overline{b}.(C^\frown Buff_n(k+1)) + Q
$$

But (noting that $1 \le k + 2 \le n$) this is evident from the equations which we obtained by expansion. We have thus shown

$$
C'^\frown Buff_n(k+1) = \tau.(C^\frown Buff_n(k+2))
$$

and this completes our inductive proof of $(*)$; it also completes our inductive proof that

$$
C^{(n+1)} = Buff_{n+1}(0)
$$

It is worth noting that we never needed to use the associativity of the linking combinator $^\frown$ in the above proof.   ∎

3.4   The static laws

We claimed at the beginning of this chapter that the static laws, relating Composition, Restriction and Relabelling, can be regarded as an algebra of flow graphs. Indeed, it is illuminating to introduce the laws in this guise, and so we begin this section by making more precise what we mean by a flow graph.

We assume that we have available a set of *Nodes*, each with a name and a set of ports with (inner) labels from $\mathcal{L}$. Nodes will be drawn as follows:

Notice that *every* port has a label; the reason for writing it inside the node will be explained shortly.

Next, we define a *flow graph* to be a set of nodes, where some pairs of ports are joined by *arcs* and some ports are assigned (outer) labels, under the following conditions:

- If two ports have outer labels ℓ and $\bar{\ell}$ then they are joined.
- If two ports are joined and one has an outer label ℓ, then the other has outer label $\bar{\ell}$.

In fact the only way in which this definition departs from the flow graphs which we have previously used is in the presence of the inner labels. The system consisting of a semaphore, all by itself, would be represented by the flow graph

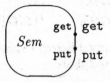

and indeed we could choose to omit an inner label – as we have hitherto done – if it is identical to the outer. But the *Hammer*, defined by

$$Hammer = Sem[\texttt{geth/get}, \texttt{puth/put}]$$

will be represented as follows

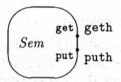

while the system $C^\frown C$ (see Example 3 in the last section) will be represented as

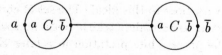

and these examples show how the inner labels may be informative in the presence of Relabelling and/or Restriction.

It is almost obvious how to define the operations of Composition, Restriction and Relabelling upon flow graphs, but let us spell it out. Let G and G' be arbitrary flow graphs. Then:

- $G|G'$ is formed by joining every pair of ports – one in G and one in G' – which have complementary outer labels;
- $G\backslash L$ is formed by erasing outer labels ℓ and $\overline{\ell}$ from G, for each $\ell \in L$;
- $G[f]$ is formed by applying the relabelling function f to all outer labels in G.

We also decree that the *sort* $\mathcal{L}(G)$ of G is just its set of outer labels, and the above rules ensure, as we would expect, that

$$\mathcal{L}(G|G') = \mathcal{L}(G) \cup \mathcal{L}(G')$$
$$\mathcal{L}(G\backslash L) = \mathcal{L}(G) - (L \cup \overline{L})$$
$$\mathcal{L}(G[f]) = f(\mathcal{L}(G))$$

Now clearly there are many different expressions for a single flow graph. In Section 1.3 we indicated that

$$(Jobber \mid Jobber \mid Hammer \mid Mallet)\backslash\{\texttt{geth},\texttt{puth},\texttt{getm},\texttt{putm}\}$$
$$= \;((Jobber \mid Jobber \mid Hammer)\backslash\{\texttt{geth},\texttt{puth}\} \mid Mallet)\backslash\{\texttt{getm},\texttt{putm}\}$$

and indeed it can easily be verified from the above formation rules that this equation holds when the expressions are interpreted as flow graphs. (Note, by the way, that it does not hold for arbitrary nodes in place of *Jobber*, *Hammer* and *Mallet*, but only holds by virtue of the sorts of these nodes.)

The ideal situation would be

- To have a set of equational axioms for the static combinators which are sound and complete for flow graphs; that is, axioms from which can be deduced exactly those equations which are true in the flow graph interpretation.
- To know that every equation which is true in the flow graph interpretation is also true in the process interpretation.

In fact, we come very close to this ideal. The set of equations we give in the rest of this section are certainly true in both interpretations; we shall prove them for the process interpretation in a later chapter, and shall leave the assiduous reader to check them for flow graphs. Moreover with a few minor variations and constraints (which may even be unnecessary) they have been proved complete for the flow graph interpretation.

We shall present the equations in three groups, concerned respectively with Composition, Restriction and Relabelling as the outermost combinator in an expression.

Proposition 8: Composition laws

(1) $P|Q = Q|P$
(2) $P|(Q|R) = (P|Q)|R$
(3) $P|0 = P$ ∎

These laws need little comment. Note that 0 (in the flow graph interpretation) stands for the empty flow graph.

Proposition 9: Restriction laws

(1) $P \backslash L = P$ if $\mathcal{L}(P) \cap (L \cup \overline{L}) = \emptyset$
(2) $P \backslash K \backslash L = P \backslash (K \cup L)$
(3) $P[f] \backslash L = P \backslash f^{-1}(L)[f]$
(4) $(P|Q) \backslash L = P \backslash L \mid Q \backslash L$ if $\mathcal{L}(P) \cap \overline{\mathcal{L}(Q)} \cap (L \cup \overline{L}) = \emptyset$ ∎

We make a few remarks to see why these laws hold for flow graphs. The
side-condition on (1) ensures that the labels L, and their complements,
do not appear as (outer) labels in the flow graph P, so the Restriction
$\backslash L$ is vacuous. (3) asserts that Restriction and Relabelling commute –
with a little adjustment. (4) is a kind of distributive law; it says that
Restriction distributes over (or 'can be pushed inside') Composition, as
long as the restricted labels are not possible vehicles of communication
between P and Q.

Proposition 10: Relabelling laws

(1) $P[Id] = P$
(2) $P[f] = P[f']$ if $f \restriction \mathcal{L}(P) = f' \restriction \mathcal{L}(P)$
(3) $P[f][f'] = P[f' \circ f]$
(4) $(P|Q)[f] = P[f] \mid Q[f]$ if $f \restriction (L \cup \overline{L})$ is one-to-one, where $L = \mathcal{L}(P|Q)$.   ∎

In (1), Id is the identity function. The side-condition on (2) ensures that
f and f' have like effect upon P (the notation $f \restriction D$ means the function
f restricted to domain D). In (4) the side-condition is needed to ensure
that when $[f]$ is applied to P and Q separately, it does not create more
complementary port-pairs than existed previously (f is *one-to-one* iff
$x \neq y$ implies $f(x) \neq f(y)$).

Mostly we shall deal with one-to one Relabellings; when we apply

$$[\ell_1'/\ell_1, \ldots, \ell_n'/\ell_n]$$

to P we shall normally have the names of ℓ_i' and ℓ_i all distinct, and the names of ℓ'_i distinct from those of $\mathcal{L}(P)$. Thus Proposition 10(4) will usually be applicable. Also, when the names of ℓ'_i and ℓ_i are all distinct, then it is easy to check that

$$(\ell'_1/\ell_1, \ldots, \ell'_n/\ell_n) = (\ell'_1/\ell_1) \circ \cdots \circ (\ell'_n/\ell_n)$$

(note that this is an equation between relabelling functions) so that

$$P[\ell'_1/\ell_1, \ldots, \ell'_n/\ell_n] = P[\ell'_1/\ell_1] \cdots [\ell'_n/\ell_n]$$

by Proposition 10(3). Hence it is convenient (and often sufficient) to deal with relabelling functions of the simple form ℓ'/ℓ. Here are a few easily-remembered consequences of our propositions, stated for simplicity in terms of names $a, b, \ldots$ rather than labels:

Corollary 11

(1) $P[b/a] = P$ if $a, \overline{a} \notin \mathcal{L}(P)$
(2) $P\backslash a = P[b/a]\backslash b$ if $b, \overline{b} \notin \mathcal{L}(P)$
(3) $P\backslash a[b/c] = P[b/c]\backslash a$ if $b, c \neq a$.

Proof

(1) By the side-condition, $(b/a)\restriction\mathcal{L}(P) = Id\restriction\mathcal{L}(P)$; hence

$$
\begin{aligned}
P[b/a] &= P[Id] \text{ by Proposition 10(2)} \\
&= P \text{ by Proposition 10(1)}
\end{aligned}
$$

(2) Let $f = b/a$ and $N = \{b\}$, whence $f^{-1}(N) = \{a, b\}$; then from Proposition 9(3) we get

$$
\begin{aligned}
P[b/a]\backslash b &= P\backslash\{a, b\}[b/a] \\
&= P\backslash b\backslash a[b/a] \text{ by Proposition 9(2)} \\
&= P\backslash a[b/a] \text{ by Proposition 9(1)}
\end{aligned}
$$

(since $b, \overline{b} \notin \mathcal{L}(P\backslash a)$ by the side-condition)

$$
\begin{aligned}
&= P\backslash a \text{ by Proposition 10(2), (1).}
\end{aligned}
$$

(3) Let $g = b/c$; then from the side-condition we have that $g^{-1}\{a\} = \{a\}$, so the result follows directly from Proposition 9(3). ∎

Notice Corollary 11(2) in particular; compare it with the rule of alpha conversion in the lambda-calculus, namely $\lambda x.E = \lambda y.(E\{y/x\})$ provided y is not free in the expression E. We see that in this respect (and also in others) Restriction behaves like a name-binding operation, one which declares a new name whose scope is the operand expression, and Relabelling behaves like substitution.

We now look at some useful applications of the static laws.

Example 6 (Linking is associative)   In Example 3 we defined linking by

$$P^\frown Q \stackrel{\text{def}}{=} (P[c/b] \mid Q[c/a])\backslash c$$

where c is chosen so that $c, \bar{c} \notin \mathcal{L}(P) \cup \mathcal{L}(Q)$. We wish to prove that $P^\frown(Q^\frown R) = (P^\frown Q)^\frown R$; it will be enough to reduce both sides to the same form. First, consider $(P^\frown Q)[d/b]$, where d is new:

$$
\begin{aligned}
(P^\frown Q)[d/b] &= (P[c/b] \mid Q[c/a])\backslash c[d/b] \\
&= (P[c/b] \mid Q[c/a])[d/b]\backslash c \text{ by Corollary 11(3)} \\
&= (P[c/b][d/b] \mid Q[c/a][d/b])\backslash c \text{ by Proposition 10(4)} \\
&= (P[c/b] \mid Q[c/a, d/b])\backslash c \text{ by Proposition 10(1)-(3)}
\end{aligned}
$$

Hence

$$
\begin{aligned}
(P^\frown Q)^\frown R &= ((P[c/b] \mid Q[c/a, d/b])\backslash c \mid R[d/a])\backslash d \\
&= ((P[c/b] \mid Q[c/a, d/b])\backslash c \mid R[d/a]\backslash c)\backslash d
\end{aligned}
$$

by Proposition 9(1) (since c may be chosen so that $c, \bar{c} \notin \mathcal{L}(R)$),

$$= (P[c/b] \mid Q[c/a, d/b] \mid R[d/a])\backslash\{c, d\} \text{ by Proposition 9(4), (2)}$$

But this is a symmetric form, to which $P^\frown(Q^\frown R)$ may be similarly reduced, so the proof is complete.   ∎

Exercise 14   The definition of linking allows c to be chosen arbitrarily, under a certain condition. Prove that the choice of c is indeed immaterial; that is, prove that

$$(P[c/b] \mid Q[c/a])\backslash c = (P[c'/b] \mid Q[c'/a])\backslash c'$$

provided that $c, \bar{c}, c', \bar{c'} \notin \mathcal{L}(P) \cup \mathcal{L}(Q)$.
Hint: $Q[c/a][c'/c] = Q[(c'/c) \circ (c/a)] = Q[c'/c, c'/a]$; then apply Proposition 10(2) to get $Q[c'/a]$.   ∎

Exercise 15   In the notation of Chapter 1, prove that

$(Jobber \mid Jobber \mid Hammer \mid Mallet)\backslash\{\texttt{geth}, \texttt{puth}, \texttt{getm}, \texttt{putm}\}$

$= ((Jobber \mid Jobber \mid Hammer)\backslash\{\texttt{geth}, \texttt{puth}\} \mid Mallet)\backslash\{\texttt{getm}, \texttt{putm}\}$

∎

After these exercises, you should have some feel for moving Restrictions and Relabellings past each other, and into and out of Compositions. One outcome of all this work is that we are able to choose an expression for a system – based upon the flow graph which represents it – which reflects best the way in which we wish to decompose it into subsystems.

Exercise 16   Consider the system S of Exercise 13(2), consisting of five cyclers. Write it first as a restricted Composition of five (relabelled) cyclers – i.e. as a standard concurrent form with five components. Then convert it, using the static laws, into the form

$$(C^{(4)} \mid C[f])\backslash L$$

where $C^{(4)}$ is the ring of four cyclers described in Exercise 13.   ■

4

Strong Bisimulation and Strong Equivalence

In this chapter we shall set up a notion of equivalence between agents, based intuitively upon the idea that we only wish to distinguish between two agents P and Q if the distinction can be detected by an external agent interacting with each of them. We may consider this agent to be ourselves – this is how we shall first look at the question – or we may consider it to be another agent of the calculus. For the entire chapter we shall treat τ, the internal action, exactly like any other action, and this will yield a rather strict equivalence relation which we shall call *strong equivalence*, in which we shall even distinguish between $a.\tau.0$ and $a.0$. But in Chapter 5 we shall take account of our intention that τ cannot be observed or detected by an external agent; this will yield a weaker notion which we shall call *observation equivalence*. We treat the stronger notion first because it is simpler, and because many of the equational laws which we wish to use in practice are valid even for strong equivalence. In particular, we shall see that it is a *congruence* relation; that is, it is preserved by all algebraic contexts. It is therefore our first proper notion of equality for the calculus. Strong equivalence will also be important in the synchronous calculus which we study in Chapter 9, where the silent action is indeed observable.

We begin in Section 1 by showing the need for a notion of equality stronger than that found in standard automata theory. Section 2 introduces the important idea of *strong bisimulation*, and strong equivalence is defined using this notion. We first meet the proof technique for establishing equivalence by using bisimulation, and find a slightly wider notion useful, namely strong bisimulation *up to strong equivalence*. The remainder of the chapter, Sections 3–6, is taken up with proving laws already stated in Chapter 3. The application-oriented reader can safely omit these sections at least at first reading, to allow him to reach the examples in Chapters 5 and 6 more quickly.

4.1   Experimenting upon agents

To explain our approach clearly it is best to work with an example. Consider two agents A and B, whose defining equations are as follows:

$$A \overset{\text{def}}{=} a.A_1 \qquad B \overset{\text{def}}{=} a.B_1 + a.B_1'$$
$$A_1 \overset{\text{def}}{=} b.A_2 + c.A_3 \quad B_1 \overset{\text{def}}{=} b.B_2 \qquad B_1' \overset{\text{def}}{=} c.B_3$$
$$A_2 \overset{\text{def}}{=} 0 \qquad B_2 \overset{\text{def}}{=} 0$$
$$A_3 \overset{\text{def}}{=} d.A \qquad B_3 \overset{\text{def}}{=} d.B$$

Then A and B may be thought of as finite-state automata over the alphabet *Act*, and their transition graphs are as follows:

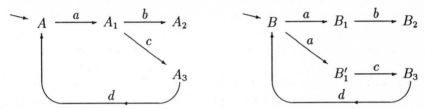

Now in standard automata theory, an automaton is interpreted as a *language*, i.e. as a set of strings over the alphabet *Act*. In this interpretation '+' stands for union of languages, '.' stands for concatenation and '0' – which would usually be written as '∧' or 'ε' – stands for the language whose only member is the empty string. Then, if we take A_2 and B_2 to be the accepting states of our two automata, we can argue as follows that A and B denote the same language:

$$\begin{aligned} A &= a.(b.0 + c.d.A) &&\text{by substitution} \\ &= a.b.0 + a.c.d.A &&\text{using the distributive law} \end{aligned}$$

(conventionally $b.0$ would be abbreviated to b, but this is irrelevant to the present argument). Hence we deduce

$$A = (a.c.d)^*.a.b.0$$

by a rule, often called Arden's rule, concerning unique solutions of equations. (S^*, for any language S, means the language gained by concatenating zero or more members of S.) Similarly

$$B = a.b.0 + a.c.d.B$$

and hence also

$$B = (a.c.d)^*.a.b.0$$

But we now argue in favour of another interpretation in which A and

B are different. According to our earlier treatment of examples, A and B are agents which may interact with their environment through the ports a, b, c, d:

We imagine an experimenter trying to interact with the agent A, or with B, through its ports; think of each port as a button which is *unlocked* if the agent can perform the associated action, and can be depressed to make it do the action, otherwise the button is *locked* and cannot be depressed.

Now at the start, only a is unlocked for each agent; we have shown this by ringing the a-port. But after the a-button is depressed a difference emerges between A and B. For A – which is deterministic – b and c will be unlocked, while for B – which is nondeterministic – sometimes only b will be unlocked and sometimes only c will be unlocked.

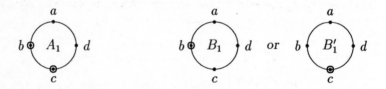

We do not know what 'determines' the outcome for B; perhaps it is the weather, and then if we try the experiment of first depressing a and then attempting to depress b under all weather conditions, on both A and B, then we shall surely distinguish A from B since the experiment will always succeed for A but will sometimes fail for B.

What allowed us, then, to deduce the equivalence of A and B according to standard automata theory? It was just one step, the use of the distributive law $a.(P+Q) = a.P + a.Q$. According to the argument of the preceding paragraph, and as already discussed in Section 3.2, this law is not faithful to the experimental idea; indeed, the idea forces us to differentiate between two very simple finite agents A' and B' whose derivation trees are

We shall even wish to distinguish between the agents A'' and B'', whose trees are

(In fact these are the derivation trees of $A'' \overset{\text{def}}{=} A'\backslash c$, $B'' \overset{\text{def}}{=} B'\backslash c$.) Here, even more clearly, we can see the reason for distinction in terms of *deadlock*; after a it is possible that B'' will be in a deadlocked state – i.e. with *all* buttons locked, while A'' will always have the button b unlocked after a.

We might conclude that two agents should be strongly equivalent iff they have identical derivation trees. But this is *too* strong, since there are cases of apparent nondeterminism which are not real. We shall want to equate the agents whose trees are as follows:

since the extra branching on the right cannot be distinguished by any conceivable experiment, if the experimenter is only able to detect which actions can occur at any stage.

4.2   Strong bisimulation

The above discussion leads us to consider an equivalence relation with the following property:

> P and Q are equivalent iff, for every action α, every α-derivative of P is equivalent to some α-derivative of Q, and conversely.

We can write this formally as follows, using $\sim$ for our equivalence relation:

$P \sim Q$ iff, for all $\alpha \in Act$,   (*)
   (i) Whenever $P \xrightarrow{\alpha} P'$ then, for some Q', $Q \xrightarrow{\alpha} Q'$ and $P' \sim Q'$
   (ii) Whenever $Q \xrightarrow{\alpha} Q'$ then, for some P', $P \xrightarrow{\alpha} P'$ and $P' \sim Q'$

We would like to adopt this as our definition of $\sim$, but unfortunately it is *not* a definition, since there are many equivalence relations $\sim$ which satisfy it! But we are presumably content to equate as many pairs of agents as possible, as long as (*) is satisfied by our equivalence relation. For example, we shall certainly expect such harmless equations as $P|Q \sim Q|P$, $P + 0 \sim P$, and a host of others. What we really want, then, is the *largest* (or *weakest*, or most generous) relation $\sim$ which satisfies the property (*). But *is* there a largest such relation?

To see that there is, we adopt an approach which may seem indirect, but which gives us much more than a positive answer to the question; it gives us a natural and powerful proof technique which will pervade our whole calculus.

Definition 1   A binary relation $\mathcal{S} \subseteq \mathcal{P} \times \mathcal{P}$ over agents is a *strong bisimulation* if $(P,Q) \in \mathcal{S}$ implies, for all $\alpha \in Act$,

   (i) Whenever $P \xrightarrow{\alpha} P'$ then, for some Q', $Q \xrightarrow{\alpha} Q'$ and $(P',Q') \in \mathcal{S}$
   (ii) Whenever $Q \xrightarrow{\alpha} Q'$ then, for some P', $P \xrightarrow{\alpha} P'$ and $(P',Q') \in \mathcal{S}$ ∎

Notice that any relation $\sim$ which satisfies (*) is a strong bisimulation. But because the condition in the definition is weaker than (*) – we have used 'implies' instead of 'iff' – there are many strong bisimulations; even the empty relation $\mathcal{S} = \emptyset$ is one!

Before developing the theory in terms of Definition 1, let us look at a simple example of a strong bisimulation. Recall the example of Section 2.2:

$$a \lhd \!\!\left(\!A\!\right)\!\!\overset{\overline{c}}{\rule{0pt}{0pt}}\!\!\rule[0.5ex]{3em}{0.4pt}\!\!\overset{c}{\rule{0pt}{0pt}}\!\!\left(\!B\!\right)\!\!\rhd \overline{b}$$

We argued there, informally in terms of derivation trees, that $(A|B)\backslash c$ behaves like an agent C_1, given by the equations

$$C_0 \overset{\text{def}}{=} \overline{b}.C_1 + a.C_2$$
$$C_1 \overset{\text{def}}{=} a.C_3$$

$$C_2 \stackrel{\text{def}}{=} \overline{b}.C_3$$
$$C_3 \stackrel{\text{def}}{=} \tau.C_0$$

Our argument was that the derivation tree of $(A|B)\backslash c$ is identical with that of C_1 – gained by unfolding the transition graph shown from the start-node C_1. Now this argument can be seen as asserting that the following relation $\mathcal{S}$, with just four member pairs, is a strong bisimulation:

$$\mathcal{S} = \{ ((A|B)\backslash c,\ C_1),$$
$$((A'|B)\backslash c,\ C_3),$$
$$((A|B')\backslash c,\ C_0),$$
$$((A'|B')\backslash c,\ C_2) \}$$

It is easy to check that this is so; one only has to check all possible derivatives of each of the eight agents – for example

As another example, recall the definition of semaphores in Chapter 1. In Section 1.4 we stated that the n-ary semaphore $Sem_n(0)$ is equivalent to a Composition of n unary semaphores,

$$\underbrace{Sem \mid Sem \mid \ldots \mid Sem}_{n \text{ times}}$$

Exercise 1   Find a bisimulation which contains the pair

$$(Sem_2(0),\ Sem|Sem)$$

thereby showing the equivalence in the case $n = 2$. Try the same for $n = 3$, i.e. find a bisimulation containing the pair

$$(Sem_3(0),\ Sem|Sem|Sem)$$ ∎

The first property which is enjoyed by the notion of strong bisimulation is that it is preserved by various operations on relations. In general, we define the *converse* $\mathcal{R}^{-1}$ of a binary relation and the *composition* $\mathcal{R}_1\mathcal{R}_2$ of two binary relations by

$$\mathcal{R}^{-1} = \{(y,x) : (x,y) \in \mathcal{R}\}$$
$$\mathcal{R}_1\mathcal{R}_2 = \{(x,z) : \text{for some } y, \ (x,y) \in \mathcal{R}_1 \text{ and } (y,z) \in \mathcal{R}_2\}$$

Proposition 1   Assume that each $\mathcal{S}_i$ $(i = 1, 2, \ldots)$ is a strong bisimulation. Then the following relations are all strong bisimulations:

(1) $Id_{\mathcal{P}}$ (3) $\mathcal{S}_1\mathcal{S}_2$
(2) $\mathcal{S}_i^{-1}$ (4) $\bigcup_{i \in I} \mathcal{S}_i$

Proof   We shall just prove (3); the others are as easy. Let us suppose that

$$(P, R) \in \mathcal{S}_1\mathcal{S}_2$$

Then for some Q we have

$$(P, Q) \in \mathcal{S}_1 \text{ and } (Q, R) \in \mathcal{S}_2$$

Now let $P \xrightarrow{\alpha} P'$. Then for some Q' we have, since $(P, Q) \in \mathcal{S}_1$,

$$Q \xrightarrow{\alpha} Q' \text{ and } (P', Q') \in \mathcal{S}_1$$

Also since $(Q, R) \in \mathcal{S}_2$ we have, for some R',

$$R \xrightarrow{\alpha} R' \text{ and } (Q', R') \in \mathcal{S}_2$$

Hence $(P', R') \in \mathcal{S}_1\mathcal{S}_2$. By similar reasoning if $R \xrightarrow{\alpha} R'$ then we can find P' such that $P \xrightarrow{\alpha} P'$ and $(P', R') \in \mathcal{S}_1\mathcal{S}_2$.   ∎

We are now ready to define strong equivalence.

Definition 2 P and Q are *strongly equivalent* or *strongly bisimilar*, written $P \sim Q$, if $(P, Q) \in \mathcal{S}$ for some strong bisimulation $\mathcal{S}$. This may be equivalently expressed as follows:

$$\sim = \bigcup\{\mathcal{S} : \mathcal{S} \text{ is a strong bisimulation}\}$$ ∎

Proposition 2

(1) $\sim$ is the largest strong bisimulation.
(2) $\sim$ is an equivalence relation.

Proof

(1) By Proposition 1(4), $\sim$ is a strong bisimulation and includes any other such.

(2) *Reflexivity*: For any P, $P \sim P$ by Proposition 1(1).
Symmetry: If $P \sim Q$, then $(P, Q) \in \mathcal{S}$ for some strong bisimulation $\mathcal{S}$. Hence $(Q, P) \in \mathcal{S}^{-1}$, and so $Q \sim P$ by Proposition 1(2).
Transitivity: If $P \sim Q$ and $Q \sim R$ then $(P, Q) \in \mathcal{S}_1$ and $(Q, R) \in \mathcal{S}_2$ for strong bisimulations $\mathcal{S}_1, \mathcal{S}_2$. So $(P, R) \in \mathcal{S}_1\mathcal{S}_2$, and so $P \sim R$ by Proposition 1(3). ∎

We still wish to verify that $\sim$ satisfies property (∗) stated at the beginning of this section. We know that half of it holds, with 'iff' replaced by 'implies', since $\sim$ is a strong bisimulation; we shall now prove the other half. We use an elementary method here; mathematical readers may prefer the method given in the last section of this chapter, in which we show that $\sim$ is the maximum fixed-point of a certain functional.

First, we define a new relation $\sim'$ in terms of $\sim$ as follows:

Definition 3 $P \sim' Q$ iff, for all $\alpha \in Act$,

(i) Whenever $P \xrightarrow{\alpha} P'$ then, for some Q', $Q \xrightarrow{\alpha} Q'$ and $P' \sim Q'$
(ii) Whenever $Q \xrightarrow{\alpha} Q'$ then, for some P', $P \xrightarrow{\alpha} P'$ and $P' \sim Q'$ ∎

Now Proposition 2(1) tells us that $\sim$ is a strong bisimulation; we then deduce from Definitions 1 and 3 that

$$P \sim Q \text{ implies } P \sim' Q \qquad\qquad \#$$

It remains to show that $P \sim' Q$ implies $P \sim Q$. The following suffices:

Lemma 3   The relation $\sim'$ is a strong bisimulation.

Proof   Let $P \sim' Q$, and let $P \xrightarrow{\alpha} P'$. It will be enough, for the lemma, to find Q' so that $Q \xrightarrow{\alpha} Q'$ and $P' \sim' Q'$. But by the definition of $\sim'$ we can indeed find Q' so that $Q \xrightarrow{\alpha} Q'$ and $P' \sim Q'$; hence also $P' \sim' Q'$ by (#), and we are done. ∎

At last, therefore, we have proved that $\sim$ satisfies property (∗):

Proposition 4 $P \sim Q$ iff, for all $\alpha \in Act$,

(i) Whenever $P \xrightarrow{\alpha} P'$ then, for some Q', $Q \xrightarrow{\alpha} Q'$ and $P' \sim Q'$
(ii) Whenever $Q \xrightarrow{\alpha} Q'$ then, for some P', $P \xrightarrow{\alpha} P'$ and $P' \sim Q'$ ∎

We conclude this section with a generalisation of the notion of strong bisimulation, which is often more useful in applications. The more general notion will be needed in the proofs of Propositions 12 and 14, and also in later chapters for applications.

Let us first see why we need a more general notion. In Exercise 1 about semaphores, you should have discovered the bisimulation

$$
\begin{aligned}
S \;=\; \{ \;&(Sem_2(0),\, Sem|Sem) \\
&(Sem_2(1),\, Sem|Sem') \\
&(Sem_2(1),\, Sem'|Sem) \\
&(Sem_2(2),\, Sem'|Sem') \;\}
\end{aligned}
$$

Now this contains what seems to be a redundancy. The second and third pairs have the same first member, and their second members are strongly equivalent (see Proposition 8(1) to follow) simply by commutativity of Composition; we feel that we should not be required to list members of a bisimulation which are identical 'up to' strong equivalence. In the above example, of course, this would save us only one pair; but in the case of $Sem_3(0)$ you can soon see that it would save four out of eight pairs, and in larger examples one can expect a proportionally greater saving.

The following definition and proposition put the idea on a firm basis. Henceforward we shall often write $P\mathcal{R}Q$ to mean $(P,Q) \in \mathcal{R}$, for any binary relation $\mathcal{R}$. Note also that $\sim S \sim$ is a composition of binary relations, so that $P \sim S \sim Q$ means that for some P' and Q' we have $P \sim P'$, $P'SQ'$ and $Q' \sim Q$.

Definition 4 S is a *strong bisimulation up to* $\sim$ if PSQ implies, for all $\alpha \in Act$,

(i) Whenever $P \xrightarrow{\alpha} P'$ then, for some Q', $Q \xrightarrow{\alpha} Q'$ and $P' \sim S \sim Q'$
(ii) Whenever $Q \xrightarrow{\alpha} Q'$ then, for some P', $P \xrightarrow{\alpha} P'$ and $P' \sim S \sim Q'$ ∎

Pictorially, clause (i) says that if PSQ and $P \xrightarrow{\alpha} P'$ then we can fill in the following diagram:

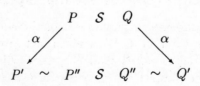

Now we shall show that, to establish $P \sim Q$, it is enough to establish that (P, Q) belongs to some strong bisimulation up to $\sim$. The crux is the following:

Lemma 5   If $\mathcal{S}$ is a strong bisimulation up to $\sim$, then $\sim\mathcal{S}\sim$ is a strong bisimulation.

Proof   Let $P \sim\mathcal{S}\sim Q$ and $P \xrightarrow{\alpha} P'$. By symmetry it will be enough to show that we can fill in the following diagram:

$$
\begin{array}{ccccc}
P & \sim & \mathcal{S} & \sim & Q \\
\alpha \big\downarrow & & & & \big\downarrow \alpha \\
P' & \sim & \mathcal{S} & \sim & Q'
\end{array}
$$

To do this, first note that, for some P_1 and Q_1, $P \sim P_1\ \mathcal{S}\ Q_1 \sim Q$. Thus we can fill in the following three diagrams in sequence, from left to right, knowing that $\mathcal{S}$ is a strong bisimulation up to $\sim$:

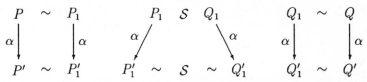

Composing these, using the transitivity of $\sim$, we easily obtain the required diagram.   ∎

It is now a short step to

Proposition 6   If $\mathcal{S}$ is a strong bisimulation up to $\sim$ then $\mathcal{S} \subseteq \sim$.

Proof   Since, by Lemma 5, $\sim\mathcal{S}\sim$ is a strong bisimulation, we have that $\sim\mathcal{S}\sim \subseteq \sim$ by definition of $\sim$. But $Id_{\mathcal{P}} \subseteq \sim$, and hence $\mathcal{S} \subseteq \sim\mathcal{S}\sim$, so we are done.   ∎

Hence, to prove $P \sim Q$, we only have to find a strong bisimulation up to $\sim$ which contains (P, Q).

4.3   Some properties of strong equivalence

We are now in a position to prove most of the equational laws which were introduced in Chapter 3. We shall in fact prove them valid when '=' is interpreted as strong equivalence; they will therefore be valid also for the weaker (larger) notion of equality introduced in the next chapter. However, Proposition 3.2 (the τ laws) is not valid for strong equivalence, but only for the weaker notion. Also, we must defer the proof of Proposition 3.4 (unique solution) until we deal with the weaker notion of equality, but Proposition 14 gives laws for recursion under strong equivalence.

Proposition 7   (implies Proposition 3.1, the monoid laws)

(1) $P + Q \sim Q + P$
(2) $P + (Q + R) \sim (P + Q) + R$
(3) $P + P \sim P$
(4) $P + 0 \sim P$

Proof   We shall only prove (2); the others are just as easy. Suppose that
$$P + (Q + R) \xrightarrow{\alpha} P'$$
Then by the semantic rules **Sum**$_j$ of Section 2.5, either $P \xrightarrow{\alpha} P'$ or $Q \xrightarrow{\alpha} P'$ or $R \xrightarrow{\alpha} P'$; in each case we easily infer by **Sum**$_j$ that $(P + Q) + R \xrightarrow{\alpha} P'$, and we know $P' \sim P'$. This establishes (i) of property (∗), and (ii) is similar.   ∎

Exercise 2   Prove at least one of the other parts of Proposition 7, by referring to the semantic rules.   ∎

Proposition 8   (implies Propositions 3.8–3.10, the static laws)

(1) $P|Q \sim Q|P$
(2) $P|(Q|R) \sim (P|Q)|R$
(3) $P|0 \sim P$
(4) $P\backslash L \sim P$ if $\mathcal{L}(P) \cap (L \cup \overline{L}) = \emptyset$
(5) $P\backslash K\backslash L \sim P\backslash(K \cup L)$
(6) $P[f]\backslash L \sim P\backslash f^{-1}(L)[f]$
(7) $(P|Q)\backslash L \sim P\backslash L \mid Q\backslash L$ if $\mathcal{L}(P) \cap \overline{\mathcal{L}(Q)} \cap (L \cup \overline{L}) = \emptyset$
(8) $P[Id] \sim P$
(9) $P[f] \sim P[f']$ if $f \upharpoonright \mathcal{L}(P) = f' \upharpoonright \mathcal{L}(P)$
(10) $P[f][f'] \sim P[f' \circ f]$
(11) $(P|Q)[f] \sim P[f] \mid Q[f]$ if $f \upharpoonright (L \cup \overline{L})$ is one-to-one, where $L = \mathcal{L}(P) \cup \mathcal{L}(Q)$

Proof   All these laws may be proved by exhibiting appropriate strong bisimulations. The hardest is (2), and we consider it first.

For (2), we need to show that $\mathcal{S}$ is a strong bisimulation, where

$$\mathcal{S} = \{(P_1|(P_2|P_3),\ (P_1|P_2)|P_3)\ :\ P_1, P_2, P_3 \in \mathcal{P}\}$$

Now suppose that $P_1|(P_2|P_3) \xrightarrow{\alpha} Q$. (This Q is nothing to do with that in the statement of the proposition.) There are three main cases, with subcases:

Case 1 $P_1 \xrightarrow{\alpha} P_1'$, and $Q \equiv P_1'|(P_2|P_3)$.
Then it is easy to show that $(P_1|P_2)|P_3 \xrightarrow{\alpha} R \equiv (P_1'|P_2)|P_3$, and clearly $(Q, R) \in \mathcal{S}$.

Case 2 $P_2|P_3 \xrightarrow{\alpha} P_{23}'$ and $Q \equiv P_1|P_{23}'$.

    Case 2.1 $P_2 \xrightarrow{\alpha} P_2'$ and $P_{23}' \equiv P_2'|P_3$.
    Then $Q \equiv P_1|(P_2'|P_3)$, and it is easy to show that $(P_1|P_2)|P_3 \xrightarrow{\alpha} R \equiv (P_1|P_2')|P_3$, and clearly $(Q, R) \in \mathcal{S}$.

    Case 2.2 $P_3 \xrightarrow{\alpha} P_3'$ and $P_{23}' \equiv P_2|P_3'$.
    Similar.

    Case 2.3 $\alpha = \tau$, $P_2 \xrightarrow{\ell} P_2'$, $P_3 \xrightarrow{\bar{\ell}} P_3'$ and $P_{23}' \equiv P_2'|P_3'$.
    Then $Q \equiv P_1|(P_2'|P_3')$, and it is easy to show that $(P_1|P_2)|P_3 \xrightarrow{\tau} R \equiv (P_1|P_2')|P_3'$, and clearly $(Q, R) \in \mathcal{S}$.

Case 3 $\alpha = \tau$, $P_1 \xrightarrow{\ell} P_1'$, $P_2|P_3 \xrightarrow{\bar{\ell}} P_{23}'$ and $Q \equiv P_1'|P_{23}'$.

    Case 3.1 $P_2 \xrightarrow{\bar{\ell}} P_2'$ and $P_{23}' \equiv P_2'|P_3$.
    Then $Q \equiv P_1'|(P_2'|P_3)$, and it is easy to show that $(P_1|P_2)|P_3 \xrightarrow{\tau} R \equiv (P_1'|P_2')|P_3$, and clearly $(Q, R) \in \mathcal{S}$.

    Case 3.2 $P_3 \xrightarrow{\bar{\ell}} P_3'$ and $P_{23}' \equiv P_2|P_3'$.
    Similar.

This proves condition (i) in Definition 1, the definition of bisimulation; condition (ii) follows by a symmetric argument, and we have then shown that $\mathcal{S}$ is a strong bisimulation.

The other parts of the proposition are handled in a similar way. For (4), we must prove that, for fixed L, the relation

$$\mathcal{S} = \{(P\backslash L, P)\ :\ P \in \mathcal{P},\ \mathcal{L}(P) \cap (L \cup \overline{L}) = \emptyset\}$$

is a strong bisimulation. Now if $(P\backslash L, P) \in \mathcal{S}$, then (by the side condition) $P \xrightarrow{\alpha} P'$ implies that $\alpha, \overline{\alpha} \notin L$; it only remains to show that $(P'\backslash L, P') \in \mathcal{S}$. But $\mathcal{L}(P') \subseteq \mathcal{L}(P)$ whenever P' is a derivative of P, by Proposition 2.2(2), so $\mathcal{L}(P') \cap (L \cup \overline{L}) = \emptyset$, and hence $(P'\backslash L, P') \in \mathcal{S}$ as required.

The remaining parts raise no significantly different issues.   ∎

Exercise 3 Prove at least one of the other parts of Proposition 8. ∎

Proposition 9 : the expansion law (implies Proposition 3.5)

Let $P \equiv (P_1[f_1] \mid \ldots \mid P_n[f_n]) \backslash L$, with $n \geq 1$. Then

$$P \ \sim \ \sum \Big\{ f_i(\alpha).(P_1[f_1] \mid \ldots \mid P_i'[f_i] \mid \ldots \mid P_n[f_n]) \backslash L \ :$$

$$P_i \xrightarrow{\alpha} P_i', f_i(\alpha) \notin L \cup \overline{L} \Big\}$$

$$+ \ \sum \Big\{ \ \tau.(P_1[f_1] \mid \ldots \mid P_i'[f_i] \mid \ldots \mid P_j'[f_j] \mid \ldots \mid P_n[f_n]) \backslash L \ :$$

$$P_i \xrightarrow{\ell_1} P_i' \ , \ P_j \xrightarrow{\ell_2} P_j' \ , \ f_i(\ell_1) = \overline{f_j(\ell_2)} \ , \ i < j \Big\}$$

Proof We shall first consider the simpler case in which there is no Relabelling or Restriction. In fact, we shall prove the following by induction on n:

If $P \equiv P_1 \mid \cdots \mid P_n$, $n \geq 1$, then   (∗)

$$P \ \sim \ \sum \{ \alpha.(P_1 \mid \cdots \mid P_i' \mid \cdots \mid P_n) \ : \ 1 \leq i \leq n, \ P_i \xrightarrow{\alpha} P_i' \}$$

$$+ \ \sum \{ \tau.(P_1 \mid \cdots \mid P_i' \mid \cdots \mid P_j' \mid \cdots \mid P_n) \ :$$

$$1 \leq i < j \leq n, \ P_i \xrightarrow{\ell} P_i', \ P_j \xrightarrow{\overline{\ell}} P_j' \}$$

For $n = 1$, we are reduced to proving $P_1 \sim \sum \{ \alpha.P_1' \ : \ P_1 \xrightarrow{\alpha} P_1' \}$, which is immediate. So assume the result for n, and consider $R \equiv P \mid P_{n+1}$. It is immediate from the semantic rules **Com₁**, **Com₂** and **Com₃** (Section 2.5) that

$$R \ \sim \ \sum \{ \alpha.(P' \mid P_{n+1}) \ : \ P \xrightarrow{\alpha} P' \}$$

$$+ \ \sum \{ \alpha.(P \mid P_{n+1}') \ : \ P_{n+1} \xrightarrow{\alpha} P_{n+1}' \}$$

$$+ \ \sum \{ \tau.(P' \mid P_{n+1}') \ : \ P \xrightarrow{\ell} P', \ P_{n+1} \xrightarrow{\overline{\ell}} P_{n+1}' \}$$

Now using the inductive assumption for $P \equiv P_1 \mid \cdots \mid P_n$, the right-hand side can be reformulated as follows (note that the first sum splits into two sums, according to whether $P \xrightarrow{\alpha} P'$ arises from an action by a single P_i or from an interaction between P_i and P_j):

$$\sum \{ \alpha.(P_1 \mid \cdots \mid P_i' \mid \cdots \mid P_n \mid P_{n+1}) \ : \ 1 \leq i \leq n, \ P_i \xrightarrow{\alpha} P_i' \}$$

$$+ \ \sum \{ \tau.(P_1 \mid \cdots \mid P_i' \mid \cdots \mid P_j' \mid \cdots \mid P_n \mid P_{n+1}) \ :$$

$$1 \leq i < j \leq n, \ P_i \xrightarrow{\ell} P_i', \ P_j \xrightarrow{\overline{\ell}} P_j' \}$$

$$+ \; \sum\{\alpha.(P_1 \mid \cdots \mid P_n \mid P'_{n+1}) \; : \; P_{n+1} \xrightarrow{\alpha} P'_{n+1}\}$$
$$+ \; \sum\{\tau.(P_1 \mid \cdots \mid P'_i \mid \cdots \mid P_n \mid P'_{n+1}) \; :$$
$$1 \le i \le n, \; P_i \xrightarrow{\ell} P'_i, \; P_{n+1} \xrightarrow{\bar{\ell}} P'_{n+1}\}$$

Now we may combine the first with the third sum, and the second with the fourth, to yield as required

$$R \;\sim\; \sum\{\alpha.(P_1 \mid \cdots \mid P'_i \mid \cdots \mid P_{n+1}) \; : \; 1 \le i \le n+1, \; P_i \xrightarrow{\alpha} P'_i\}$$
$$+ \; \sum\{\tau.(P_1 \mid \cdots \mid P'_i \mid \cdots \mid P'_j \mid \cdots \mid P_{n+1}) \; :$$
$$1 \le i < j \le n+1, \; P_i \xrightarrow{\ell} P'_i, \; P_j \xrightarrow{\bar{\ell}} P'_j\}$$

It will now be enough just to outline the steps from ($*$) to the full theorem. First we can add the Relabellings, by considering $P_i \equiv Q_i[f_i]$ in ($*$), and observing that P_i has a transition $P_i \xrightarrow{\alpha} P'_i$ iff $Q - i$ has a transition $Q_i \xrightarrow{\beta} Q'_i$ such that $\alpha = f(\beta)$ and $P'_i = Q'_i[f_i]$. Then we can add the Restriction, using the strong equivalence

$$Q \backslash L \;\sim\; \sum\{\beta.(Q' \backslash L) \; : \; Q \xrightarrow{\beta} Q', \; \beta \notin L \cup \bar{L}\}$$

where $Q \equiv Q_1[f_1] \mid \cdots \mid Q_n[f_n]$. ∎

Exercise 4   Prove the above strong equivalence for arbitrary Q. ∎

We have now proved all the laws of Chapter 3 which we intended to prove, with $\sim$ in place of $=$. However, we also wish to establish the property of $\sim$ which entitles us to call it a *congruence* relation; that is, we wish to establish that if E is any agent expression containing the variable X, and $P \sim Q$, then $E\{P/X\} \sim E\{Q/X\}$.

4.4   Strong congruence

This section is devoted to showing that strong equivalence is substitutive under all our combinators, and also under recursive definition.

Proposition 10   Let $P_1 \sim P_2$. Then

(1) $\alpha.P_1 \sim \alpha.P_2$
(2) $P_1 + Q \sim P_2 + Q$
(3) $P_1 \mid Q \sim P_2 \mid Q$
(4) $P_1 \backslash L \sim P_2 \backslash L$
(5) $P_1[f] \sim P_2[f]$

Proof   For (1), we can easily deduce conditions (i) and (ii) of Proposition 4, with $\alpha.P$ and $\alpha.Q$ in place of P and Q.

The proof of (2) is similar.

For (3), we shall show that $\mathcal{S}$ is a strong bisimulation, where

$$\mathcal{S} = \{(P_1|Q, P_2|Q) \; : \; P_1 \sim P_2\}$$

Now suppose $(P_1|Q, P_2|Q) \in \mathcal{S}$. Let $P_1|Q \xrightarrow{\alpha} R$. There are three cases:

Case 1 $P_1 \xrightarrow{\alpha} P_1'$, and $R \equiv P_1'|Q$.

Then because $P_1 \sim P_2$ we have $P_2 \xrightarrow{\alpha} P_2'$ with $P_1' \sim P_2'$; hence also $P_2|Q \xrightarrow{\alpha} P_2'|Q$, and $(P_1'|Q, P_2'|Q) \in \mathcal{S}$.

Case 2 $Q \xrightarrow{\alpha} Q'$, and $R \equiv P_1|Q'$.

Then also $P_2|Q' \xrightarrow{\alpha} P_2|Q'$ and $(P_1|Q', P_2|Q') \in \mathcal{S}$.

Case 3 $\alpha = \tau$, $P_1 \xrightarrow{\ell} P_1'$, $Q \xrightarrow{\bar{\ell}} Q'$ and $R \equiv P_1'|Q'$.

Then because $P_1 \sim P_2$, we have $P_2 \xrightarrow{\ell} P_2'$ with $P_1' \sim P_2'$; hence also $P_2|Q \xrightarrow{\tau} P_2'|Q'$, and $(P_1'|Q', P_2'|Q') \in \mathcal{S}$.

By a symmetric argument, we complete the proof that $\mathcal{S}$ is a strong bisimulation.

The proofs of (4) and (5) are similar.   ∎

Hitherto we have only defined strong equivalence over *agents* – i.e. expressions with no variables. To remedy this, we naturally extend the definition of $\sim$ as follows:

Definition 5   Let E and F contain variables $\tilde{X}$ at most. Then $E \sim F$ if, for all indexed sets $\tilde{P}$ of agents, $E\{\tilde{P}/\tilde{X}\} \sim F\{\tilde{P}/\tilde{X}\}$.

We shall also use $\tilde{E} \sim \tilde{F}$ to mean component-wise congruence between $\tilde{E}$ and $\tilde{F}$.   ∎

Exercise 5   Prove that Proposition 10 generalises to agent expressions; e.g. prove that $E_1 \sim E_2$ implies $\alpha.E_1 \sim \alpha.E_2$, where E_1 and E_2 may contain variables.   ∎

Before showing that definition by recursion preserves strong equivalence, we have to prepare the ground. Our proposition will state in a simple case that, if $A \overset{\text{def}}{=} E\{A/X\}$, $B \overset{\text{def}}{=} F\{B/X\}$ and $E \sim F$, then $A \sim B$. Before proving the proposition, let us look at why we need it. What does the above simple case of it mean? Well, if we have defined

$$A \overset{\text{def}}{=} b.0 + a.(A \mid c.0)$$

for example, then we surely demand the right to manipulate the right-hand side according to known rules of equivalence without affecting the meaning of the agent defined. In particular, we expect that the definition

$$B \stackrel{\text{def}}{=} a.(c.0 \mid B) + b.0$$

should make B equivalent to A; indeed it would be intolerable if it gave a meaning different from A. Why will our proposition ensure that $A \sim B$? Because the two definitions can be written

$$A \stackrel{\text{def}}{=} E\{A/X\} \text{ where } E \equiv b.0 + a.(X \mid c.0)$$

$$B \stackrel{\text{def}}{=} F\{B/X\} \text{ where } F \equiv a.(c.0 \mid X) + b.0$$

and our laws (namely Propositions 7, 8 and 10 with Definition 5) ensure that indeed $E \sim F$, so the proposition to follow does the rest.

First, we prove a simpler result:

Proposition 11   If $\tilde{A} \stackrel{\text{def}}{=} \tilde{P}$, then $\tilde{A} \sim \tilde{P}$.

Proof   By the rule **Con** for defining Constants (Section 2.5) we see that for each i, A_i and P_i have exactly the same derivatives, and the result follows directly.   ∎

Now we are ready to show that $\sim$ is preserved by recursive definition.

Proposition 12   Let $\tilde{E}$ and $\tilde{F}$ contain variables $\tilde{X}$ at most. Let $\tilde{A} \stackrel{\text{def}}{=} \tilde{E}\{\tilde{A}/\tilde{X}\}$, $\tilde{B} \stackrel{\text{def}}{=} \tilde{F}\{\tilde{B}/\tilde{X}\}$ and $\tilde{E} \sim \tilde{F}$. Then $\tilde{A} \sim \tilde{B}$.

Proof   We shall deal only with the case of single recursion equations, thus replacing $\tilde{E}, \tilde{F}, \tilde{A}, \tilde{B}$ by E, F, A, B. So assume

$$E \sim F$$
$$A \stackrel{\text{def}}{=} E\{A/X\}$$
$$B \stackrel{\text{def}}{=} F\{B/X\}$$

It will be enough to show that $\mathcal{S}$ is a strong bisimulation up to $\sim$, where

$$\mathcal{S} = \{(G\{A/X\}, G\{B/X\}) \; : \; G \text{ contains at most the variable } X\}$$

For then, by taking $G \equiv X$, it follows that $A \sim B$.

To show this, it will be enough to prove that

If $G\{A/X\} \stackrel{\alpha}{\rightarrow} P'$ then, for some Q' and Q'',   (∗)
   $G\{B/X\} \stackrel{\alpha}{\rightarrow} Q'' \sim Q'$, with $(P', Q') \in \mathcal{S}$

We shall prove (∗) by transition induction, on the depth of the inference by which the action $G\{A/X\} \xrightarrow{\alpha} P'$ is inferred. We argue by cases on the form of G:

Case 1 $G \equiv X$.

Then $G\{A/X\} \equiv A$, so $A \xrightarrow{\alpha} P'$, hence also $E\{A/X\} \xrightarrow{\alpha} P'$ by a shorter inference. Hence, by induction

$$E\{B/X\} \xrightarrow{\alpha} Q'' \sim Q', \text{ with } (P', Q') \in \mathcal{S}$$

But $E \sim F$, so $F\{B/X\} \xrightarrow{\alpha} Q''' \sim Q'$, and since $B \overset{\text{def}}{=} F\{B/X\}$

$$G\{B/X\} \equiv B \xrightarrow{\alpha} Q''' \sim Q' \text{ with } (P', Q') \in \mathcal{S}$$

as required.

Case 2 $G \equiv \alpha.G'$.

Then $G\{A/X\} \equiv \alpha.G'\{A/X\}$, so $P' \equiv G'\{A/X\}$; also

$$G\{B/X\} \equiv \alpha.G'\{B/X\} \xrightarrow{\alpha} G'\{B/X\}$$

and clearly $(G'\{A/X\}, G'\{B/X\}) \in \mathcal{S}$ as required.

Case 3 $G \equiv G_1 + G_2$.

This is simpler than the following case, and we omit the proof.

Case 4 $G \equiv G_1 \mid G_2$.

Then $G\{A/X\} \equiv G_1\{A/X\} \mid G_2\{A/X\}$. There are three cases for the action $G\{A/X\} \xrightarrow{\alpha} P'$, according to whether it arises from one or other component alone or from a communication. We shall treat only the case in which $\alpha = \tau$, and

$$G_1\{A/X\} \xrightarrow{\ell} P_1' \ , \ G_2\{A/X\} \xrightarrow{\bar{\ell}} P_2'$$

where $P' \equiv P_1' \mid P_2'$. Now each component action has a shorter inference, so by induction

$$G_1\{B/X\} \xrightarrow{\ell} Q_1'' \sim Q_1' \ , \text{ with } (P_1', Q_1') \in \mathcal{S}$$
$$G_2\{B/X\} \xrightarrow{\bar{\ell}} Q_2'' \sim Q_2' \ , \text{ with } (P_2', Q_2') \in \mathcal{S}$$

Hence, setting $Q' \equiv Q_1' \mid Q_2'$ and $Q'' \equiv Q_1'' \mid Q_2''$,

$$G\{B/X\} \equiv G_1\{B/X\} \mid G_2\{B/X\} \xrightarrow{\tau} Q'' \sim Q'$$

It remains to show that $(P', Q') \in \mathcal{S}$. But $(P_i', Q_i') \in \mathcal{S}$ ($i = 1, 2$) so for some H_i, $P_i' \equiv H_i\{A/X\}$ and $Q_i' \equiv H_i\{B/X\}$ ($i = 1, 2$); thus if we set $H \equiv H_1 \mid H_2$ we have

$$(P', Q') \equiv (H\{A/X\}, H\{B/X\}) \in \mathcal{S}$$

Case 5 $G \equiv G_1 \backslash L$, or $G_1[R]$.

These cases are simpler than Case 4, and we omit the proof.

Case 6 $G \equiv C$, an agent Constant with associated definition $C \stackrel{\text{def}}{=} R$.

Then, since X does not occur, $G\{A/X\}$ and $G\{B/X\}$ are identical with C and hence *both* have α-derivative P' ; clearly

$$(P', P') \equiv (P'\{A/X\}, P'\{B/X\}) \in \mathcal{S} \qquad \blacksquare$$

This proof is one of the longest that we shall meet in the book. But please bear in mind that recursion, represented by the definition of Constants, is the only feature of the calculus which gives us agents with the power to compute infinitely; more than that, it gives our calculus the full power of Turing machines or any other basis for computation, so we should expect to spend some effort in showing that it behaves properly.

We have fulfilled the aim of this section, which was to show that if any subexpression of an expression E is replaced by a strongly equivalent subexpression, then the resulting E' will be strongly equivalent to E.

Exercise 6   Complete the proof of Case 5 in Proposition 14. $\blacksquare$

4.5   Unique solution of equations

We continue this chapter with a version of Proposition 3.4, but for the strong congruence in place of the notion of equality which we shall eventually use. The main conclusion we reach is that, under a certain condition on the expression E, there is a unique P (up to $\sim$) such that

$$P \sim E\{P/X\}$$

That solution is, naturally, the agent A defined by $A \stackrel{\text{def}}{=} E\{A/X\}$.

Clearly this cannot be true for all E; in the case where E is just X, for example, *every* agent P satisfies the equation, because the equation is just $P \sim P$. But we shall see that the conclusion holds provided that X is weakly guarded in E, according to the following definition.

Definition 6 X is *weakly guarded* in E if each occurrence of X is within some subexpression $\alpha.F$ of E. $\blacksquare$

(Note that X is weakly guarded, but not guarded, in $\tau.X$.) Thus we shall be able to conclude, for example, that there is a unique P (up to $\sim$) such that $P \sim \tau.P + b.0$.

We must first prove a lemma. It states in effect that if X is weakly guarded in E, then the 'first move' of E is independent of the agent substituted for X.

Lemma 13 If the variables $\tilde{X}$ are weakly guarded in E, and $E\{\tilde{P}/\tilde{X}\} \overset{\alpha}{\to} P'$, then P' takes the form $E'\{\tilde{P}/\tilde{X}\}$ (for some expression E'), and moreover, for any $\tilde{Q}$, $E\{\tilde{Q}/\tilde{X}\} \overset{\alpha}{\to} E'\{\tilde{Q}/\tilde{X}\}$.

Proof We proceed by transition induction on the depth of the inference of $E\{\tilde{P}/\tilde{X}\} \overset{\alpha}{\to} P'$. Consider the cases for E:

Case 1 $E \equiv Y$, a variable.

Then $Y \notin \tilde{X}$, since the variables $\tilde{X}$ are weakly guarded in E. But then $Y\{\tilde{P}/\tilde{X}\} \equiv Y$ has no derivatives, so this case is impossible.

Case 2 $E \equiv \beta.F$.

Then we must have $\alpha = \beta$, and $P' \equiv F\{\tilde{P}/\tilde{X}\}$; also clearly $E\{\tilde{Q}/\tilde{X}\} \equiv \beta.F\{\tilde{Q}/\tilde{X}\} \overset{\beta}{\to} F\{\tilde{Q}/\tilde{X}\}$. The result follows by choosing E' to be F.

Case 3 $E \equiv E_1 + E_2$.

Then either $E_1\{\tilde{P}/\tilde{X}\} \overset{\alpha}{\to} P'$ or $E_2\{\tilde{P}/\tilde{X}\} \overset{\alpha}{\to} P'$ by a shorter inference; we may therefore apply the lemma in either case, and the result follows easily.

Case 4 $E \equiv E_1 | E_2$.

There are three possibilities. First, we may have $E_1\{\tilde{P}/\tilde{X}\} \overset{\alpha}{\to} P'_1$, with $P' \equiv P'_1 | (E_2\{\tilde{P}/\tilde{X}\})$; then (since the inference is shorter) we apply the lemma to show that P'_1 is of form $E'_1\{\tilde{P}/\tilde{X}\}$ and that, for any Q, $E_1\{\tilde{Q}/\tilde{X}\} \overset{\alpha}{\to} E'_1\{\tilde{Q}/\tilde{X}\}$. Hence P' is of the form $(E'_1|E_2)\{\tilde{P}/\tilde{X}\}$; also, for any Q, $E\{\tilde{Q}/\tilde{X}\} \equiv E_1\{\tilde{Q}/\tilde{X}\} \mid E_2\{\tilde{Q}/\tilde{X}\} \overset{\alpha}{\to} (E'_1|E_2)\{\tilde{Q}/\tilde{X}\}$. The result follows by choosing E' to be $E'_1|E'_2$.

The second possibility is $E_2\{P/X\} \overset{\alpha}{\to} P'_2$, with $P' \equiv E_1\{P/X\} \mid P'_2$, and this is handled similarly. The third possibility is that $\alpha = \tau$, $E_1\{P/X\} \overset{\ell}{\to} P'_1$, and $E_2\{P/X\} \overset{\bar{\ell}}{\to} P'_2$. In this case we have two shorter inferences, and we apply the lemma for both of them; the details are not hard.

Case 5 $E \equiv F[R]$ or $F\backslash L$.

These cases are handled in a similar way to Case 4.

Case 6 $E \equiv C$, an agent Constant defined by $C \overset{\text{def}}{=} R$.

Then X does not occur in E, so we have $C \overset{\alpha}{\to} P'$; the result follows easily taking E' to be P' itself.   ∎

We are now ready to prove the following, the main proposition of this section. For convenience we also restate Proposition 11 as its first part.

Proposition 14

(1) If $\tilde{A} \stackrel{\text{def}}{=} \tilde{P}$, then $\tilde{A} \sim \tilde{P}$.

(2) Let the expressions E_i ($i \in I$) contain at most the variables X_i ($i \in I$), and let each X_j ($j \in I$) be weakly guarded in each E_i. Then

$$\text{If } \tilde{P} \sim \tilde{E}\{\tilde{P}/\tilde{X}\} \text{ and } \tilde{Q} \sim \tilde{E}\{\tilde{Q}/\tilde{X}\} \text{ then } \tilde{P} \sim \tilde{Q}$$

Proof   (1) See Proposition 11.

(2) We want to prove $P_i \sim Q_i$ ($i \in I$), and this will follow (by taking $E \equiv X_i$) if we can show that

$$\mathcal{S} = \{(E\{\tilde{P}/\tilde{X}\}, E\{\tilde{Q}/\tilde{X}\}) \; : \; Vars(E) \subseteq \tilde{X}\} \cup Id_{\mathcal{P}}$$

is a strong bisimulation up to $\sim$. By symmetry it will be enough to prove that

$$\text{If } E\{\tilde{P}/\tilde{X}\} \stackrel{\alpha}{\to} P', \text{ then } E\{\tilde{Q}/\tilde{X}\} \stackrel{\alpha}{\to} Q' \text{ with } P' \sim\mathcal{S}\sim Q' \qquad (*)$$

As in Lemma 13, we argue by transition induction on the depth of the inference of $E\{\tilde{P}/\tilde{X}\} \stackrel{\alpha}{\to} P'$. Consider the cases for E:

Case 1 $E \equiv X_i$.

Then we have $E\{\tilde{P}/\tilde{X}\} \equiv P_i \stackrel{\alpha}{\to} P'$, so since $P_i \sim E_i\{\tilde{P}/\tilde{X}\}$ we have $E_i\{\tilde{P}/\tilde{X}\} \stackrel{\alpha}{\to} P'' \sim P'$. But the $\tilde{X}$ are weakly guarded in E_i, so by the lemma $P'' \equiv E'\{\tilde{P}/\tilde{X}\}$ and $E_i\{\tilde{Q}/\tilde{X}\} \stackrel{\alpha}{\to} E'\{\tilde{Q}/\tilde{X}\}$. But $E\{\tilde{Q}/\tilde{X}\} \equiv X_i\{\tilde{Q}/\tilde{X}\} \equiv Q_i \sim E_i\{\tilde{Q}/\tilde{X}\}$, so $E\{\tilde{Q}/\tilde{X}\} \stackrel{\alpha}{\to} Q' \sim E'\{\tilde{Q}/\tilde{X}\}$. Hence $P' \sim\mathcal{S}\sim Q'$.

Case 2 $E \equiv \alpha.F$.

This case is very easy.

Case 3 $E \equiv E_1 + E_2$.

Then from the assumption of $(*)$ we have $E_i\{\tilde{P}/\tilde{X}\} \stackrel{\alpha}{\to} P'$ (for $i = 1, 2$) by a shorter inference. Hence we can use $(*)$ to deduce $E_i\{\tilde{Q}/\tilde{X}\} \stackrel{\alpha}{\to} Q'$ with $P' \sim\mathcal{S}\sim Q'$, and the result follows easily.

Case 4 $E \equiv E_1|E_2$, or $F\backslash L$, or $F[R]$, or C (an agent Constant).

In all these cases the argument is quite routine, following the style of these cases in the lemma.

This concludes the proof that $\mathcal{S}$ is a strong bisimulation up to $\sim$, and the proof of the proposition.   ∎

Exercise 7   Complete the proof of Case 2, and of $E \equiv E_1 | E_2$ in Case 4 of the proposition.   ∎

4.6   Strong bisimulation as a fixed-point

In this short section we give an alternative proof that $\sim$ satisfies the property (∗) of Section 4.2. We include it for readers with more mathematical interests, since it indicates that we are dealing with a simple application of fixed-point theory; but this section is not needed for anything which follows.

Definition 7   We define the function $\mathcal{F}$, over subsets of $\mathcal{P} \times \mathcal{P}$ (i.e. binary relations over agents), as follows. If $\mathcal{R} \subseteq \mathcal{P} \times \mathcal{P}$, then $(P, Q) \in \mathcal{F}(R)$ iff for all $\alpha \in Act$:

(i) Whenever $P \xrightarrow{\alpha} P'$ then, for some Q', $Q \xrightarrow{\alpha} Q'$ and $P'\mathcal{R}Q'$

(ii) Whenever $Q \xrightarrow{\alpha} Q'$ then, for some P', $P \xrightarrow{\alpha} P'$ and $P'\mathcal{R}Q'$ ∎

Notice that $\mathcal{F}$ operates upon *any* R, but we are interested in using $\mathcal{F}$ to say more succinctly what a strong bisimulation is.

Proposition 15

(1) $\mathcal{F}$ is monotonic; that is, if $R_1 \subseteq R_2$ then $\mathcal{F}(R_1) \subseteq \mathcal{F}(R_2)$

(2) $\mathcal{S}$ is a strong bisimulation iff $\mathcal{S} \subseteq \mathcal{F}(\mathcal{S})$

Proof   (1) follows directly from Definition 7. (2) is simply a reformulation of Definition 1; note that 'implies' is reformulated as '$\subseteq$'.   ∎

We call $\mathcal{R}$ a *fixed-point* of $\mathcal{F}$ if $\mathcal{R} = \mathcal{F}(\mathcal{R})$. Similarly, we say that $\mathcal{R}$ is a *pre-fixed-point* of $\mathcal{F}$ if $\mathcal{R} \subseteq \mathcal{F}(\mathcal{R})$. So strong bisimulations are exactly the pre-fixed-points of $\mathcal{F}$, and we wish to show that $\sim$, the largest pre-fixed-point, is a fixed-point of $\mathcal{F}$. This is an instance of a general property in fixed-point theory, but for completeness we prove it here.

Proposition 16   Strong equivalence is a fixed-point of $\mathcal{F}$; that is, $\sim = \mathcal{F}(\sim)$. Moreover, it is the largest fixed-point of $\mathcal{F}$.

Proof   Since $\sim$ is a strong bisimulation, $\sim \subseteq \mathcal{F}(\sim)$. Hence, because $\mathcal{F}$ is monotonic, $\mathcal{F}(\sim) \subseteq \mathcal{F}(\mathcal{F}(\sim))$, i.e. $\mathcal{F}(\sim)$ is also a pre-fixed-point of $\mathcal{F}$. But $\sim$ is the largest pre-fixed-point of $\mathcal{F}$, hence it includes $\mathcal{F}(\sim)$, i.e. $\mathcal{F}(\sim) \subseteq \sim$. Hence $\sim = \mathcal{F}(\sim)$. Moreover $\sim$ must be the largest fixed-point of $\mathcal{F}$ since it is the largest pre-fixed-point.   ∎

Thus we have shown that $\sim$ is the largest relation satisfying property $(*)$ given at the start of Section 4.2.

5

Bisimulation and Observation Equivalence

In Section 4.2 we introduced the notion of strong bisimulation, in which every α action of one agent must be matched by an α action of the other – even for τ actions. Here we relax the requirement, only as far as τ actions are concerned; this yields a weaker notion of bisimulation. More precisely, we merely require that each τ action be matched by zero or more τ actions.

Sections 1 and 2 introduce weak bisimulation and weak (or observation) equivalence in a way which closely parallels the development in Sections 4.1 and 4.2. Section 3 briefly presents enough properties to enable applications, deferring proofs until Chapter 7. The remainder of the chapter is devoted to non-trivial examples of proof that systems satisfy their specifications. In Section 5 we specify and implement a scheduling process, and prove that the implementation is bisimilar to the specification; in Section 6 we verify the jobshop of Chapter 1. In both these systems there are many internal τ actions.

5.1 The definition of bisimulation

A few preliminary definitions are needed.

Definition 1 If $t \in Act^*$, then $\hat{t} \in \mathcal{L}^*$ is the sequence gained by deleting all occurrences of τ from t. ∎

Note, in particular, that $\widehat{\tau^n} = \varepsilon$ (the empty sequence).

Definition 2 If $t = \alpha_1 \cdots \alpha_n \in Act^*$, then we write $E \xrightarrow{t} E'$ if $E \xrightarrow{\alpha_1} \cdots \xrightarrow{\alpha_n} E'$. We shall also write $E \xrightarrow{t}$ to mean that $E \xrightarrow{t} E'$ for some E'. ∎

We now define a new labelled transition system

$$(\mathcal{E} \,,\, \mathcal{L}^* \,,\, \{\overset{s}{\Rightarrow} \,:\, s \in \mathcal{L}^*\})$$

over agent expressions, in which the transition relations $\overset{s}{\Rightarrow}$ are defined as follows. For convenience we actually define $\overset{t}{\Rightarrow}$ for all $t \in Act^*$, i.e. for sequences which may contain τ:

Definition 3   If $t = \alpha_1 \cdots \alpha_n \in Act^*$, then $E \overset{t}{\Rightarrow} E'$ if

$$E(\overset{\tau}{\rightarrow})^* \overset{\alpha_1}{\rightarrow} (\overset{\tau}{\rightarrow})^* \cdots (\overset{\tau}{\rightarrow})^* \overset{\alpha_n}{\rightarrow} (\overset{\tau}{\rightarrow})^* E'$$

We shall also write $E \overset{t}{\Rightarrow}$ to mean that $E \overset{t}{\Rightarrow} E'$ for some E'.   ∎

Thus $E \overset{ab}{\Rightarrow} E'$ means that $E \overset{\tau^p}{\rightarrow}\overset{a}{\rightarrow}\overset{\tau^q}{\rightarrow}\overset{b}{\rightarrow}\overset{\tau^r}{\rightarrow} E'$ for some $p, q, r \geq 0$. Note also that $E \overset{\varepsilon}{\Rightarrow} E'$ iff $E \overset{\tau^n}{\rightarrow} E'$ for some $n \geq 0$.

We now introduce a notion analogous to derivative.

Definition 4   If $t \in Act^*$, then E' is a *t-descendant* of E iff $E \overset{\hat{t}}{\Rightarrow} E'$.∎

Note that if $t \in \mathcal{L}^*$ this just means $E \overset{t}{\Rightarrow} E'$, since $t = \hat{t}$ in this case. But notice that E' is a τ-descendant of E iff $E \overset{\tau^n}{\rightarrow} E'$ for some $n \geq 0$, and this includes the case $n = 0$ in which $E' \equiv E$.

At this point, let us summarise the difference between the three relations $\overset{t}{\rightarrow}$, $\overset{t}{\Rightarrow}$ and $\overset{\hat{t}}{\Rightarrow}$, for $t \in Act^*$. Each specifies an action-sequence with exactly the same observable content as t, but the possibilities for intervening τ actions are different:

$\overset{t}{\rightarrow}$ specifies *exactly* the τ actions occurring in t;

$\overset{t}{\Rightarrow}$ specifies *at least* the τ actions occurring in t;

$\overset{\hat{t}}{\Rightarrow}$ specifies nothing about τ actions.

Thus $P \overset{t}{\rightarrow} P'$ implies $P \overset{t}{\Rightarrow} P'$, and $P \overset{t}{\Rightarrow} P'$ implies $P \overset{\hat{t}}{\Rightarrow} P'$.

So, bearing in mind what we said about matching a τ action by *zero or more* τ actions, we want a notion of equivalence – which we shall call *observation equivalence* – with the following property:

> P and Q are observation-equivalent iff, for every action α, every α-derivative of P is observation-equivalent to some α-descendant of Q, and similarly with P and Q interchanged.

By analogy with our treatment of strong equivalence, we write this formally as follows using '$\approx$' to stand for observation equivalence:

$P \approx Q$ iff, for all $\alpha \in Act$,   (*)

(i) Whenever $P \xrightarrow{\alpha} P'$ then, for some Q', $Q \xRightarrow{\hat{\alpha}} Q'$ and $P' \approx Q'$

(ii) Whenever $Q \xrightarrow{\alpha} Q'$ then, for some P', $P \xRightarrow{\hat{\alpha}} P'$ and $P' \approx Q'$

As before, we want the *largest* relation with this property; so we proceed via an analogous definition:

Definition 5   A binary relation $S \subseteq \mathcal{P} \times \mathcal{P}$ over agents is a (*weak*) *bisimulation* if $(P, Q) \in S$ implies, for all $\alpha \in Act$,

(i) Whenever $P \xrightarrow{\alpha} P'$ then, for some Q', $Q \xRightarrow{\hat{\alpha}} Q'$ and $(P', Q') \in S$

(ii) Whenever $Q \xrightarrow{\alpha} Q'$ then, for some P', $P \xRightarrow{\hat{\alpha}} P'$ and $(P', Q') \in S$ ■

Example 1   In Section 2.2 we discussed two agents C_0 and D, which are represented by the following transition graphs:

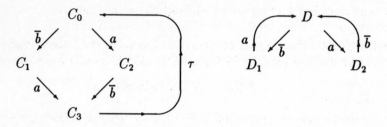

One can easily check that

$$S = \{(C_0, D), (C_1, D_1), (C_2, D_2), (C_3, D)\}$$

is a bisimulation, though there can be no *strong* bisimulation containing the pair (C_3, D). Note particularly that since $(C_3, D) \in S$, and $C_3 \xrightarrow{\tau} C_0$, we have to find D' such that $D \xRightarrow{\hat{\tau}} D'$ and $(C_0, D') \in S$. But $\hat{\tau} = \varepsilon$, so we can take D' to be D itself. If we had used $\xRightarrow{\alpha}$ instead of $\xRightarrow{\hat{\alpha}}$ in defining bisimulation (Definition 5) then there would be no bisimulation containing (C_0, D), since it would have also to contain the pair (C_3, D), so we would have to find D' such that $D \xRightarrow{\tau} D'$, and this is impossible.■

Example 2   If $P \equiv a.0 + b.0$ and $Q \equiv a.0 + \tau.b.0$, then (P, Q) cannot be in *any* bisimulation, assuming that $a \neq b$. For if $(P, Q) \in S$ (S a bisimulation) then, since $Q \xrightarrow{\tau} b.0$, we would require $(P', b.0) \in S$ for some P' such that $P \xRightarrow{\varepsilon} P'$. But the only such P' is P itself, and clearly $(P, b.0)$ can be in no bisimulation, since $P \xrightarrow{a} 0$, while $b.0$ has no a-descendant.   ■

Example 3 Consider the agents defined as follows:

$$A_0 \stackrel{\mathrm{def}}{=} a.A_0 + b.A_1 + \tau.A_1$$
$$A_1 \stackrel{\mathrm{def}}{=} a.A_1 + \tau.A_2 \qquad\qquad B_1 \stackrel{\mathrm{def}}{=} a.B_1 + \tau.B_2$$
$$A_2 \stackrel{\mathrm{def}}{=} b.A_0 \qquad\qquad\qquad\; B_2 \stackrel{\mathrm{def}}{=} b.B_1$$

Then it can be shown that the following is a bisimulation:

$$\mathcal{S} = \{\ (A_0, B_1)\ ,\ (A_1, B_1)\ ,\ (A_2, B_2)\ \}$$

In particular, consider the action $A_0 \stackrel{b}{\to} A_1$; we must find a b-descendant of B_1 to match it, and this descendant must be again B_1 since the only 'mate' for A_1 in $\mathcal{S}$ is B_1. And indeed you can check that $B_1 \stackrel{b}{\Rightarrow} B_1$. ∎

Exercise 1 Draw the transition graphs for A_0 and B_1, and prove in detail that $\mathcal{S}$ is a bisimulation. ∎

We can now define observation equivalence, or bisimilarity:

Definition 6 P and Q are *observation-equivalent* or (*weakly*) *bisimilar*, written $P \approx Q$, if $(P, Q) \in \mathcal{S}$ for some (weak) bisimulation $\mathcal{S}$. That is,

$$\approx\ =\ \bigcup\{\mathcal{S}\ :\ \mathcal{S} \text{ is a bisimulation}\} \qquad\qquad ∎$$

In the next section we prove a few simple properties of $\approx$, analogous with similar properties of $\sim$. In Section 3 we then state without proof some further properties; their proofs will be dealt with in Chapter 7. This order of presentation allows us to devote most of the present chapter to some non-trivial examples of bisimulation; in this way we hope to motivate the theoretical development of Chapter 7.

5.2 Basic properties of bisimilarity

Throughout this section we proceed by analogy with the treatment of strong equivalence of Section 4.2; we even match the numbering of propositions in that section. The analogy saves us from exhibiting proofs, except for one or two details of difference.

Proposition 1 Assume that each $\mathcal{S}_i$ ($i = 1, 2, \ldots$) is a bisimulation. Then the following are all bisimulations:

(1) $Id_{\mathcal{P}}$ (3) $\mathcal{S}_1 \mathcal{S}_2$

(2) $\mathcal{S}_i^{-1}$ (4) $\bigcup_{i \in I} \mathcal{S}_i$

Proof   Similar to Proposition 4.1; in (3), we also need the auxiliary result that if $(Q, R) \in \mathcal{S}_i$ and $Q \stackrel{\hat{a}}{\Rightarrow} Q'$ then, for some R', $R \stackrel{\hat{a}}{\Rightarrow} R'$ and $(Q', R') \in \mathcal{S}_i$. This is straightforward. ∎

Proposition 2

(1) $\approx$ is the largest bisimulation.

(2) $\approx$ is an equivalence relation.

Proof   Based on Proposition 1, just as Proposition 4.2 is based on Proposition 4.1. ∎

We continue the analogy by showing that $\approx$ satisfies property (∗) of the previous section.

First, we define a new relation $\approx'$ in terms of $\approx$ as follows:

Definition 7 $P \approx' Q$ iff, for all $\alpha \in Act$,

(i) Whenever $P \stackrel{\alpha}{\to} P'$ then, for some Q', $Q \stackrel{\hat{\alpha}}{\Rightarrow} Q'$ and $P' \approx Q'$

(ii) Whenever $Q \stackrel{\alpha}{\to} Q'$ then, for some P', $P \stackrel{\hat{\alpha}}{\Rightarrow} P'$ and $P' \approx Q'$ ∎

Now Proposition 2(1) tells us that $\approx$ is a bisimulation; we then deduce from Definitions 5 and 7 that $P \approx Q$ implies $P \approx' Q$, so it remains to show that $P \approx' Q$ implies $P \approx Q$. For this, the following suffices:

Lemma 3   The relation $\approx'$ is a weak bisimulation.

Proof   Analogous to Lemma 4.3. ∎

Now, therefore, we have proved that $\approx$ satisfies property (∗):

Proposition 4 $P \approx Q$ iff, for all $\alpha \in Act$,

(i) Whenever $P \stackrel{\alpha}{\to} P'$ then, for some Q', $Q \stackrel{\hat{\alpha}}{\Rightarrow} Q'$ and $P' \approx Q'$

(ii) Whenever $Q \stackrel{\alpha}{\to} Q'$ then, for some P', $P \stackrel{\hat{\alpha}}{\Rightarrow} P'$ and $P' \approx Q'$ ∎

Thus we have shown that $\approx$ is the largest relation satisfying property (∗) in the previous section.

We conclude our analogy by introducing the notion of bisimulation up to $\approx$. This is even more important than *strong* bisimulation up to $\sim$. In realistic systems we find many states which are bisimilar but not identical, due to the presence of τ actions; it would be tedious if we could not *treat* them as identical when we exhibit weak bisimulations.

Definition 8 S is a (*weak*) *bisimulation up to* $\approx$ if PSQ implies, for all α,

(i) Whenever $P \xrightarrow{\alpha} P'$ then, for some Q', $Q \xRightarrow{\hat{\alpha}} Q'$ and $P' \approx S \approx Q'$

(ii) Whenever $Q \xrightarrow{\alpha} Q'$ then, for some P', $P \xRightarrow{\hat{\alpha}} P'$ and $P' \approx S \approx Q'$ ∎

Now we shall show that, to establish $P \approx Q$, it is enough to establish that (P, Q) belongs to some bisimulation up to $\approx$. The crux is the following:

Lemma 5   If S is a bisimulation up to $\approx$, then $\approx S \approx$ is a bisimulation.

Proof   Analogous to Lemma 4.5.   ∎

It is now a short step to:

Proposition 6   If S is a bisimulation up to $\approx$ then $S \subseteq \approx$.

Proof   Since, by Lemma 5, $\approx S \approx$ is a bisimulation, we have that $\approx S \approx \subseteq \approx$ by definition of $\approx$. But $S \subseteq \approx S \approx$, so we are done.   ∎

Hence, to prove $P \approx Q$, we only have to find a bisimulation up to $\approx$ which contains (P, Q).

Thus we can see that, as far as elementary properties are concerned, $\approx$ and $\sim$ behave in a very similar way.

Exercise 2   Complete the proof of Proposition 1(3), taking care with the auxiliary result needed. This is the one place at which the six propositions of this section need rather more care than Props 4.1–4.6; it is Proposition 1(3) which ensures that $\approx$ is transitive (see Proposition 2(2)), so the care is rewarded!   ∎

5.3   Further properties of bisimilarity

We now turn to further properties of $\approx$. We start with the property which distinguishes $\approx$ from $\sim$ most sharply.

Proposition 7 $P \approx \tau.P$

Proof   Since we have shown that $\approx$ and $\approx'$ are identical, we shall prove $P \approx' \tau.P$. First, consider any action $P \xrightarrow{\alpha} P'$ of P; clearly

$\tau.P \xrightarrow{\tau} P \xrightarrow{\alpha} P'$, so $\tau.P \overset{\widehat{\alpha}}{\Rightarrow} P'$, and we know that $P' \approx P'$. On the other hand consider the only action $\tau.P \xrightarrow{\tau} P$ of $\tau.P$; it is clearly matched by the null action $P \overset{\varepsilon}{\Rightarrow} P$ of P, since $\widehat{\tau} = \varepsilon$. So $P \approx' \tau.P$ and hence $P \approx \tau.P$. ∎

This is perhaps the source of all the power (and the subtlety!) of bisimilarity. It allows τ to be ignored – to some extent – in investigating bisimilarity.

On the other hand, we can see that (unlike $\sim$) $\approx$ is not preserved by Summation; and this is due to the pre-emptive power of τ which was pointed out in Section 2.3. For we have $b.0 \approx \tau.b.0$ by Proposition 7, but from Example 2 we see that

$$a.0 + b.0 \not\approx a.0 + \tau.b.0$$

Thus $\approx$ is *not* the notion of equality $=$ which we promised in Chapter 3. The definition of $=$ will be given in Chapter 7; here we state a few properties which show that $\approx$ and $=$ are very close, leaving the proofs until Chapter 7.

Proposition 8 $P \sim Q$ implies $P = Q$, and $P = Q$ implies $P \approx Q$. ∎

Thus all our equational laws for $\sim$ and $=$ hold also for bisimilarity, though the converse is not true; from Proposition 7 we have $P \approx \tau.P$ but we know that in general $P \neq \tau.P$.

The next two propositions show how equality may be deduced from bisimilarity; they are crucial in applications.

Definition 9 P is *stable* if P has no τ-derivative. ∎

Proposition 9   If $P \approx Q$ and both are stable, then $P = Q$. ∎

Thus it appears that the difference between $\approx$ and $=$ is only a matter of the initial actions of agents. The next result underlines this:

Proposition 10   If $P \approx Q$ then $\alpha.P = \alpha.Q$. ∎

This implies that bisimilarity is preserved – even strengthened – by the Prefix combinator. It is also preserved by every other combinator, except Summation:

Proposition 11   The static combinators preserve bisimilarity; that is, if $P \approx Q$ then $P|R \approx Q|R$, $P\backslash L \approx Q\backslash L$ and $P[f] \approx Q[f]$.   ∎

It is important to realise that this only holds because the silent τ action can neither be restricted nor relabelled.

Exercise 3   Let P be $\sum_{i \in I} \alpha_i.P_i$ and Q be $\sum_{i \in I} \alpha_i.Q_i$. Show that if $P_i \approx Q_i$ for all $i \in I$, then $P \approx Q$. With Props 10 and 11, this shows that $\approx$ is a congruence if we limit the use of Summation to *guarded sums*, like P and Q here. In fact, in applications we hardly ever use Summation in any other way.   ∎

We now have all the properties we need to explore some applications. We shall see that the big strength of observation equivalence, or bisimilarity, lies in the convenient proof technique which we have for establishing $P \approx Q$; namely, we only have to exhibit a bisimulation $\mathcal{S}$ which contains the pair (P, Q). We did this in Example 1. Often $\mathcal{S}$ can be described quite simply; in Example 1 it was actually small and finite.

Exercise 4   Prove $P \approx \tau.P$ by finding a bisimulation containing the pair $(P, \tau.P)$. What is the smallest bisimulation which contains *all* such pairs?   ∎

5.4   Specifying a simple scheduler

Suppose that a set of agents P_i, $1 \leq i \leq n$, is to be scheduled in performing a certain task. More precisely, each agent P_i wishes to perform the task repeatedly, and a scheduler is required to ensure that they begin the task in cyclic order starting with P_1. The different task-performances need not exclude each other in time – for example P_2 can begin before P_1 finishes – but the scheduler is required to ensure that each agent finishes one performance before it begins another.

We suppose that P_i requests task initiation by $\overline{a_i}$, and signals completion by $\overline{b_i}$, assuming that the names a_i and b_i are all distinct. Thus our scheduler has sort $\tilde{a} \cup \tilde{b}$, where $\tilde{a} = \{a_1, \ldots, a_n\}$ and $\tilde{b} = \{b_1, \ldots, b_n\}$, and the informal specification of the scheduler is

(1) It must perform $a_1, \ldots, a_n$ cyclically, starting with a_1.

(2) It must perform a_i and b_i alternately, for each i.

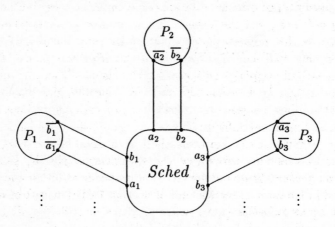

However, a scheduler which imposes a fixed sequence – say $a_1 b_1 a_2 b_2 \cdots$ – is not good enough; the scheduler must allow *any* sequence of initiations and completions compatible with the conditions (1) and (2) above.

It is worth reflecting a moment upon the vagueness of the last sentence! We can soon see that it has various interpretations. For example, we may naturally expect that *Sched* has the following partial derivation tree:

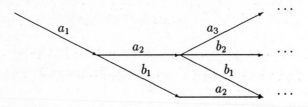

which (suitably developed) will contain all admissible action sequences. But then consider also the following tree:

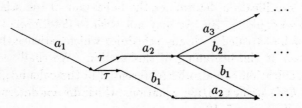

– exactly like the first but with τ actions inserted in some places. This tree still contains all admissible sequences. However, the upper of the τ actions shown represents an autonomous commitment by the scheduler to do a_2 *before* b_1, and the lower τ action represents the opposite commitment. Such a nondeterministic scheduler runs the risk of causing deadlock; this will occur for example if the scheduler makes the first commitment (the upper τ action) while the agents P_1 and P_2 agree between them that P_2 will delay its start $(\overline{a_2})$ until P_1 has finished $(\overline{b_1})$! (Our system does not preclude these inter-process negotiations.)

Thus we find a real difficulty in specifying our scheduler using natural language. In this case, however, there is a good alternative, which is to use the calculus to express the specification (in the same way that *Strongjobber | Strongjobber* served as a specification for the system described in Chapter 1; see the end of Section 1.4). Let us consider the abstract agent $Schedspec(i, X)$, where $1 \leq i \leq n$ and $X \subseteq \{1, \cdots, n\}$, standing for the scheduler in the state when

(1) It is P_i's turn to initiate next;
(2) The agents $\{P_j : j \in X\}$ are currently performing the task.

In this state, clearly any P_j $(j \in X)$ may terminate; also P_i may initiate provided that $i \notin X$. Thus our specification is that the scheduler should be equal to the abstract agent $Schedspec(1, \emptyset)$, defined as follows (where we adopt the convention that $i + 1, i - 1$ etc. are calculated modulo n):

$$(i \in X) \qquad Schedspec(i, X) \;\overset{\text{def}}{=}\; \sum_{j \in X} b_j.Schedspec(i, X - \{j\})$$

$$(i \notin X) \qquad Schedspec(i, X) \;\overset{\text{def}}{=}\; a_i.Schedspec(i + 1, X \cup \{i\})$$
$$+ \sum_{j \in X} b_j.Schedspec(i, X - \{j\})$$

We have dwelt a little upon this specification question, because specifications are of so many varieties. We have chosen one here which can well be expressed as an equation in our calculus, i.e. $Sched = Schedspec(1, \emptyset)$, where $Sched$ is the (concrete) scheduler which we wish to build. This specification determines the behaviour of the scheduler *completely*, up to equality. But we may not wish to determine it completely; we may be satisfied with any scheduler which satisfies the two conditions stated at the beginning of this section. We shall see that this weaker specification can also be represented in the calculus, by requiring that $Sched$ satisfies certain equations which do *not* determine it completely; see Exercises 7–10.

5.5   Implementing the scheduler

We choose to build our scheduler, *Sched*, as a ring of n cells each linked
to one of the agents P_i:

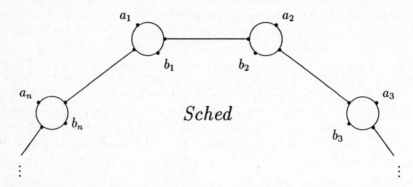

This has the advantage of distributing the scheduling computation, and
if we make the cells identical and independent of n then schedulers of
different size n can be built from the same 'kit'.

Let a, b, c, d be distinct names. As a first attempt at the scheduler
we may choose a cycler cell

$$A \overset{\text{def}}{=} a.c.b.d.A$$

which fires its ports in clockwise order. If (as here) we ring any port
which can fire immediately, then the initial state of the scheduler will
be as follows:

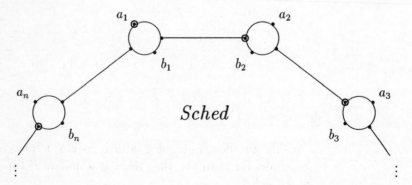

where each cell but the first is waiting to be fired by its left neighbour. This appears to work; after a_1 and a_2 for example we have

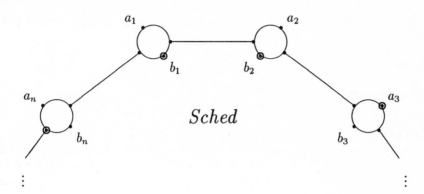

showing that P_3 may initiate, and either P_1 or P_2 may terminate. But it doesn't quite work; if you draw the state, in similar fashion, after $P_1, \cdots, P_n$ have all initiated but none has terminated you will find that P_n cannot terminate before P_1 has terminated – and this violates our specification since $Schedspec(1, \{1, \cdots, n\})$ allows any b_i, even b_n, as the next action! This small bug is typical of the faulty design of concurrent systems. It may take a long time to detect this bug in use, since the phenomenon in which it is P_1's turn, but P_1 has not terminated, may perhaps occur only rarely – and even then a deadlock would only occur if P_n and P_1 had agreed, via some other communication, that P_n should terminate first.

Exercise 5   What slight modification to *Schedspec* would yield a specification satisfied by this scheduler? You cannot expect to be certain of the answer, but make an intelligent guess.   ∎

To recover from this mistake, let us try modifying the cell so that b and d can occur in either order:

$$A \overset{\text{def}}{=} a.c.(b.d.A + d.b.A)$$

or, for convenience of reference:

$$A = a.C, \quad C = c.E, \quad E = b.D + d.B, \quad B = b.A, \quad D = d.A$$

Now let us define the relabelling functions $f_i = (a_i/a, b_i/b, c_i/c, \overline{c_{i-1}}/d)$, and set $A_i = A[f_i]$, $C_i = C[f_i]$ etc:

Then our scheduler is given by

$$Sched \stackrel{\text{def}}{=} (A_1 \mid D_2 \mid \cdots \mid D_n)\backslash \tilde{c}$$

We shall often use the notation $\Pi_{i \in I} P_i$ for the Composition of all the agents P_i, $i \in I$, so we can rewrite the scheduler as

$$Sched = (A_1 \mid \Pi_{j \neq 1} D_j)\backslash \tilde{c}$$

which we note is stable, since no component can perform c_i for any i.

We now conjecture the following significance of states of the ith cell:

A_i	means	P_i's turn and P_i ready to initiate
B_i	means	P_i's turn and P_i not ready to initiate
D_i	means	not P_i's turn and P_i ready to initiate
E_i	means	not P_i's turn and P_i not ready to initiate

If this is correct, then we should be able to show that, under the following definition, the system states $Sched(i, X)$, for each i and each $X \subseteq \{1, \cdots, n\}$, are in bisimulation with $Schedspec(i, X)$:

$$Sched(i, X) \stackrel{\text{def}}{=} \begin{cases} (B_i \mid \Pi_{j \notin X} D_j \mid \Pi_{j \in X - \{i\}} E_j)\backslash \tilde{c} & \text{if } i \in X \\ (A_i \mid \Pi_{j \notin X \cup \{i\}} D_j \mid \Pi_{j \in X} E_j)\backslash \tilde{c} & \text{if } i \notin X \end{cases}$$

More exactly, we shall show that the relation

$$\mathcal{S} = \{(Sched(i, X), Schedspec(i, X)) : 1 \leq i \leq n, \ X \subseteq \{1, \cdots, n\}\}$$

is a bisimulation up to $\approx$. Note that our initial state $Sched$ defined above is just $Sched(1, \emptyset)$, so it will follow that

$$Sched \ \approx \ Schedspec(1, \emptyset)$$

and equality follows from Proposition 9 since both are stable. Note also that the states $Sched(i, X)$ are *all* stable; the absence of any component C_j shows that no component can perform the action c_j, so no internal communication is possible in these states.

The proof of bisimulation is mainly a matter of careful case analysis, and one has to keep track – using the Π notation – of the states of the several components. In a single action of $Sched(i, X)$ only one component changes state, since the agent is stable; but there are two key points in the proof where the derivative of a visible action is unstable.

We therefore begin with a lemma which shows that the small subsystem which is in each case responsible for this instability – two neighbouring cells – is actually equivalent to a stable subsystem.

Lemma

(1) $(C_i|D_{i+1})\backslash c_i \approx (E_i|A_{i+1})\backslash c_i$
(2) $(C_i|E_{i+1})\backslash c_i \approx (E_i|B_{i+1})\backslash c_i$

Proof   (1) By expansion we easily get $(C_i|D_{i+1})\backslash c_i = \tau.(E_i|A_{i+1})\backslash c_i$, and Proposition 7 does the rest. (2) By expansion:

$$
\begin{aligned}
(C_i|E_{i+1})\backslash c_i &= b_{i+1}.(C_i|D_{i+1})\backslash c_i + \tau.(E_i|B_{i+1})\backslash c_i \\
&= b_{i+1}.(E_i|A_{i+1})\backslash c_i + \tau.(b_{i+1}.(E_i|A_{i+1})\backslash c_i + \cdots)
\end{aligned}
$$

by (1), using also Proposition 10 and partial expansion;

$$
= \tau.(E_i|B_{i+1})\backslash c_i
$$

since $P + \tau.(P + Q) = \tau.(P + Q)$ (Corollary 3.3);

$$
\approx (E_i|B_{i+1})\backslash c_i
$$

by Proposition 7.   ∎

When we use this lemma in the proof to follow, Proposition 11 is crucial: it is essential to know that substituting an equivalent subsystem yields an equivalent system, just because the static combinators preserve equivalence.

We now embark upon the main proof, that $\mathcal{S}$ is a bisimulation. Consider then the derivatives of $Sched(i, X)$.

Case $i \in X$:   First, we have

$$
\begin{aligned}
Sched(i, X) &\xrightarrow{b_i} (A_i \mid \Pi_{j\notin X}D_j \mid \Pi_{j\in X-\{i\}}E_j)\backslash\tilde{c} \\
&= Sched(i, X - \{i\})
\end{aligned}
$$

and to match this we have as required

$$
Schedspec(i, X) \xrightarrow{b_i} Schedspec(i, X - \{i\})
$$

Second, for each $k \in X - \{i\}$ we have

$$
\begin{aligned}
Sched(i, X) &\xrightarrow{b_k} (B_i \mid \Pi_{j\notin X}D_j \mid D_k \mid \Pi_{j\in X-\{i,k\}}E_j)\backslash\tilde{c} \\
&= (B_i \mid \Pi_{j\notin X-\{k\}}D_j \mid \Pi_{j\in X-\{i,k\}}E_j)\backslash\tilde{c} \\
&= Sched(i, X - \{k\})
\end{aligned}
$$

and to match this we have also

$$Schedspec(i, X) \xrightarrow{b_k} Schedspec(i, X - \{k\})$$

These are all the derivatives of $Sched\,(i, X)$, and in matching them we have also matched all the derivatives of $Schedspec\,(i, X)$.

Case $i \notin X$: First, we have for each $k \in X$

$$
\begin{aligned}
Sched(i, X) &\xrightarrow{b_k} (A_i \mid \Pi_{j \notin X \cup \{i\}} D_j \mid D_k \mid \Pi_{j \in X - \{k\}} E_j) \backslash \tilde{c} \\
&= (A_i \mid \Pi_{j \notin (X - \{k\}) \cup \{i\}} D_j \mid \Pi_{j \in X - \{k\}} E_j) \backslash \tilde{c} \\
&= Sched(i, X - \{k\})
\end{aligned}
$$

and to match this we have as before

$$Schedspec(i, X) \xrightarrow{b_k} Schedspec(i, X - \{k\})$$

thus matching up all the b_k derivatives of both agents. Second, we have

$$Sched(i, X) \xrightarrow{a_i} (C_i \mid \Pi_{j \notin X \cup \{i\}} D_j \mid \Pi_{j \in X} E_j) \backslash \tilde{c}$$

and we distinguish two subcases:

Subcase $i + 1 \in X$: then the a_i-derivative

$$= ((C_i | E_{i+1}) \backslash c_i \mid \Pi_{j \notin X \cup \{i\}} D_j \mid \Pi_{j \in X - \{i+1\}} E_j) \backslash \tilde{c}$$

by moving $\backslash c_i$ inwards, using the static laws Proposition 3.9;

$$\approx ((E_i | B_{i+1}) \backslash c_i \mid - - -- \mid - - --) \backslash \tilde{c}$$

by the lemma, and by Proposition 11;

$$= (B_{i+1} \mid \Pi_{j \notin X \cup \{i\}} D_j \mid \Pi_{j \in X \cup \{i\} - \{i+1\}} E_j) \backslash \tilde{c}$$

by the static laws again;

$$= Sched(i + 1, X \cup \{i\}) \quad (\text{recalling } i + 1 \in X)$$

and this is matched (up to $\approx$) by

$$Schedspec(i, X) \xrightarrow{a_i} Schedspec(i + 1, X \cup \{i\})$$

Subcase $i + 1 \notin X$: then the a_i-derivative

$$= ((C_i | D_{i+1}) \backslash c_i \mid \Pi_{j \notin X \cup \{i, i+1\}} D_j \mid \Pi_{j \in X} E_j) \backslash \tilde{c}$$

by moving $\backslash c_i$ inwards as before;

$$\approx ((E_i | A_{i+1}) \backslash c_i \mid - - -- \mid - - --) \backslash \tilde{c}$$

by the lemma and Proposition 11;

$$= (A_{i+1} \mid \Pi_{j \notin X \cup \{i\} \cup \{i+1\}} D_j \mid \Pi_{j \in X \cup \{i\}} E_j) \backslash \tilde{c}$$

by the static laws again;

$$= Sched(i + 1, X \cup \{i\}) \quad (\text{recalling } i + 1 \notin X)$$

which again is matched (up to $\approx$) by

$$Schedspec(i, X) \xrightarrow{a_i} Schedspec(i + 1, X \cup \{i\})$$

Thus we have shown $\mathcal{S}$ to be a bisimulation up to $\approx$ as required.   ∎

An important detail of the above proof is that we could only prove bisimulation *up to* $\approx$; this was because the a_i derivative of $Sched(i, X)$ in the case $i \notin X$ is unstable, and the lemma was needed to show it bisimilar to the a_i derivative of $Schedspec(i, X)$.

It is also interesting to note that there is an alternative proof, in which we prove $Sched(i, X) = Schedspec(i, X)$ by proving that the agents $Sched(i, X)$ satisfy the defining equations of $Schedspec(i, X)$. This proof proceeds by applying the expansion law to $Sched(i, X)$; but, since the expansion law is just a way of exhibiting all the derivatives of an agent, the details are really much the same as in the given proof.

Exercise 6   Write out the details of this alternative proof.   ∎

Let us now consider the looser specification of a scheduler, i.e. the requirement that the scheduler satisfies the two conditions:

(1) The actions $a_i, \ldots, a_n$ are performed cyclically, starting with a_1;
(2) For each i, the actions a_i and b_i are performed alternately.

Thus a scheduler should satisfy the specification if, for example, it can perform the sequence $a_1 b_1 a_2 b_2 \cdots$ and no other.

To formulate this specification, we need two definitions.

Definition 10   Let $s = \alpha_1 \cdots \alpha_{\!,} \in Act^*$. Then $Ever(s)$ is the agent defined by

$$Ever(s) = \alpha_1. \cdots . \alpha_n . Ever(s)$$

That is, $Ever(s)$ performs the sequence s for ever.   ∎

Next, we need the idea of *Hiding* a set L of visible actions; by this we mean replacing each $\ell \in L$ by τ. This can be achieved by supplying an agent which is always ready to complement ℓ by $\bar{\ell}$, so we arrive at the following:

Definition 11 The combinator $/L$, called *Hiding*, is defined by

$$P/L \stackrel{\text{def}}{=} (P \mid Ever(\bar{\ell}_1) \mid \cdots \mid Ever(\bar{\ell}_n))\backslash L$$

where $L = \{\ell_1, \cdots, \ell_n\}$.   ∎

Here, each $Ever(\bar{\ell}_i)$ acts as an absorber for any ℓ_i performed by P.

Now we can formulate conditions (1) and (2) as equations to be satisfied by a scheduler *Sched*:

(1) $Sched/\tilde{b} \approx Ever(a_1 \cdots a_n)$
(2) $Sched/(\tilde{a} - \{a_i\})/(\tilde{b} - \{b_i\}) \approx Ever(a_i b_i)$ $(1 \leq i \leq n)$

Let us consider how to prove (1), for our scheduler

$$Sched \quad = (A_1 \mid D_2 \mid \cdots \mid D_n)\backslash \tilde{c}$$

We first observe that the Hiding $/\tilde{b}$, applied to *Sched*, can be distributed over the components so that the Hiding $/b_i$ is applied to the ith component. That is:

$$Sched/\tilde{b} = (A_1/b_1 \mid D_2/b_2 \mid \cdots \mid D_n/b_n)\backslash \tilde{c}$$

Exercise 7 Prove this equation by appealing to the definition of Hiding and by using the static laws.   ∎

To continue, we would first like to simplify the components $A_1/b_1, D_2/b_2, \cdots$. In fact let us define a simpler cell A', of sort $\{a, c, d\}$, as follows:

$$A' \stackrel{\text{def}}{=} Ever(acd) , \quad \text{or } A' = a.C', \; C' = c.D', \; D' = d.A'$$

Then we can prove that $A/b = A'$, $C/b = C'$, $D/b = D'$.

Exercise 8 Prove these equations, using the τ laws (Proposition 3.2 and Corollary 3.3), by showing that A/b satisfies the defining equations for A'.   ∎

Thus we are left with proving that

$$(A_1' \mid D_2' \mid \cdots \mid D_n')\backslash \tilde{c} = Ever(a_1 \cdots a_n)$$

where of course $A_1' = A'[f_1]$ etc.

Exercise 9   Prove this equation; use the expansion law, about $2n$ times, to show that the left-hand side satisfies the defining equation of $Ever(a_1 \cdots a_n)$.   ■

Exercise 10   Prove condition (2) of the specification similarly.   ■

This looser specification is interesting as an example of specifications expressed by equations which do not determine the behaviour of an agent completely. How many specifications of this kind can be expressed by equations is an intriguing question. We would not claim that equations are always the most natural way of expressing a specification – it may often be better to use some logical formalism – but in the above example the equational method seems quite direct and succinct.

5.6   Proving the jobshop correct

We now turn to a proof of the equation

$$Jobshop = Strongjobber \mid Strongjobber$$

which was claimed in Section 1.4. This is an example of a straightforward bisimulation proof, without the need for any intermediate results about subsystems. First, recall the definition of *Jobshop*:

$$Jobshop \; = \; (Jobber \mid Jobber \mid Ham \mid Mal) \setminus L,$$

where $L = \{\texttt{geth}, \texttt{puth}, \texttt{getm}, \texttt{putm}\}$, and its flow graph:

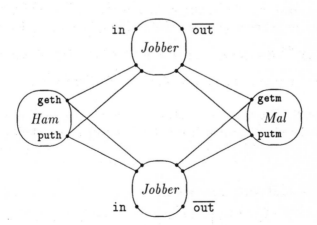

In the equation and the flow graph we have abbreviated *Hammer, Mallet*

to *Ham*, *Mal* and also inserted some inner labels (see Section 3.4) for clarity. We shall actually write *Jobshop* as

$$Jobber|Jobber \parallel Ham|Mal$$

where we understand $P \parallel Q$ to mean $(P \mid Q)\backslash L$; this use of '$\parallel$' (with weaker binding power than '$\mid$') is often useful provided the Restriction-set L is understood from context.

For convenience, we give the definitions of the components again, introducing a few more auxiliary agent names than in Chapter 1 (and shortening some others):

$$Ham \ \stackrel{\mathrm{def}}{=} \ \mathrm{geth}.Ham'$$
$$Ham' \ \stackrel{\mathrm{def}}{=} \ \mathrm{puth}.Ham$$

$$Mal \ \stackrel{\mathrm{def}}{=} \ \mathrm{getm}.Mal'$$
$$Mal' \ \stackrel{\mathrm{def}}{=} \ \mathrm{putm}.Mal$$

$$Jobber \ \stackrel{\mathrm{def}}{=} \ \mathrm{in}(j).Start(j)$$
$$Start(j) \ \stackrel{\mathrm{def}}{=} \ \textbf{if } easy(j) \textbf{ then } Finish(j)$$
$$\textbf{else if } hard(j) \textbf{ then } Useh(j)$$
$$\textbf{else } Usetool(j)$$
$$Usetool(j) \ \stackrel{\mathrm{def}}{=} \ Useh(j) \ + \ Usem(j)$$
$$Useh(j) \ \stackrel{\mathrm{def}}{=} \ \overline{\mathrm{geth}}.Usingh(j)$$
$$Usingh(j) \ \stackrel{\mathrm{def}}{=} \ \overline{\mathrm{puth}}.Finish(j)$$
$$Usem(j) \ \stackrel{\mathrm{def}}{=} \ \overline{\mathrm{getm}}.Usingm(j)$$
$$Usingm(j) \ \stackrel{\mathrm{def}}{=} \ \overline{\mathrm{putm}}.Finish(j)$$
$$Finish(j) \ \stackrel{\mathrm{def}}{=} \ \overline{\mathrm{out}}(done(j)).Jobber$$

and for the specification:

$$Strongjobber \ \stackrel{\mathrm{def}}{=} \ \mathrm{in}(j).Doing(j)$$
$$Doing(j) \ \stackrel{\mathrm{def}}{=} \ \overline{\mathrm{out}}(done(j)).Strongjobber$$

In this system, as in most examples from now on, we are using the full value-passing calculus introduced in Section 2.8. Thus we should think of $\mathrm{in}(j).Start(j)$ as short for $\sum_j \mathrm{in}_j.Start(j)$, where j ranges over all possible jobs. So *Jobber* has the action $\xrightarrow{\mathrm{in}_j}$ for any job j; in keeping with our convention we shall also write the action as $\xrightarrow{in(j)}$.

Now we shall exhibit the relation S which we wish to prove is a bisimulation up to $\approx$. In this case, because of the presence of two identical agents *Jobber*, working 'up to $\approx$' saves us almost half of the writing, since for example

$$Jobber \mid Usingh(j) = Usingh(j) \mid Jobber$$

Note that certain 'states' of the *Jobshop*, for example

$$Jobber \mid Usingh(j) \parallel Ham' \mid Mal$$

can only occur (i.e. are only reachable from the initial state) under a certain condition on the parameter; in this case $\neg easy(j)$ is the condition. But we include this state (paired with $Strongjobber \mid Doing(j)$) in S, because it is simpler to do so and because to include more pairs in a bisimulation does no harm – provided it *is* a bisimulation.

Pairs in S, for all jobs j and j'

(1)	$Jobber \mid Jobber \parallel Ham \mid Mal$,	$Strongjobber \mid Strongjobber$
(2)	$Jobber \mid Start(j) \parallel Ham \mid Mal$,	$Strongjobber \mid Doing(j)$
(3)	$Jobber \mid Usingh(j) \parallel Ham' \mid Mal$,	$Strongjobber \mid Doing(j)$
(4)	$Jobber \mid Usingm(j) \parallel Ham \mid Mal'$,	$Strongjobber \mid Doing(j)$
(5)	$Jobber \mid Finish(j) \parallel Ham \mid Mal$,	$Strongjobber \mid Doing(j)$
(6)	$Start(j') \mid Start(j) \parallel Ham \mid Mal$,	$Doing(j') \mid Doing(j)$
(7)	$Start(j') \mid Usingh(j) \parallel Ham' \mid Mal$,	$Doing(j') \mid Doing(j)$
(8)	$Start(j') \mid Usingm(j) \parallel Ham \mid Mal'$,	$Doing(j') \mid Doing(j)$
(9)	$Start(j') \mid Finish(j) \parallel Ham \mid Mal$,	$Doing(j') \mid Doing(j)$
(10)	$Usingh(j') \mid Usingm(j) \parallel Ham' \mid Mal'$,	$Doing(j') \mid Doing(j)$
(11)	$Usingh(j') \mid Finish(j) \parallel Ham' \mid Mal$,	$Doing(j') \mid Doing(j)$
(12)	$Usingm(j') \mid Finish(j) \parallel Ham \mid Mal$,	$Doing(j') \mid Doing(j)$
(13)	$Finish(j') \mid Finish(j) \parallel Ham \mid Mal$,	$Doing(j') \mid Doing(j)$

Now to check that S is a bisimulation up to $\approx$ is a fairly routine exercise (in systems much larger than this we should want computer assistance in the task, to be sure no cases are left unconsidered). Let us take a few examples:

Pair (1)   Consider the action

$$Jobber \mid Jobber \parallel Ham \mid Mal \xrightarrow{in(j)} Start(j) \mid Jobber \parallel Ham \mid Mal$$

This can be matched by

$$Strongjobber \mid Strongjobber \xrightarrow{in(j)} Doing(j) \mid Strongjobber$$

and the derivatives of these two actions are paired in pair (2) (up to $\approx$). Every other action of each member of pair (1) is similarly matched by an action of the other member – that is, the derivatives of the corresponding actions appear as a pair in S. (In fact the only possible actions for pair (1) are of the form $in(j)$.)

Pair (2) Consider the actions of the left member, depending upon the difficulty of the job j.

Case $easy(j)$: in this case $Start(j) = Finish(j)$, so it is enough to check pair (5).

Case $hard(j)$: in this case $Start(j) = Useh(j)$, so the left member has two actions:

$$Jobber|Start(j) \parallel Ham|Mal \xrightarrow{in(j')} Start(j')|Start(j) \parallel Ham|Mal$$
$$Jobber|Start(j) \parallel Ham|Mal \xrightarrow{\tau} Jobber|Usingh(j) \parallel Ham'|Mal$$

These are respectively matched by

$$Strongjobber \mid Doing(j) \xrightarrow{in(j')} Doing(j') \mid Doing(j)$$
$$Strongjobber \mid Doing(j) \xrightarrow{\varepsilon} Strongjobber \mid Doing(j)$$

and we refer to pair (6) and pair (3) respectively.

Case $\neg easy(j)$ and $\neg hard(j)$: in this case $Start(j) = Usetool\ (j)$, so the left member has the two actions of the previous case, and in addition

$$Jobber|Start(j) \parallel Ham|Mal \xrightarrow{\tau} Jobber|Usingm(j) \parallel Ham|Mal'$$

and this is matched again by

$$Strongjobber \mid Doing(j) \xrightarrow{\varepsilon} Strongjobber \mid Doing(j)$$

so we refer this time to pair (4).

In the opposite direction, we still have to match the action

$$Strongjobber \mid Doing(j) \xrightarrow{\overline{out(j)}} Strongjobber \mid Strongjobber$$

by a derivative of the left member of pair (2). In the case $hard(j)$ this must take the form of the second $Jobber$ picking up the $Hammer$, putting it down, and outputting the job; in fact we can readily discover the composite action

$$Jobber|Start(j) \parallel Ham|Mal \xrightarrow{\overline{\text{out}}(j)} Jobber|Jobber \parallel Ham|Mal$$

so we refer to pair (1) again.

The above cases have been enough to illustrate the procedure, and we leave the rest to the reader.

Exercise 11   Check two or three more pairs. Do pair (7) in particular; notice that when you refer to pair (10) you must use (10) with j and j' interchanged; this is admissible, because pair (10) is in $\mathcal{S}$ for *every pair of values* j and j'.   ∎

Exercise 12   Consider the left member of each pair. In each case, give the condition (on j and j') under which the state is reachable from the initial state, *Jobshop*.   ∎

Having finished the proof that $\mathcal{S}$ is a bisimulation up to $\approx$, we must not forget that we have only proved the *bisimilarity*, not equality,

$$Jobshop \approx Strongjobber \mid Strongjobber$$

But we immediately gain equality, by Proposition 9, since both sides are stable.

Exercise 13   As a much simpler exercise, investigate whether the following agent *Twojobber*, analogous to a buffer of capacity two, is equal to *Strongjobber* | *Strongjobber*:

$$Twojobber \stackrel{\text{def}}{=} \text{in}(j).Doingone(j)$$

$$Doingone(j) \stackrel{\text{def}}{=} \text{in}(j').Doingtwo(j,j') + \overline{\text{out}}(done(j)).Twojobber$$

$$Doingtwo(j,j') \stackrel{\text{def}}{=} \overline{\text{out}}(done(j)).Doingone(j')$$

Give a proof or a disproof, and in the latter case modify *Twojobber* so that it *is* equal to *Strongjobber* | *Strongjobber*.   ∎

In this example we have *checked* that a *given* relation is indeed a bisimulation. The question arises what general procedure exists for *finding* a bisimulation, containing a given pair (P,Q) of agents. We shall not go into detail here, but there are reasonable procedures of this kind, and for finite-state agents there is a complete procedure which takes time which is a polynomial function of the number of states. (For those who are familiar with theory of finite-state automata, we may mention that the method is close to the standard algorithm for determining whether two automata accept the same input language, except that it does not incur the exponential penalty of that algorithm since it need not initially convert each automaton to a deterministic one.) The procedures are suitable for mechanisation.

6

Further Examples

In this chapter we study a variety of examples, which illustrate both equational reasoning and the method of finding bisimulations. We begin by considering different ways in which agents can change their structure dynamically; we illustrate this particularly with counters and stacks. We then look at an example in which a family of sorting networks, each with fixed structure, is defined inductively; this allows us to illustrate proof of correctness of the whole family by mathematical induction. As an exercise, we ask for the design of a family of read-only memories. Finally, we tackle the verification of a communications protocol which is designed to work in the presence of faulty media.

We shall continue to use the full value-passing calculus introduced in Section 2.8, when convenient. In this calculus, the convention is that value-variables are bound by positive labels, e.g. x is bound by a in $ax.P$, and this turns the expansion law into an example of the instantiation of bound variables, very much like the conversion rule $(\lambda x.M)N \to M\{N/x\}$ in the lambda-calculus. For example, the agent

$$(\overline{a}v.P \mid ax.Q)\backslash a$$

(where v is a value) is an abbreviation for

$$(\overline{a_v}.P \mid \sum_{u \in V} a_u.Q\{u/x\})\backslash\{a_u : u \in V\}$$

So the expansion law in this simple case finds a_v to be the only possible label for communication, and therefore yields the equivalent form

$$\tau.(P \mid Q\{v/x\})\backslash a$$

For full comparison with the reduction rule in λ-calculus, we should write this as an action:

$$(\overline{a}v.P \mid ax.Q)\backslash a \xrightarrow{\tau} (P \mid Q\{v/x\})\backslash a$$

The expansion law states also that this is the *only* possible action.

We shall often use the expansion law in this way. In more complex cases, the direction in which a value passes between two agents may depend upon which of several possible communications occurs, as the following example shows:

$$((\bar{a}e_1.P_1 + by.P_2) \mid (ax.Q_1 + \bar{b}e_2.Q_2))\backslash a\backslash b$$
$$= \tau.(P_1 \mid Q_1\{e_1/x\})\backslash a\backslash b + \tau.(P_2\{e_2/y\} \mid Q_2)\backslash a\backslash b$$

(Recall also that the values qualified by negative labels may be denoted by arbitrary value expressions, such as e_1, e_2 here.)

6.1   Systems with evolving structure

Consider a system
$$S \equiv (P \mid Q \mid R)\backslash L$$
with $P : \{a, b, c\}$, and $b, c \in L$ but $a \notin L$.

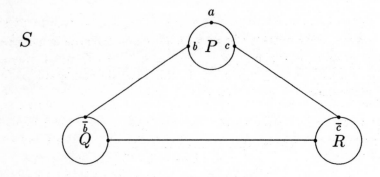

Now consider an action $P \xrightarrow{a} P'$. Then also $S \xrightarrow{a} S'$, where

$$S' \equiv (P' \mid Q \mid R)\backslash L$$

We have hitherto dealt with systems in which the sort of P' is the same as that of P, and in which we do not expect P' to have a more complex spatial structure than P; in these cases the flow graph for S' looks just like that for S.

Interesting differences in structure can arise between S and S', however. Here are some possibilities, depending on the nature of P':

Loss of an arc   This can arise if $P' : \{a, b\}$; for example, we may have $P \equiv a.(a.\mathbf{0} + b.\mathbf{0}) + c.\mathbf{0}$, so that $P' \equiv a.\mathbf{0} + b.\mathbf{0}$. Then the flow graph of S' would be as follows:

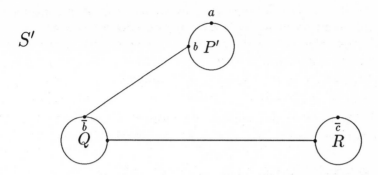

Loss of a node   This arises if $P' : \emptyset$; for example, $P' \equiv \mathbf{0}$. In this case, since $S' = (Q|R)\backslash L$, the flow graph of S' would reduce to

Development of a node   A single node may become a composite flow graph; for example, $P \equiv a.P'$ and $P' \equiv (P_1|P_2)\backslash d$, where $P_1 : \{a, b, d\}$ and $P_2 : \{a, c, \overline{d}\}$. In this case the flow graph of S' would expand to

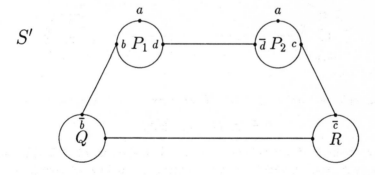

All of these dynamic variations of structure can clearly be represented in the calculus. In fact, with the help of recursion, we can model agents whose 'size', or number of components, can increase unboundedly. This takes us out of the realm of direct descriptions of physical systems, and opens up the possibility of more abstract descriptions such as the generation of tasks in a parallel programming language. In Chapter 8 we shall indeed study such a language; for the present we give a simple example of an agent which can expand indefinitely. It consists of a counter, which can assume any of the natural numbers as its 'state', by increment and decrement actions. It is specified as follows:

$$Count_0 \overset{\text{def}}{=} \text{inc}.Count_1 + \text{zero}.Count_0$$

$$Count_n \overset{\text{def}}{=} \text{inc}.Count_{n+1} + \text{dec}.Count_{n-1} \qquad (n > 0)$$

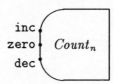

An agent using the counter and wishing to perform a test-and-decrement action would take the form $\overline{\text{zero}}.P + \overline{\text{dec}}.P'$; this would enter P if the counter were zero, and would otherwise decrement the counter and enter P'.

We shall implement the counter by linking together several copies of an agent C and one B, with the following interfaces:

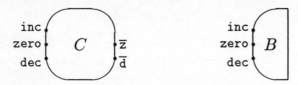

The definitions of C and B are as follows:

$$C \overset{\text{def}}{=} \text{inc}.(C^\frown C) + \text{dec}.D$$

$$D \overset{\text{def}}{=} \overline{\text{d}}.C + \overline{\text{z}}.B$$

$$B \overset{\text{def}}{=} \text{inc}.(C^\frown B) + \text{zero}.B$$

Note that B cannot perform dec initially, but after inc – which turns B into $C^\frown B$ – it will be able to perform dec. The definition of the appropriate linking combinator is as follows:

$$P^\frown Q = (P[\text{i}'/\text{i}, \text{z}'/\text{z}, \text{d}'/\text{d}] \mid Q[\text{i}'/\text{inc}, \text{z}'/\text{zero}, \text{d}'/\text{dec}]) \backslash \{\text{i}', \text{z}', \text{d}'\}$$

It is exactly analogous to our original linking combinator (Section 3.3, Example 3), except that it links three pairs of ports instead of one; in particular, it can be proved associative as in Section 3.4, Example 6. Note one point particularly: C has no port labelled $\bar{\text{i}}$, and so the linking combination $C^\frown B$, which would link such a port (if it existed) to the inc port of B, merely has the effect of restricting the latter port completely. (When we have defined the counter below, you may like to consider why

C possesses a $\overline{\mathsf{d}}$ port but no $\overline{\mathsf{i}}$ port.) So we now define our composite counter, in state n, by

$$C^{(n)} = \overbrace{C^\frown \cdots {}^\frown C}^{n \text{ times}} {}^\frown B$$

and we wish to prove that the agents $C^{(n)}$ ($n \geq 0$) satisfy the defining equations for $Count_n$.

In fact, for $n = 0$ we see immediately that

$$C^{(0)} = \mathsf{inc}.C^{(1)} + \mathsf{zero}.C^{(0)}$$

by definition, since $C^{(0)} = B$ and $C^{(1)} = C^\frown B$. For $n > 0$ we have

$$
\begin{aligned}
C^{(n)} &= C^\frown C^{(n-1)} \\
&= \mathsf{inc}.((C^\frown C)^\frown C^{(n-1)}) + \mathsf{dec}.(D^\frown C^{(n-1)}) \quad \text{by Expansion} \\
&= \mathsf{inc}.C^{(n+1)} + \mathsf{dec}.(D^\frown C^{(n-1)})
\end{aligned}
$$

where, in the last step, we have used the associativity of linking. So we are done if we can show that $D^\frown C^{(n)} \approx C^{(n)}$ for all $n \geq 0$, with the help of Proposition 5.10.

Exercise 1   Complete the proof by first proving the following:

$$
\begin{aligned}
D^\frown C &\approx C^\frown D \\
D^\frown B &\approx B^\frown B \\
B^\frown B &= B
\end{aligned}
$$

For the third result, you only need to use the static laws.   ∎

Exercise 2   Instead of the unary counter above, can you build a binary counter to match exactly the same specification?
Hint: Give the cell C four states, instead of two (C and D); two of the states represent 0 and 1, and the other two represent 'carry' and 'borrow'. The left-most cell will represent the least significant bit of the stored number. The right-most cell, B, will be the most significant bit. You should be able to find a small list of equations – as in Exercise 1 – which represent the process of carrying or borrowing, and thus prove your system correct.   ∎

It is quite easy to convert the unary counter into a pushdown stack. First we have to modify the specification, since its parameter, i.e. its 'state', is no longer an integer but a sequence of values. We now define $Stack\langle v_1, \ldots, v_n \rangle$, which specifies a stack containing n values, with v_1 topmost. Using s for an arbitrary value sequence, ε for the empty sequence and ':' for sequence concatenation, we define

$$Stack(\varepsilon) \stackrel{\mathrm{def}}{=} \mathrm{push}(x).Stack\langle x \rangle + \mathrm{empty}.Stack(\varepsilon)$$

$$Stack(v\!:\!s) \stackrel{\mathrm{def}}{=} \mathrm{push}(x).Stack(x\!:\!v\!:\!s) + \overline{\mathrm{pop}}(v).Stack(s)$$

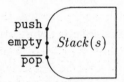

The implementation can be done using cells as in the counter, but storing and transmitting values, and the linking combinator is just the same except that we have changed the port labels to suit the stack better:

$$C(x) \stackrel{\mathrm{def}}{=} \mathrm{push}(y).(C(y)^\frown C(x)) + \overline{\mathrm{pop}}(x).D$$

$$D \stackrel{\mathrm{def}}{=} \mathrm{o}(x).C(x) + \overline{\mathrm{e}}.B$$

$$B \stackrel{\mathrm{def}}{=} \mathrm{push}(y).(C(y)^\frown B) + \mathrm{empty}.B$$

Then we implement the stack holding the sequence $s = \langle v_1, \ldots, v_n \rangle$ by

$$Cells\langle v_1, \ldots, v_n \rangle \stackrel{\mathrm{def}}{=} C(v_1)^\frown C(v_2)^\frown \cdots ^\frown C(v_n)^\frown B$$

Finally, by a proof very similar to that for the counter, we show that for all s

$$Cells(s) \;=\; Stack(s)$$

Exercise 3 Carry out this proof, by first proving a small set of equations analogous to those in Exercise 1. ∎

Exercise 4 Can you modify the system to meet the specification of a queue (FIFO) rather than a stack (LIFO)?

$$Queue(\varepsilon) \overset{\text{def}}{=} \text{in}(x).Queue\langle x \rangle + \text{empty}.Queue(\varepsilon)$$

$$Queue(s\!:\!v) \overset{\text{def}}{=} \text{in}(x).Queue(x\!:\!s\!:\!v) + \overline{\text{out}}(v).Queue(s)$$

Keep the structure similar (i.e. both input and output occurring at the left-most cell), but find a way in which the last input value can percolate to the right-hand end.

Compare the *Queue* specification with the bounded buffer defined in Section 1.2. What is the difference?   ■

We conclude this section with an important theoretical consequence of the ability to define systems with evolving structure, and stacks in particular. (Readers who are not interested in the theoretical question of a decision procedure for observation equivalence may safely skip to the next section.) The consequence is that observation equivalence ($\approx$) and the two congruence relations ($\sim$ and $=$) are undecidable. This holds even for the basic the calculus confined to finite expressions – that is, forbidding infinite Summation.

To see this, first notice that our implementation of *Stack*, if we were to translate it into the basic calculus, would involve expressions like

$$\sum_{v \in V} \text{push}_v.(C_v^\frown C_u)$$

in place of $\text{push}(y).(C(y)^\frown C(x))$. So, assuming the set V of values is *finite*, the stack can be implemented in the basic calculus without value-passing, using only finite Summation and finitely many Constants (such as C_v). But a Turing machine – whose alphabet is always finite – can be simulated by two stacks together with a finite-state control mechanism. Thus we can find a uniform way of constructing a finite definition in the basic calculus of an agent TM_i, corresponding to the ith Turing machine (in some enumeration), with the property that $TM_i \approx \mathbf{0}$ if and only if the ith Turing machine does not halt on blank tape, – and also that TM_i outputs (in some way) the value sequence s iff the ith Turing machine halts with value sequence s upon the tape. We conclude that in a natural sense our calculus has full computational power, and that the relation $\approx$ is undecidable since we know that the halting problem is undecidable.

Exercise 5

(1) Prove further that the relation $=$, observation congruence, is also

undecidable.

Hint: Find an equation $\cdots = \cdots$ which holds iff $TM_i \approx 0$.

(2) (a little harder) By another adaptation in the same spirit, prove that $\sim$, strong bisimilarity, is also undecidable. ∎

6.2 Systems with inductive structure

As a further illustration of the variety of applications and the pitfalls of design, we include here two examples of systems which are of fixed but arbitrary size, in contrast to the systems of varying size in the previous section. Both examples in this section are such that the system of size $n+1$ can be defined in terms of the system of size n (where the measure of size is obvious in each case). They are both amenable to analysis either by bisimulation or by purely equational reasoning, and they are both easy to get wrong. Although real-life systems may not be as elegant as these, they certainly throw up design problems of the kind illustrated here.

Example 1: a sorting machine   We would like to build a sorting machine $Sorter_n$, for each $n \geq 0$, capable of sorting n-length sequences of positive integers. We suppose $Sorter_n$ has sort $\{\text{in}, \overline{\text{out}}\}$. It must accept exactly n integers one by one at in; then it must deliver them up one by one in descending order at $\overline{\text{out}}$, terminated by a zero. After that, it must return to its start state.

This specification can be varied, of course, and the problem becomes subtly different with each variation. We have chosen a version which is amenable to recursive construction.

Let us first write the specification, *Sortspec*. In this we shall use *multisets* of positive integers. A multiset is like a set, but the multiplicity of elements is significant; thus $\{1,2,2\} = \{2,1,2\} \neq \{1,2\}$. We use S to range over multisets, and $max\,S, min\,S$ are the maximum and minimum elements of S. Here is the specification:

$$Sortspec_n \stackrel{\text{def}}{=} \text{in}\,x_1.\cdots.\text{in}\,x_n.Hold_n\{x_1,\ldots,x_n\}$$
$$Hold_n(S) \stackrel{\text{def}}{=} \overline{\text{out}}(max\,S).Hold_n(S - \{max\,S\})\ (S \neq \emptyset)$$
$$Hold_n(\emptyset) \stackrel{\text{def}}{=} \overline{\text{out}}\,0.Sortspec_n$$

Exercise 6   Vary the specification so that it will sort sequences of length m, for any $m \leq n$, assuming that the end of the input sequence is marked by a zero. ∎

In building the sorter we wish to use n identical cells C, linked together as in the counter of Section 1; but, unlike the counter, the system will be of fixed size. It is important that C is independent of n; we think of C as a hardware component of fixed finite size which can be used to build sorting machines of any size. To be precise, we shall link together n copies of C and a single barrier cell B:

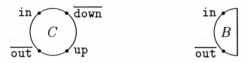

We shall also use the obvious linking combinator $\frown$, linking $\overline{\text{down}}$ to in and up to $\overline{\text{out}}$. So our problem is to define C and B in such a way that, if we set

$$Sorter_n \overset{\text{def}}{=} \overbrace{C^\frown \cdots ^\frown C}^{n \text{ times}} {}^\frown B$$

then we have

$$Sorter_n = Sortspec_n$$

We shall wish to prove this by induction on n, so we immediately see that for the case $n = 0$ we must have

$$B = Sortspec_0$$

and this fixes B. Now we have

$$Sorter_{n+1} = C^\frown Sorter_n$$

so the inductive step amounts to showing that

$$Sortspec_{n+1} = C^\frown Sortspec_n$$

So, with this in mind, let us try to define the cell C.

The idea in designing C is first that it should have storage capacity for two numbers, and be able to compare them. Second, its behaviour must have two phases. In the first phase it receives inputs at in and puts them out at $\overline{\text{down}}$; but since it does not know the size of the sorter, it must be ready to change at any moment to its second phase, in which it receives inputs at up and (using comparison) puts them out at $\overline{\text{out}}$. The delicacy is that some cells will still be in the first phase while others are in the second. Here is the definition:

$$C \overset{\text{def}}{=} \text{in } x.C'(x)$$

$$C'(x) \overset{\text{def}}{=} \overline{\text{down}}\, x.C + \text{up } y.\overline{\text{out}}(max\{x, y\}).C''(min\{x, y\})$$

$$C''(x) \overset{\text{def}}{=} \text{if } x = 0 \text{ then } \overline{\text{out}}\, 0.C \text{ else } C'(x)$$

The job of B is simple; it simply delivers a 0 whenever required to do so, thereby triggering a phase-change in its neighbour, which will then perform the same service for its own neighbour, and so on.

$$B \stackrel{\text{def}}{=} \overline{\text{out}}\, 0.B$$

Before proceeding to the proof of correctness, the reader may like to experiment with $Sorter_3$, say, to get a feel for how it works.

Exercise 7 Can you find an alternative solution, which performs comparison and exchange during the first phase? ∎

Exercise 8 Prove $B = Sortspec_0$, the inductive basis. ∎

Now, for the inductive step, it will be enough to show that $C^\frown Sortspec_n$ satisfies the defining equation of $Sortspec_{n+1}$, which can be rewritten as follows:

$$Sortspec_{n+1} = \text{in}\, x_1.\cdots.\text{in}\, x_{n+1}.Hold_{n+1}\{x_1,\ldots,x_{n+1}\}$$
$$Hold_{n+1}\{y_1,\ldots,y_{n+1}\} = \overline{\text{out}}\, y_1.\cdots.\overline{\text{out}}\, y_{n+1}.\overline{\text{out}}\, 0.Sortspec_{n+1}$$
$$(\text{assuming that } y_1 \geq \cdots \geq y_{n+1})$$

So now let us outline the proof. Essentially, we just apply the expansion law to $C^\frown Sortspec_n$ many times, and generate a computation which follows the phases of C's behaviour.

$$
\begin{aligned}
C^\frown Sortspec_n &= (\text{in}\, x_1.C'(x_1))^\frown(\text{in}\, z_1.\cdots.\text{in}\, z_n.Hold_n\{z_1,\ldots,z_n\})\\
&= \text{in}\, x_1.((\overline{\text{down}}\, x_1.C + \cdots)^\frown\\
&\qquad (\text{in}\, z_1.\cdots.\text{in}\, z_n.Hold_n\{z_1,\ldots,z_n\}))\\
&= \text{in}\, x_1.\tau.(C^\frown(\text{in}\, z_2.\cdots.\text{in}\, z_n.Hold_n\{x_1,z_2,\ldots,z_n\})\\
&\qquad (x_1 \text{ has entered, and we continue similarly})\\
&= \text{in}\, x_1.\cdots.\text{in}\, x_n.\text{in}\, x_{n+1}.(C'(x_{n+1})^\frown Hold_n\{x_1,\ldots,x_n\})
\end{aligned}
$$

At this point, we make use of a lemma whose proof we leave as an exercise:

Lemma If S is any multiset of size k, and if $\{x\} \cup S = \{y_1,\ldots,y_{k+1}\}$ where $y_1 \geq \cdots \geq y_{k+1}$, then

$$C'(x)^\frown Hold_n(S) = \tau.\overline{\text{out}}\, y_1.\cdots.\overline{\text{out}}\, y_{k+1}.\overline{\text{out}}\, 0.(C^\frown Sortspec_n)$$ ∎

Exercise 9 Prove the lemma by induction on k. ∎

Now all that remains is to apply the lemma with $k = n$, at the point where we left off, to obtain finally that $C^\frown Sortspec_n$ satisfies the defining equation of $Sortspec_{n+1}$ as required.   ∎

Example 2: a read-only memory   A read-only memory holds 2^k values $\tilde{v} = v_0, v_1, \ldots, v_{2^k-1}$. It has two ports, address and deliver, and it works as follows:

- At address it receives k bits in sequence, most significant first, representing the index i of the value v_i to be delivered.
- It then delivers the value v_i at $\overline{\text{deliver}}$, ignoring any further bits which arrive at address before delivery occurs.
- After delivery, it returns immediately to its starting state.

We can transform this informal description into a precise definition of the memory's behaviour, in the same sort of way as for the sorting machine:

$$Memspec_k(\tilde{v}) \;\overset{\text{def}}{=}\; \text{address}(b_k). \cdots$$
$$\cdots.\text{address}(b_1).Fetch_k(\tilde{v}, 0 + b_1 + \cdots + 2^{k-1}b_k)$$
$$Fetch_k(\tilde{v}, i) \;\overset{\text{def}}{=}\; \text{address}(b).Fetch_k(\tilde{v}, i) + \overline{\text{deliver}}(v_i).Memspec_k(\tilde{v})$$

Note that in the degenerate case $k = 0$, in which $\tilde{v}$ consists of a single value v_0, we just have

$$Memspec_0(v_0) = \text{address}(b).Memspec_0(v_0) + \overline{\text{deliver}}(v_0).Memspec_0(v_0)$$

Now suppose that the agent $Mem_k(\tilde{v})$ is to be built to meet this specification, using 2^k copies of *Cell* (each holding a value) and $2^k - 1$ copies of *Node*, arranged as a binary tree. The flow graph for the case $k = 2$ is shown on the next page. Just as with the sorting machine, the *Node* must be independent of the size of the memory; it should transmit relevant address bits to its appropriate son along one line, and be ready to receive a value from that son along the other line. Particular care must be taken to meet the specification exactly, as far as ignoring superfluous address bits is concerned. We leave the design as a phased exercise:

Exercise 10

(1) Express $Mem_{k+1}(\tilde{u}\tilde{v})$ in terms of one *Node* and two copies of Mem_k, assuming that $\tilde{u}$ and $\tilde{v}$ are both of size 2^k.
(2) Now define the agents *Node* and *Cell*, to achieve the right behaviour. (Assume that *Node* has only storage capacity for one address bit and one value.) What is $Mem_0(v_0)$?

(3) Finally, prove by induction on k that for all $k \geq 0$

$$Mem_k(\tilde{v}) = Memspec_k(\tilde{v})$$

Your proof can follow the same style as the previous example. ∎

Exercise 11

(1) Modify the specification and implementation of the memory so that values can be both read from it, as above, and also written into it. You will need more ports, of course.
(2) Modify your proof of correctness from Exercise 10. ∎

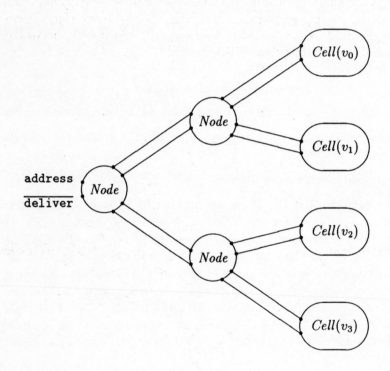

A tree-structured read-only memory

6.3   The alternating-bit protocol

A communications protocol is a discipline for transmission of messages from a source to a destination. Sometimes the protocol is designed to perform routing through large networks; sometimes it is designed to ensure reliable transmission under possibly adverse conditions. Typically, the adverse conditions pertain to the transmission medium, which may lose, duplicate or corrupt messages; for example, the sender cannot assume that a transmission was successful until an acknowledgment is obtained from the receiver. The problem is further compounded if acknowledgments themselves may be lost, duplicated or corrupted.

Here we are interested in a system where the transmission medium consists of communication lines which behave as unbounded buffers (see Section 1.1), except that they are unreliable. The transmission system may be depicted by the following flow graph, in which we indicate the direction of information flow by arrows:

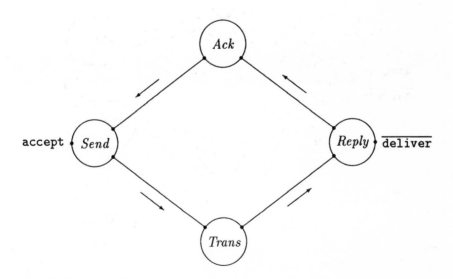

The source (to the left) and the destination (to the right) are not shown. Here *Trans* and *Ack* are the unreliable communication lines, while *Send* and *Reply* are the agents which represent the protocol or discipline.

A famous protocol is called the Alternating-Bit (AB) protocol, and we shall now give a simple narrative description of it. We shall assume that the *Trans* and *Ack* lines may lose or duplicate (but not corrupt) messages, and are 'buffers' with an unbounded message capacity. (Other versions may take them to have bounded capacity.) The name of the protocol refers to the method used; messages are sent tagged with the bits 0 and 1 alternately, and these bits also constitute the acknowledgments.

The sender works as follows. After accepting a message, it sends it with bit b along the *Trans* line and sets a timer. There are then three possibilities:

- it may get a 'time-out' from the timer, upon which it sends the message again with b;
- it may get an acknowledgment b from the *Ack* line, upon which it is ready to accept another message (which it will send with bit $\hat{b} = 1 - b$);
- it may get an acknowledgment $\hat{b}$ (resulting from a superfluous retransmission of the previous message) which it ignores.

The replier works in a dual manner. After delivering a message it acknowledges it with bit b along the *Ack* line and sets a timer. There are then three possibilities:

- it may get a 'time-out' from the timer, upon which it acknowledges again with b;
- it may get a new message with bit $\hat{b}$ from the *Trans* line, upon which it is ready to deliver the new message (which it will acknowledge with bit $\hat{b}$);
- it may get a superfluous transmission of the previous message with bit b, which it ignores.

There are subtle variations of the discipline. In one, which was the original design, the replier sets no timer and only returns one acknowledgment per message received. This is simpler, but loses the pleasant duality which we prefer to keep.

It is easy to specify how this protocol, and others, should behave – namely, it should simply accept and deliver messages alternately. This is just to say that it should behave like a perfect buffer of capacity one. This we shall prove. (As an exercise later, we raise the question of whether the buffer capacity need be exactly one.) First, of course, we have to define the system as a composite agent of our calculus. The flow graph is as follows:

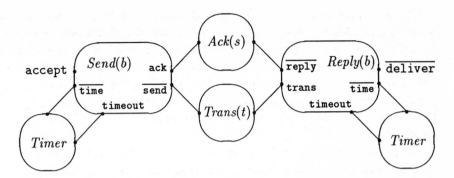

Note that each agent (except *Timer*) is parameterised. *Send*(b) and *Reply*(b) are sending and replying with bit b; *Trans*(t) and *Ack*(s) are currently holding bit-sequences $t, s \in \{0,1\}^*$. Since the content of messages is unimportant for the discipline, we are omitting this content (otherwise, of course, each member of t would be a message tagged with a bit).

We now give the definitions, which you should compare with the informal description given earlier. We choose not to use the variable binding convention in this example, since the only values involved are boolean; thus, for example, we write $\overline{\texttt{send}}_b$ rather than $\overline{\texttt{send}}(b)$.

$$Send(b) \stackrel{\text{def}}{=} \overline{\texttt{send}_b}.\texttt{time}.Sending(b)$$

$$Sending(b) \stackrel{\text{def}}{=} \texttt{timeout}.Send(b) + \texttt{ack}_b.\texttt{timeout}.Accept(\hat{b})$$
$$+ \ \texttt{ack}_{\hat{b}}.Sending(b)$$

$$Accept(b) \stackrel{\text{def}}{=} \texttt{accept}.Send(b)$$

$$Reply(b) \stackrel{\text{def}}{=} \overline{\texttt{reply}_b}.\texttt{time}.Replying(b)$$

$$Replying(b) \stackrel{\text{def}}{=} \texttt{timeout}.Reply(b) + \texttt{trans}_{\hat{b}}.\texttt{timeout}.Deliver(\hat{b})$$
$$+ \ \texttt{trans}_b.Replying(b)$$

$$Deliver(b) \stackrel{\text{def}}{=} \overline{\texttt{deliver}}.Reply(b)$$

$$Timer \stackrel{\text{def}}{=} \texttt{time}.\overline{\texttt{timeout}}.Timer$$

If we were to use the variable binding convention, then the second equation would be written

$$Sending(b) \stackrel{\text{def}}{=} \texttt{timeout}.Send(b) + \texttt{ack}(x).Check(x, b)$$

$$Check(x, b) \stackrel{\text{def}}{=} \textbf{if } x = b \textbf{ then } \texttt{timeout}.Accept(\hat{b}) \textbf{ else } Sending(b)$$

We now turn to the communication lines. Instead of defining *Trans* and *Ack* by equations – although this is not difficult – it is a little easier to define them by giving all their transitions. In the following, we shall represent concatenation of sequences by juxtaposition; so by sbt, for example, we mean the concatenation of s, b and t (where $s, t \in \{0,1\}^*$, $b \in \{0,1\}$).

$$Ack(bs) \xrightarrow{\overline{\text{ack}_b}} Ack(s) \qquad\qquad Trans(sb) \xrightarrow{\overline{\text{trans}_b}} Trans(s)$$
$$Ack(s) \xrightarrow{\text{reply}_b} Ack(sb) \qquad\qquad Trans(s) \xrightarrow{\text{send}_b} Trans(bs)$$
$$Ack(sbt) \xrightarrow{\tau} Ack(st) \qquad\qquad Trans(tbs) \xrightarrow{\tau} Trans(ts)$$
$$Ack(sbt) \xrightarrow{\tau} Ack(sbbt) \qquad\qquad Trans(tbs) \xrightarrow{\tau} Trans(tbbs)$$

The last two lines represent loss and duplication, respectively, of any bit in transit.

First we shall compose $Send(b)$ with its *Timer*, and likewise $Reply(b)$, since this leads to a simplification. It is easy to show that, if we define

$$Send'(b) \stackrel{\text{def}}{=} (Send(b) \mid Timer)\backslash\{\texttt{time}, \texttt{timeout}\}$$

(with similar priming of the other compositions) then the following equations hold among $Send'(b)$, $Sending'(b)$ and $Accept'(b)$ – in which we now drop the primes:

$$
\begin{aligned}
Send(b) &= \overline{\text{send}_b}.Sending(b) \\
Sending(b) &= \tau.Send(b) + \text{ack}_b.Accept(\hat{b}) + \text{ack}_{\hat{b}}.Sending(b) \\
Accept(b) &= \texttt{accept}.Send(b)
\end{aligned}
$$

and similarly, by composing the *Timer* into $Reply(b)$:

$$
\begin{aligned}
Reply(b) &= \overline{\text{reply}_b}.Replying(b) \\
Replying(b) &= \tau.Reply(b) + \text{trans}_{\hat{b}}.Deliver(\hat{b}) + \text{trans}_b.Replying(b) \\
Deliver(b) &= \overline{\texttt{deliver}}.Reply(b)
\end{aligned}
$$

Exercise 12   Derive these equations by expansion.   ∎

We are now ready to build the complete system, in which we imagine that a message has just been delivered, a new message is just about to be accepted, and the lines are empty:

$$AB \stackrel{\text{def}}{=} Accept(\hat{b}) \parallel Trans(\varepsilon) \parallel Ack(\varepsilon) \parallel Reply(b)$$

where ε is the empty sequence, and $\parallel$ denotes restricted Composition as usual.

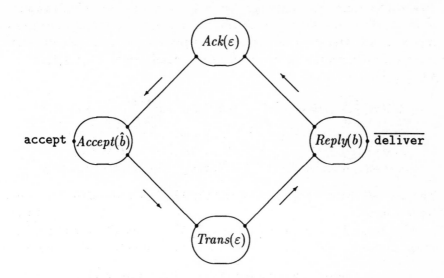

Now we define the protocol specification to be a buffer as follows:

$$Buff \stackrel{\text{def}}{=} \text{accept}.Buff'$$
$$Buff' \stackrel{\text{def}}{=} \overline{\text{deliver}}.Buff$$

and to prove that AB meets its specification, we require

$$AB \approx Buff$$

Note however that $AB \neq Buff$, since AB is unstable.

6.4   Proof of the protocol

We want to find a bisimulation containing the pair $(AB, Buff)$. At first
sight it appears that the state-space, and hence the bisimulation, will
be horribly large because the lines may contain arbitrary bit-sequences.
But the *reachable* state-space is not so large. A little thought shows
that, however many bits may be in transit on either line, there can be
at most one sign-change in the bit-sequence on each line. We do not
have to *prove* this first; it will be a consequence of finding a bisimulation
which only contains such states. Here is our candidate bisimulation $\mathcal{S}$,
partitioned into twelve groups indexed by $m, n, p, q \geq 0$ and by $b \in \{0, 1\}$:

$$AB \text{ states} \qquad\qquad\qquad\qquad Buff \text{ states}$$

$$Accept(\hat{b}) \parallel Trans(b^n) \parallel Ack(b^p) \parallel \left\{ \begin{array}{l} Reply(b) \\ Replying(b) \end{array} \right. \qquad Buff$$

$$\left. \begin{array}{l} Send(\hat{b}) \\ Sending(\hat{b}) \end{array} \right\} \parallel Trans(\hat{b}^m b^n) \parallel Ack(b^p) \parallel \left\{ \begin{array}{l} Reply(b) \\ Replying(b) \end{array} \right. \qquad Buff'$$

$$\left. \begin{array}{l} Send(\hat{b}) \\ Sending(\hat{b}) \end{array} \right\} \parallel Trans(\hat{b}^m) \parallel Ack(b^p) \parallel Deliver(\hat{b}) \qquad Buff'$$

$$\left. \begin{array}{l} Send(\hat{b}) \\ Sending(\hat{b}) \end{array} \right\} \parallel Trans(\hat{b}^m) \parallel Ack(b^p \hat{b}^q) \parallel \left\{ \begin{array}{l} Reply(\hat{b}) \\ Replying(\hat{b}) \end{array} \right. \qquad Buff$$

The twelve groups arise by choosing either of each pair of bracketed alternatives. To check that S is a bisimulation, let us start by considering one group of pairs, say the pairs

$$(\; Sending(\hat{b}) \parallel Trans(\hat{b}^m b^n) \parallel Ack(b^p) \parallel Reply(b), \; Buff' \;)$$

for all values of the bit b and the integers m, n and p. Consider the actions of the left member.

(1) There are τ actions corresponding to loss or duplication by *Trans* or *Ack*; the derivatives of these actions belong to the same group, and we choose *Buff'* again as the corresponding τ-descendant of *Buff'*.

(2) The τ action

$$Sending(\hat{b}) \xrightarrow{\tau} Send(\hat{b})$$

takes us into another group, also paired with *Buff'* (its own τ-descendant).

(3) The $\overline{\text{ack}_b}$ action by $Sending(b)$ complements the ack_b action of $Ack(b^p)$ $(p > 0)$, yielding a τ-action returning to the same group, and again we choose *Buff'* as descendant.

(4) Finally, the $\overline{\text{reply}_b}$ action by $Reply(b)$ complements the reply_b action of $Ack(b^p)$, taking us into another group paired with *Buff'* (its own τ-descendant).

On the other hand, the only action of the right member is

$$Buff' \xrightarrow{\overline{\text{deliver}}} Buff$$

and can be matched by allowing $Reply(b)$ to do $\overline{reply_b}$, then do $trans_b$ n times, then $trans_{\bar{b}}$ – all these yielding τ-actions of the left member – and finally $\overline{deliver}$, yielding the $\overline{deliver}$-descendant

$$Sending(\hat{b}) \parallel Trans(\hat{b}^{m-1}) \parallel Ack(b^{p+1}) \parallel Reply(\hat{b})$$

paired with $Buff$. (In the case that $m = 0$, $Sending(\hat{b})$ must also contribute a $\overline{send_{\hat{b}}}$!)

Exercise 13   Consider one or two other groups, being careful to deal with the cases in which m, n, p, q take the value 0.   ■

By this exhaustive case analysis, it can indeed be verified that $\mathcal{S}$ is a bisimulation; we have therefore completed the correctness proof for the alternating-bit protocol. This example lies quite near the limit beyond which a proof by 'hand', i.e. by pencil and paper, becomes unreliable.

Exercise 14   Redesign the $Reply$ agent, along the lines suggested at the beginning of the previous section. It should not use a timer; it should perform $\overline{reply_b}$ only once after $\overline{deliver}$, until a further (superfluous) $trans_b$ is received, instead of performing $\overline{reply_b}$ in response to a timeout. Adjust the bisimulation $\mathcal{S}$ (if necessary) to accommodate the change, and check it.   ■

Exercise 15   As another variant – a simpler one – examine the case in which the Ack and $Trans$ lines have capacity for at most one bit, and can only lose (not duplicate) a message. Take care; a deadlock could arise because a bounded buffer cannot always accept input!   ■

Exercise 16   Our definition of the AB protocol has been shown equivalent to a buffer of capacity one. But this appears to be due to the (somewhat arbitrary) decision to acknowledge a message before delivering it. Adjust $Reply$ so that delivery occurs *after* acknowledgment. Then investigate whether or not this makes AB equivalent to a buffer of capacity two rather than one.   ■

There are several points to discuss about this kind of proof. First, there is a question whether the result is even valid! The doubt arises from the fact that the system AB contains τ-cycles, because of the possibility of indefinite loss and retransmission and the possibility of indefinite duplication. Alternate loss and retransmission shows up in the following fragment of the transition graph of the $Sending(b) \parallel Trans(\varepsilon)$

subsystem:

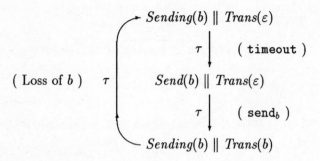

$$(\text{Loss of } b)$$

$$\begin{array}{c} \xrightarrow{\hspace{1em}} Sending(b) \parallel Trans(\varepsilon) \\[0.5em] \tau \Big\downarrow \quad (\text{ timeout }) \\[0.5em] Send(b) \parallel Trans(\varepsilon) \\[0.5em] \tau \Big\downarrow \quad (\text{ send}_b) \\[0.5em] Sending(b) \parallel Trans(b) \end{array}$$

On the other hand $Buff$ – the 'specification' of AB – contains no τ-cycles. This presence of a τ-cycle in one agent, and absence in another, does not prevent their bisimilarity; indeed the following two simple systems are bisimilar (though not equal):

and the following two are not only bisimilar, but equal:

Even more: we shall show in the next chapter that *every* system containing τ-cycles is equal to one without; there is a procedure for excising τ-cycles. One may adopt the point of view that the definitions of bisimulation and equality should be strengthened to preclude this possibility. Such stronger definitions exist, but they have the awkward consequence that if P is *convergent* (i.e. has no τ-cycles) then

$$P \mid Ever(\tau) \not\approx P$$

where $Ever(\tau) \stackrel{\text{def}}{=} \tau.Ever(\tau)$ is the *divergent* agent which is just a single τ-cycle. This is hard to accept, since P should not be considered any less convergent just because a τ-cycle is running by its side!

Our point of view, in defence of the present definition of bisimulation, is this:

(1) That the theory is somewhat simpler than one which takes care of divergence;

(2) That in a theory which equates two agents even when the proportion between their speeds may vary unboundedly, it is natural to allow this proportion to be infinite;

(3) That the convergence of an agent can often be ascertained by a separate argument, in which extra conditions may be assumed.

The second aspect of our proof which deserves comment is that – in full – it requires a tedious case analysis.

To some extent, case analysis is inescapable in handling realistic systems, but the more it obtrudes the less one finds that the proof embodies a real understanding of the system. (It is revealing to consider the dismay with which some mathematicians greeted the proof of the four-colour conjecture!) There are indeed proofs of correctness of the AB protocol which reveal more understanding, by the use of arguments which – if formalised – require a richer medium of expression than our calculus. One suitable vehicle for formalisation is temporal logic.

Without denying the value of these more intuitive proofs, we can claim two advantages for the bisimulation approach. First, it is entirely conducted within a simple calculus. Second, it is easy to mechanise; this is partly because the calculus is simple, and partly because the checking of a bisimulation is a purely routine matter. Indeed, the search for a bisimulation is itself not hard to automate, particularly for the pure calculus without value-passing. Several programs have already been written which will guarantee to find a bisimulation, if it exists, in the case of finite-state systems at least.

7

The Theory of Observation Congruence

This chapter completes the basic algebraic theory. Readers mainly interested in applications can confidently omit this Chapter at least at first reading, and proceed to the study of a programming language in Chapter 8.

We begin by giving another way of defining the notion of bisimulation, and then we prove that bisimilarity is preserved by all the basic combinators except Summation. Then the long-awaited definition of equality, =, is given (Definition 2), followed by all outstanding proofs of Propositions stated in earlier chapters. In particular, it is shown that equality is indeed a congruence relation, which justifies all the normal algebraic manipulations (substitution of equals for equals) which has been done in examples. Also the τ laws, stated as Proposition 3.2, are proved, and so is the important property stated as Proposition 3.4(2) that certain equations have unique solutions. Finally, Sections 4 and 5 give equational axioms which are *complete* (i.e. from which all valid equations can be derived) for two subclasses of agents: the finite agents and the finite-state agents.

7.1 Experiments and substitutivity

In Chapter 5 we defined the concept of bisimulation, and in particular the largest bisimulation relation $\approx$, which we call observation equivalence or bisimilarity; we also proved its elementary properties and stated others which remain to be established. Some of these relate it to the notion of equality, =, which we still have to define; others pertain to $\approx$ alone, and this section is concerned with the latter. We begin by giving another characterisation of bisimulation, in terms of the notion of *experiment*. We consider $P \overset{s}{\Rightarrow} P'$, where $s \in \mathcal{L}^*$, to be an experiment upon P; it consists of running P a little and observing the action sequence $s = \ell_1 \cdots \ell_n$. If $s = \varepsilon$, we also write $P \Rightarrow P'$; if P is unstable then this may involve one or more (unobserved) τ actions. $P \Rightarrow P'$ is still an experiment, and must play a part in our theory, because P' may admit fewer experiments than P does; consider $P \equiv a.0 + \tau.0$ for example; it admits an a-experiment, but $P \Rightarrow 0$ which does not admit an a-experiment.

Proposition 1 $\mathcal{S}$ is a bisimulation iff, for all $(P,Q) \in \mathcal{S}$ and $s \in \mathcal{L}^*$,

(i) Whenever $P \stackrel{s}{\Rightarrow} P'$ then, for some Q', $Q \stackrel{s}{\Rightarrow} Q'$ and $P'\mathcal{S}Q'$

(ii) Whenever $Q \stackrel{s}{\Rightarrow} Q'$ then, for some P', $P \stackrel{s}{\Rightarrow} P'$ and $P'\mathcal{S}Q'$

Proof ($\Longrightarrow$)   Assume that $\mathcal{S}$ is a bisimulation. Let $P \stackrel{s}{\Rightarrow} P'$, so that $P \stackrel{t}{\rightarrow} P'$ where $t = \alpha_1 \cdots \alpha_n \in Act^*$ and $\hat{t} = s$. Then $P \stackrel{\alpha_1}{\rightarrow} P_1 \stackrel{\alpha_2}{\rightarrow} \cdots \stackrel{\alpha_n}{\rightarrow} P'$, and since $\mathcal{S}$ is a bisimulation we also have $Q \stackrel{\widehat{\alpha_1}}{\Rightarrow} Q_1 \stackrel{\widehat{\alpha_2}}{\Rightarrow} \cdots \stackrel{\widehat{\alpha_n}}{\Rightarrow} Q'$ with $P'\mathcal{S}Q'$. Hence $Q \stackrel{\hat{t}}{\Rightarrow} Q'$, i.e. $Q \stackrel{s}{\Rightarrow} Q'$.

($\Longleftarrow$)   Assuming (i), Let $P \stackrel{\alpha}{\rightarrow} P'$. If $\alpha = \tau$ then $P \stackrel{\varepsilon}{\Rightarrow} P'$, so by (i) $Q \stackrel{\varepsilon}{\Rightarrow} Q'$ with $P'\mathcal{S}Q'$; but $\hat{\alpha} = \varepsilon$, so $Q \stackrel{\hat{\alpha}}{\Rightarrow} Q'$ as required. If $\alpha = \ell$, then $P \stackrel{\ell}{\Rightarrow} P'$, and by (i) $Q \stackrel{\ell}{\Rightarrow} Q'$ with $P'\mathcal{S}Q'$; but $\hat{\ell} = \ell$, so $Q \stackrel{\hat{\alpha}}{\Rightarrow} Q'$ as required. Assuming (ii), we similarly derive the second condition for bisimulation.   ∎

One may ask why the empty experiment $P \Rightarrow P'$, with $s = \varepsilon$, must be allowed in the two clauses of Proposition 1. Without it, one can easily see that $a.0 + \tau.0$ would be bisimilar with $a.0$, which is certainly false by our original definition. Furthermore, if we adopted the two clauses of Proposition 1, omitting the case $s = \varepsilon$, as the definition of bisimulation, then bisimilarity would not be preserved either by Prefix or by Composition; we would have

$$a.0 + \tau.0 \approx a.0$$

but

$$b.(a.0 + \tau.0) \;\not\approx\; b.a.0$$
$$b.0 \mid (a.0 + \tau.0) \;\not\approx\; b.0 \mid a.0$$

For if we let P_1 and P_2 stand for the two left-hand sides then $P_1 \stackrel{b}{\Rightarrow} 0$ and $P_2 \stackrel{b}{\Rightarrow} 0|0$ respectively; on the other hand if we let Q_1 and Q_2 stand for the two right-hand sides then their only b actions are $Q_1 \stackrel{b}{\Rightarrow} a.0$ and $Q_2 \stackrel{b}{\Rightarrow} 0|a.0$ respectively, and in each case the derivative of Q_i admits an a-experiment while the derivative of P_i does not.

We now look at the substitutivity of $\approx$. We saw in Section 5.3 that $\approx$ is *not* in general preserved by Summation; in fact,

$$b.0 \approx \tau.b.0$$

while

$$a.0 + b.0 \not\approx a.0 + \tau.b.0$$

On the other hand, in Proposition 5.10 we saw that the Prefix combinator actually strengthens bisimilarity to equality; this will be proved later, when we have defined equality. For now, we wish to prove what was claimed in Chapter 5:

Proposition 2 Bisimilarity is preserved by Composition, Restriction and Relabelling; that is, if $P \approx Q$ then $P|R \approx Q|R$, $P \backslash L \approx Q \backslash L$ and $P[S] \approx Q[S]$. (This is also Proposition 5.11.)

Proof We shall only prove the result for Composition; the other two are easier, and can be done by the same method. It will be enough to show that

$$\mathcal{S} = \{(P|R, Q|R) \; : \; P, Q, R \in \mathcal{P} \text{ and } P \approx Q\}$$

is a bisimulation. So let $P|R \xrightarrow{\alpha} P'|R'$ (since every derivative must have this form).

Case 1 $P \xrightarrow{\alpha} P'$ and $R \equiv R'$.
Then $Q \overset{\hat{\alpha}}{\Rightarrow} Q'$ for some Q' with $P' \approx Q'$, so $Q|R \overset{\hat{\alpha}}{\Rightarrow} Q'|R$, and $(P'|R, Q'|R) \in \mathcal{S}$ as required.

Case 2 $R \xrightarrow{\alpha} R'$ and $P \equiv P'$.
Then also $Q|R \xrightarrow{\alpha} Q|R'$, and $(P|R', Q|R') \in \mathcal{S}$ as required.

Case 3 $\alpha = \tau$, $P \xrightarrow{\ell} P'$ and $R \xrightarrow{\bar{\ell}} R'$.
Then $Q \overset{\ell}{\Rightarrow} Q'$ for some Q' with $P' \approx Q'$, so $Q|R \overset{\tau}{\Rightarrow} Q'|R'$, and $(P'|R', Q'|R') \in \mathcal{S}$ as required.

Hence, by a symmetric argument, $\mathcal{S}$ is a bisimulation.   ∎

We shall sometimes need to consider bisimilarity of expressions E containing variables. We therefore extend the definition, just as we did for strong bisimilarity in Definition 4.5, as follows:

Definition 1 Let the variables which occur in E or in F be $\tilde{X}$. Then $E \approx F$ if, for all $\tilde{P}$, $E\{\tilde{P}/\tilde{X}\} \approx F\{\tilde{P}/\tilde{X}\}$.   ∎

7.2   Equality and its basic properties

We have seen that $\approx$ is not fully substitutive; $P \approx Q$ does not imply $P + R \approx Q + R$. We want a notion of equality, $P = Q$, which implies $P \approx Q$ and which *is* fully substitutive; that is, we want a congruence relation. It should be the largest congruence relation included in $\approx$. We define it as follows, and devote this section to its basic properties.

Definition 2 P and Q are *equal* or (*observation-*)*congruent*, written $P = Q$, if for all α

(i) Whenever $P \overset{\alpha}{\to} P'$ then, for some Q', $Q \overset{\alpha}{\Rightarrow} Q'$ and $P' \approx Q'$;

(ii) Whenever $Q \overset{\alpha}{\to} Q'$ then, for some P', $P \overset{\alpha}{\Rightarrow} P'$ and $P' \approx Q'$. ∎

Note that the two clauses differ from those for $\approx$ only in one respect: $\overset{\alpha}{\Rightarrow}$ appears in place of $\overset{\hat{\alpha}}{\Rightarrow}$. Thus each action of P or Q must be matched by *at least* one action of the other. Note also that this applies only to the first actions of P and Q; we require only $P' \approx Q'$, not $P' = Q'$, for their corresponding derivatives.

We also extend equality to expressions, in the same way as bisimilarity:

Definition 3   Let the variables which occur in E or in F be $\tilde{X}$. Then $E = F$ if, for all $\tilde{P}$, $E\{\tilde{P}/\tilde{X}\} = F\{\tilde{P}/\tilde{X}\}$. ∎

We can immediately obtain a characterisation of equality which shows how close it is to bisimilarity:

Proposition 3   Assume[1] that $\mathcal{L}(P) \cup \mathcal{L}(Q) \neq \mathcal{L}$. Then $P = Q$ iff, for all R, $P + R \approx Q + R$.

Proof   ($\Longrightarrow$) It is easy to show that the following is a bisimulation:

$$\{(P + R, Q + R) : P, Q, R \in \mathcal{P} \text{ and } P = Q\} \cup \approx$$

---

[1]Because of infinite Summation, it is possible that P and Q use *all* the labels in $\mathcal{L}$, even though $\mathcal{L}$ is infinite. We do not yet know if Proposition 3 holds without the assumption. Whether it does or not, one way of ensuring that the assumption *must* hold is to declare at the outset that the 'set' $\mathcal{A}$ of names is always extensible – which is to say that we can always construct a new name no matter how many we have used. (A logician would achieve this by making $\mathcal{A}$ a *class* rather than a *set*.) We have not wished to burden the less mathematical reader with such niceties; in fact, every later result whose proof depends upon Proposition 3 can also be proved without it.

($\Longleftarrow$) We prove the contrapositive. Suppose that $P \neq Q$. Then, for example, there are α and P' such that $P \xrightarrow{\alpha} P'$ but whenever $Q \overset{\alpha}{\Rightarrow} Q'$ then $P' \not\approx Q'$. Now choose $R \equiv \ell.0$, where ℓ is not in the sort of P or Q. Clearly $P + R \xrightarrow{\alpha} P'$; so we must show that whenever $Q + R \overset{\hat{\alpha}}{\Rightarrow} Q'$ then $P' \not\approx Q'$. If $\alpha = \tau$ and $Q' \equiv Q + R$, then $P' \not\approx Q'$ since Q' has a ℓ action and P' has none; otherwise $Q + R \overset{\alpha}{\Rightarrow} Q'$, and hence $Q \overset{\alpha}{\Rightarrow} Q'$ (since $R \overset{\alpha}{\Rightarrow} Q'$ is impossible because $\alpha \neq \ell$), so again $P' \not\approx Q'$.   ∎

Now we can easily show that equality lies between strong congruence and bisimilarity:

Proposition 4 $P \sim Q$ implies $P = Q$, and $P = Q$ implies $P \approx Q$. (This is also Proposition 5.8.)

Proof   First note that $P \sim Q$ implies $P \approx Q$; this follows directly from the fact that every strong bisimulation is also a bisimulation, which can be checked directly from the definitions. Now, to see that $P \sim Q$ implies $P = Q$, use property ($*$) of strong bisimilarity (Section 4.2) together with the definition of equality.

For the second part, from Proposition 3 above we have that $P = Q$ implies $P + 0 \approx Q + 0$; but $P + 0 \sim P$ so $P + 0 \approx P$, and $P \approx Q$ follows.   ∎

Exercise 1   Establish the bisimulation which proves the first part of Proposition 3 above. Also find a proof of the second part of Proposition 4 which does not use Proposition 3.   ∎

Exercise 2   Give simple examples of P and Q for which

(1) $P = Q$ but $P \not\sim Q$
(2) $P \approx Q$ but $P \neq Q$ ∎

The first step in proving that equality is a congruence is:

Proposition 5   Equality is an equivalence relation.

Proof   The easiest way is to use Proposition 3, together with the fact that $\approx$ is an equivalence.   ∎

Next, we show that Prefix strengthens bisimilarity to equality:

Proposition 6   If $P \approx Q$ then $\alpha.P = \alpha.Q$. (This is also Proposition 5.10.)

Proof   Direct from the definition of equality.   ∎

Now we prove that all combinators preserve equality:

Proposition 7   If $P = Q$ then $\alpha.P = \alpha.Q$, $P+R = Q+R$, $P|R = Q|R$, $P\backslash L = Q\backslash L$ and $P[f] = Q[f]$.

Proof   The first follows from Proposition 6. For the second, we require $(P+R)+R' \approx (Q+R)+R'$ for all R'; but we know that $P+(R+R') \approx Q+(R+R')$, since $P = Q$, and associativity holds for $\approx$ because it holds for $\sim$.

The remaining proofs are straightforward from direct application of equality. For Composition, a case analysis similar to the proof of Proposition 2 is required; the other two are more direct.   ∎

We have one further obligation to meet, to ensure that equality is a congruence. We need to know that if we transform the defining expression P in a recursive definition $A \overset{\text{def}}{=} P$, using laws of equality, then the meaning of A is unchanged up to equality. See also the discussion preceding Proposition 4.12; the following proposition is analogous.

Proposition 8   Let $\tilde{E} = \tilde{F}$, where $Vars(\tilde{E})$, $Vars(\tilde{F}) \subseteq \tilde{X}$, and let the Constants $\tilde{A}, \tilde{B}$ be defined by the equations $\tilde{A} \overset{\text{def}}{=} \tilde{E}\{\tilde{A}/\tilde{X}\}$, $\tilde{B} \overset{\text{def}}{=} \tilde{F}\{\tilde{B}/\tilde{X}\}$. Then $\tilde{A} = \tilde{B}$.

Proof   For simplicity we shall only consider the case of a single equation, thus omitting all tildes (˜). So assume

$$
\begin{aligned}
E &= F \\
A &\overset{\text{def}}{=} E\{A/X\} \\
B &\overset{\text{def}}{=} F\{B/X\}
\end{aligned}
$$

Now it will be nearly enough to show that $\mathcal{S}$ is a bisimulation up to $\approx$, where

$$\mathcal{S} = \{(G\{A/X\}, G\{B/X\})\ :\ G \text{ contains at most } X \text{ free}\}$$

for this would establish $A \approx B$ by taking $G \equiv X$. To achieve $A = B$, we actually prove that $\mathcal{S}$ has a stronger property:

$$
\begin{aligned}
&\text{if }\ G\{A/X\} \overset{\alpha}{\to} P' \text{ then, for some } Q', \qquad\qquad (*)\\
&\qquad G\{B/X\} \overset{\alpha}{\Rightarrow} Q' \text{ and } P'\mathcal{S} \approx Q'
\end{aligned}
$$

The use of $\overset{\alpha}{\Rightarrow}$ rather than $\overset{\hat{\alpha}}{\Rightarrow}$ is important. It is clear that $(*)$ makes $\mathcal{S}$ a bisimulation up to $\approx$, and hence $P'\mathcal{S} \approx Q'$ implies $P' \approx Q'$; thus by choosing $G \equiv X$ we deduce $A = B$ from $(*)$ together with the definition of equality, Definition 2.

The proof of $(*)$ is by induction on the inference of $G\{A/X\} \overset{\alpha}{\to} P'$; we omit it, since the details are close to those of Proposition 4.12.   ∎

Now, at last, we are able to discharge our debt to Chapter 3. First, we prove the τ laws.

Proposition 9   (This is also Proposition 3.2, the τ laws.)

(1) $\alpha.\tau.P = \alpha.P$
(2) $P + \tau.P = \tau.P$
(3) $\alpha.(P + \tau.Q) + \alpha.Q = \alpha.(P + \tau.Q)$ ∎

Proof   Direct, from the definition of equality. Note that, in (1) only, we need to use $P \approx \tau.P$.   ∎

Exercise 3   Prove

(1) $P|\tau.Q \approx P|Q$
(2) $P|\tau.Q \neq P|Q$
(3) $P|\tau.Q = \tau.(P|Q)$ ∎

We finish this section with two further results which underline how close bisimilarity comes to equality. First, we discharge our one remaining debt to Chapter 5.

Proposition 10   If $P \approx Q$ and both are stable then $P = Q$. (This is also Proposition 5.9.)

Proof   Let $P \overset{\alpha}{\to} P'$, which implies $\alpha \neq \tau$ (by stability); then $Q \overset{\hat{\alpha}}{\Rightarrow} Q'$ with $P' \approx Q'$. But then $Q \overset{\alpha}{\Rightarrow} Q'$ since $\overset{\hat{\alpha}}{\Rightarrow}$ and $\overset{\alpha}{\Rightarrow}$ coincide when $\alpha \neq \tau$, and $P = Q$ follows by definition.   ∎

Finally, we prove a beautiful and rather unexpected result which was first proved in a special case by Matthew Hennessy. We shall find a use for it in proving the completeness of a set of equational laws in Section 7.4 below.

Proposition 11 $P \approx Q$ iff $(P = Q$ or $P = \tau.Q$ or $\tau.P = Q)$.

Proof($\Longleftarrow$) We know that $P = Q$ implies $P \approx Q$ from Proposition 4, and the other implications follow from $P \approx \tau.P$.

($\Longrightarrow$) Assume $P \approx Q$, and consider three cases. First, suppose that $P \xrightarrow{\tau} P' \approx Q$ for some P'; then it is easy to show that $P = \tau.Q$. Second, suppose that $Q \xrightarrow{\tau} Q' \approx P$ for some Q'; then similarly we show that $\tau.P = Q$. If neither of these conditions holds, then we can show that $P = Q$ as follows. First, let $P \xrightarrow{\ell} P'$; then since $P \approx Q$ we have $Q \xLeftarrow{\hat{}} Q' \approx P'$, i.e. $Q \xRightarrow{\ell} Q' \approx P'$ as required. On the other hand if $P \xrightarrow{\tau} P'$ then $Q \Rightarrow Q' \approx P'$, and Q' cannot be Q itself by assumption, so $Q \xRightarrow{\tau} Q' \approx P'$ as required. By symmetry, $P = Q$ follows. ∎

Exercise 4 Complete the proof of the first case above, working directly from the definition of equality, Definition 2. ∎

The outcome of this section is that we have a notion of equality which is completely substitutive, and very close to bisimilarity. But we should not conclude that bisimilarity is redundant! The proof techniques which establish bisimilarity are often more convenient; establishing a bisimulation is a quite natural and sometimes mechanisable task, and the fact that $P \approx \tau.P$ – together with the substitutivity of $\approx$ in many contexts – makes bisimilarity quite tractable. The examples of Chapter 5 are good evidence of this, and they also show that equality can often be deduced 'at the end' by stability (Proposition 5.9) and because $P \approx Q$ implies $\alpha.P = \alpha.Q$ (Proposition 5.10).

7.3   Unique solutions of equations

In this section we give the proof of Proposition 3.4(2) concerning unique solution of equations. We first recall two definitions:

Definition 4 X is *sequential in E* if every subexpression of E which contains X, apart from X itself, is of the form $\alpha.F$ or $\sum \tilde{F}$. ∎

Definition 5 X is *guarded in E* if each occurrence of X is within some subexpression of E of the form $\ell.F$. ∎

Thus, for example,

- X is sequential but not guarded in $\tau.X + a.\mathbf{0}$;
- X is guarded but not sequential in $a.X|b.\mathbf{0}$;
- X is both guarded and sequential in $\tau.(a.(P_1|P_2) + b.X)$.

Our proposition will assert that a set of equations $\tilde{X} = \tilde{E}$, where the variables $\tilde{X}$ are guarded and sequential in $\tilde{E}$, has a unique solution up to equality. We shall sometimes say that E is *guarded* (resp. *sequential*) if each variable is guarded (resp. sequential) in E.

The most important property of a guarded and sequential expression is that its action behaviour, until and including the first non-τ action, is completely independent of whatever we may substitute for its free variables. Intuitively, the guardedness ensures that the variables (or rather, whatever agents may replace them) cannot affect behaviour until a guarding ℓ action is performed. The following lemma states this precisely.

Lemma 12   Let G be guarded and sequential, $Vars(G) \subseteq \tilde{X}$, and let $G\{\tilde{P}/\tilde{X}\} \xrightarrow{\alpha} P'$. Then there is an expression H such that $G \xrightarrow{\alpha} H$, $P' \equiv H\{\tilde{P}/\tilde{X}\}$ and, for any $\tilde{Q}$, $G\{\tilde{Q}/\tilde{X}\} \xrightarrow{\alpha} H\{\tilde{Q}/\tilde{X}\}$. Moreover H is sequential, $Vars(H) \subseteq \tilde{X}$, and if $\alpha = \tau$ then H is also guarded.

Proof   We proceed by induction on the structure of G. If G is a Constant, a Composition, a Restriction or a Relabelling then it contains no variables, since G is sequential, and hence $G \xrightarrow{\alpha} P'$; then the result is immediate by taking $H \equiv P'$. If G is a Summation the result is easy by induction. If G is a Prefix, $G \equiv \beta.H$ say, then $\beta = \alpha$ and clearly $P' \equiv H\{\tilde{P}/\tilde{X}\}$ and the result is immediate, noting that H must also be guarded if $\alpha = \tau$. Finally, G cannot be a variable since it is guarded. ∎

Now we consider a set of equations $\tilde{X} = \tilde{E}$, where the expressions $\tilde{E}$ have free variables $\subseteq \tilde{X}$ and are guarded and sequential. We show that they have a unique solution up to equality.

Proposition 13   Let $\tilde{E}$ be guarded and sequential expressions with free variables $\subseteq \tilde{X}$, and let $\tilde{P} = \tilde{E}\{\tilde{P}/\tilde{X}\}$, $\tilde{Q} = \tilde{E}\{\tilde{Q}/\tilde{X}\}$. Then $\tilde{P} = \tilde{Q}$.

Proof   For simplicity, let us drop the tildes (˜) and prove the case for a single equation $X = E$; the general case is a routine adaptation. We shall write $H(P)$ for $H\{P/X\}$ to ease the notation. So we assume

$$P = E(P)$$
$$Q = E(Q)$$

Also, we shall repeatedly use equations like $H(P) = H(E(P))$, justified by the substitutivity of equality (Proposition 7). The method is rather like that for Proposition 8; we shall prove for the relation

$$\mathcal{S} = \{(H(P), H(Q)) \; : \; H \text{ sequential}\}$$

that

$$\text{if} \quad H(P) \overset{\alpha}{\to} P' \text{ then, for some } Q', \qquad\qquad (*)$$
$$H(Q) \overset{\hat{\alpha}}{\Rightarrow} Q' \text{ and } P' \approx\mathcal{S}\approx Q'$$

By symmetry this makes $\mathcal{S}$ a bisimulation up to $\approx$, and the main result $P = Q$ follows by taking $H \equiv X$.

We find it convenient to prove first a version of $(*)$ involving only τ actions:

$$\text{if} \quad H(P) \Rightarrow P' \text{ then, for some } Q', \qquad\qquad (**)$$
$$H(Q) \Rightarrow Q' \text{ and } P' \approx\mathcal{S}\approx Q'$$

So let $H(P) \Rightarrow P'$. Now $H(P) = H(E(P))$, so for some P''

$$H(E(P)) \Rightarrow P'' \approx P'$$

But $H(E)$ is guarded and sequential, so by Lemma 12 there is a sequential H' for which

$$P'' \equiv H'(P) \text{ and } H(E(Q)) \Rightarrow H'(Q)$$

and since $H(Q) = H(E(Q))$ we also have for some Q'

$$H(Q) \Rightarrow Q' \approx H'(Q)$$

Summarising, we now have

$$P' \approx P'' \equiv H'(P) \; \mathcal{S} \; H'(Q) \approx Q'$$

This establishes $(**)$, and we can now use it to prove $(*)$.

Let $H(P) \overset{\alpha}{\to} P'$. Then

$$H(E(P)) \Rightarrow\overset{\alpha}{\to}\Rightarrow P'' \approx P'$$

Now by applying Lemma 12 repeatedly, taking us through $\Rightarrow\overset{\alpha}{\to}$, we find a sequential H' such that

$$H(E(P)) \Rightarrow\overset{\alpha}{\to} H'(P) \Rightarrow P'' \approx P'$$

and also, matching each single action,

$$H(E(Q)) \Rightarrow\overset{\alpha}{\to} H'(Q)$$

which we can complete, using $(**)$, by the derivation

$$H'(Q) \Rightarrow Q'' \text{ with } P'' \approx\mathcal{S}\approx Q''$$

Finally, since $H(Q) = H(E(Q))$, we deduce

$$H(Q) \stackrel{\alpha}{\Rightarrow} Q' \approx Q''$$

So $P' \approx S \approx Q'$ and the proof of $(*)$ is complete. ∎

This proof depends crucially upon our ability to 'unwind' P into $E(P)$ at any stage, converting $H(P)$ into the *guarded* form $H(E(P))$ so that Lemma 12 can be used.

7.4   Axioms for finite agents

Definition 6   An agent expression is *finite* if it contains only finite Summations, and no Constants (or Recursions). ∎

It is clear that the derivation tree of a finite agent is finite. It is also clear that, by use of the expansion law, any finite agent can be equated to one which contains no Composition, Restriction or Relabelling.

Definition 7   An agent expression E is *serial* if it contains no Composition, Restriction or Relabelling, and also the defining equation of any Constant in E contains no Composition, Restriction or Relabelling. ∎

Thus by expansion every finite agent can be equated to a finite serial agent.

Now the only laws we have which involve only Summation (including **0**, the empty sum) and Prefix are those of Propositions 3.1 and 3.2, which we shall now consider as axioms. We therefore consider two axiom systems:

Axioms $\mathcal{A}_1$

A1 $P + Q = Q + P$
A2 $P + (Q + R) = (P + Q) + R$
A3 $P + P = P$
A4 $P + 0 = P$

The second axiom system contains also the τ laws:

Axioms $\mathcal{A}_2$

A1–A4
A5 $\alpha.\tau.P = \alpha.P$
A6 $P + \tau.P = \tau.P$
A7 $\alpha.(P + \tau.Q) + \alpha.Q = \alpha.(P + \tau.Q)$

We already know that the following is a consequence of $\mathcal{A}_2$:

$$\textbf{A6'} \quad P + \tau.(P + Q) = \tau.(P + Q)$$

Now the τ laws appear at first sight to be a rather arbitrary collection; they are unlike other axiom systems, and one might expect that other laws for Prefix and Summation may be valid which cannot be deduced solely from the axioms $\mathcal{A}_2$. We aim in this section to show that this is not the case, at least for finite agents – that is that with the help of the expansion law *any* valid equation between finite agents follows from $\mathcal{A}_2$. This means that we have a *complete* axiomatisation for finite agents, and from what we have already said it will be enough to show that axioms $\mathcal{A}_2$ are complete for finite serial agents.

In what follows we shall use $P = Q$ to mean that P and Q are equal by our definition (Definition 2) of equality, while $\mathcal{A} \vdash P = Q$ will mean that the equality can be proved by equational reasoning from axioms $\mathcal{A}$. If $\mathcal{A}$ is understood from the context, we shall sometimes write $\vdash P = Q$. As always, we shall use $\equiv$ for syntactic identity. Unless otherwise stated, we shall assume all agents to be finite and serial.

First, we shall consider the power of $\mathcal{A}_1$.

Definition 8 P is a *standard form*, or is *in standard form*, if

$$P \equiv \sum_{i=1}^{m} \alpha_i.P_i$$

where each P_i is also in standard form.   ∎

Note that $\mathbf{0}$ is a standard form, by taking $m = 0$. Note also that the order and grouping of terms in $\alpha_1.P_1 + \cdots + \alpha_n.P_n$ may be ignored by virtue of axioms **A1**, **A2**. Other examples of standard form are $a.\mathbf{0}$, $a.\mathbf{0} + b(c.\mathbf{0} + \tau.\mathbf{0})$; but $\mathbf{0} + b.\mathbf{0}$ and $a.(\mathbf{0} + b.\mathbf{0})$ are not standard forms.

Lemma 14   For any P, there is a standard form P' such that

$$\mathcal{A}_1 \vdash P = P'$$

Proof   By use of $\mathcal{A}_1$, the term $\mathbf{0}$ may be eliminated from any Summation $\cdots + \mathbf{0} + \cdots$, and this results in a standard form.   ∎

Our first result is very simple, and shows that axioms $\mathcal{A}_1$ are both sound and complete for strong congruence.

Proposition 15　$P \sim Q$ iff $\mathcal{A}_1 \vdash P = Q$

Proof　($\Longleftarrow$) This is the soundness part. All we need to observe is that all of the axioms **A1–A4** are true if we replace $=$ by $\sim$; this was proved in Proposition 4.7.

($\Longrightarrow$) This is the completeness part. Assume $P \sim Q$, and also (relying on Lemma 14) that P and Q are both in standard form, $P \equiv \sum_{i=1}^{m} \alpha_i.P_i$ and $Q \equiv \sum_{j=1}^{n} \beta_j.Q_j$. We prove the result by induction on the maximum depth of P and Q, where the depth of P is defined to be the maximum number of nested Prefixes in P.

If the maximum depth is 0 then P and Q are both **0** (since they are standard), and equational reasoning ensures that $\mathcal{A}_1 \vdash \mathbf{0} = \mathbf{0}$ (reflexivity is part of equational reasoning!).

Otherwise let $\alpha.P'$ be summand of P. Then $P \xrightarrow{\alpha} P'$, so since $P \sim Q$ there is some Q' such that $Q \xrightarrow{\alpha} Q' \sim P'$. But Q is a standard form, so $\alpha.Q'$ is a summand of Q, and by induction $\mathcal{A}_1 \vdash P' = Q'$, so the summand $\alpha.P'$ of P can be proved equal to a summand of Q. Similarly, every summand $\beta.Q'$ of Q can be proved equal to a summand of P. It follows that $\mathcal{A}_1 \vdash P = Q$, by using **A3** to eliminate duplicate summands (and **A1** and **A2** to reorder and regroup summands as necessary). ∎

Now there are standard forms which are significantly different, but are equal (though not strongly congruent). An example is any non-trivial instance of **A7**, say

$$P \equiv a.(b.\mathbf{0} + \tau.\mathbf{0}), \quad Q \equiv a(b.\mathbf{0} + \tau.\mathbf{0}) + a.\mathbf{0}$$

Now Q has a property which is not possessed by P, namely that if $Q \xRightarrow{a} Q'$ then also $Q \xrightarrow{a} Q'$. Note that $P \xRightarrow{a} \mathbf{0}$, but not $P \xrightarrow{a} \mathbf{0}$. Another example is an instance of **A6**:

$$P \equiv \tau.a.\mathbf{0}, \quad Q \equiv \tau.a.\mathbf{0} + a.\mathbf{0}$$

Again, $P \xRightarrow{a} \mathbf{0}$ but not $P \xrightarrow{a} \mathbf{0}$. We are led to strengthen our notion of standard form as follows:

Definition 9　P is a *full* standard form if

(i) $P \equiv \sum_{i=1}^{m} \alpha_i.P_i$, where each P_i is in full standard form;
(ii) Whenever $P \xRightarrow{\alpha} P'$ then $P \xrightarrow{\alpha} P'$. ∎

We can think of a full standard form as *saturated* in the following sense: whenever $P \xRightarrow{a} P'$ then $\alpha.P'$ appears as a summand of P. Our next aim is to show that every standard form can be saturated, by using $\mathcal{A}_2$. In each of the above examples, P can be saturated to Q yield by using just one axiom, but in general more are needed.

Exercise 5   Consider $P \equiv \tau.(a.(\tau.0 + b.0))$. Note that neither P nor its subagent $P' \equiv a.(\tau.0 + b.0)$ is in full standard form; for example $P \overset{a}{\Rightarrow} 0$ but not $P \overset{a}{\to} 0$. Use axioms **A6** (or **A6′**) and **A7** to expand P to full standard form.

Hint: The form is perhaps larger than you think; it actually contains nine occurrences of Prefix.   ■

The essence of the saturation process is captured by the following lemma:

Lemma 16 (saturation)   If $P \overset{\alpha}{\Rightarrow} P'$, then $\mathcal{A}_2 \vdash P = P + \alpha.P'$.

Proof   By induction on the structure of P. Consider three cases for $P \overset{\alpha}{\Rightarrow} P'$:

Case 1 $\alpha.P'$ is a summand of P. Then the conclusion holds by **A3**.

Case 2 $\alpha.Q$ is a summand of P and $Q \overset{\tau}{\Rightarrow} P'$. Then by induction $\mathcal{A}_2 \vdash Q = Q + \tau.P'$, so

$$
\begin{aligned}
\mathcal{A}_2 \vdash P &= P + \alpha.Q && \text{by } \mathbf{A3} \\
&= P + \alpha.(Q + \tau.P') && \\
&= P + \alpha.(Q + \tau.P') + \alpha.P' && \text{by } \mathbf{A7} \\
&= P + \alpha.P' && \text{by previous steps reversed}
\end{aligned}
$$

Case 3 $\tau.Q$ is a summand of P and $Q \overset{\alpha}{\Rightarrow} P'$. Then by induction $\mathcal{A}_2 \vdash Q = Q + \alpha.P'$, so

$$
\begin{aligned}
\mathcal{A}_2 \vdash P &= P + \tau.Q && \text{by } \mathbf{A3} \\
&= P + \tau.Q + Q && \text{by } \mathbf{A6} \\
&= P + \tau.Q + Q + \alpha.P' && \\
&= P + \alpha.P' && \text{by previous steps reversed}
\end{aligned}
$$

This completes the proof.   ■

With the help of this, we can convert any standard form into a full standard form:

Lemma 17   For any standard form P there is a full standard form P' of equal depth, such that $\mathcal{A}_2 \vdash P = P'$.

Proof   By induction on the structure of P. For the base case, $P \equiv 0$,

P is already a full standard form. Otherwise, for each summand $\beta.Q$ of P we can assume by induction that Q has already been converted by $\mathcal{A}_2$ into a full standard form, without depth increase. Now consider all pairs (α_i, P_i), $1 \le i \le k$, such that $P \overset{\alpha_i}{\Rightarrow} P_i$ but not $P \overset{\alpha_i}{\rightarrow} P_i$. Each P_i must be in full standard form since it must be a subexpression of some summand $\beta.Q$ of P. Hence

$$P' \equiv P + \alpha_1.P_1 + \cdots + \alpha_k.P_k$$

is a full standard form of equal depth to P, and by Lemma 16 we have $\mathcal{A}_2 \vdash P = P'$.   ∎

We are now ready to prove the main result of this section, that $\mathcal{A}_2$ is sound and complete for equality of finite serial agents.

Proposition 18 $P = Q$ iff $\mathcal{A}_2 \vdash P = Q$

Proof   ($\Longleftarrow$) For soundness, we merely need to observe that axioms **A1–A7** are all true, when $=$ is understood as equality, as defined by Definition 2.

($\Longrightarrow$) We can assume, by Lemmas 14 and 17, that P and Q are in full standard form; the proof proceeds by induction on the sum of the depths of P and Q.

When both depths are 0 we have $P \equiv \mathbf{0} \equiv Q$, so the result is trivial. Otherwise assume $P = Q$, and let $\alpha.P'$ be a summand of P. We aim to prove that Q has a summand provably equal to $\alpha.P'$. Now $P \overset{\alpha}{\rightarrow} P'$, so there is a Q' such that $Q \overset{\alpha}{\Rightarrow} Q'$ and $P' \approx Q'$. Moreover $Q \overset{\alpha}{\rightarrow} Q'$ since Q is a full standard form, so $\alpha.Q'$ is a summand of Q.

We cannot use induction immediately, since we only know $P' \approx Q'$, not $P' = Q'$. But by Hennessy's theorem, Proposition 11, we know that $P' = Q'$ or $P' = \tau.Q'$ or $\tau.P' = Q'$.

In the first case, since P' and Q' are full standard forms, and of lesser depth than P and Q, by induction $\mathcal{A}_2 \vdash P' = Q'$, so $\mathcal{A}_2 \vdash \alpha.P' = \alpha.Q'$. In the second case we must first convert $\tau.Q'$ to full standard form before applying induction. From Lemma 17 there is a full standard form Q'', of equal depth to $\tau.Q'$, such that $\mathcal{A}_2 \vdash \tau.Q' = Q''$; but the sum of depths of P' and Q'' is one less than the sum of depths of P and Q, so by induction we infer that $\mathcal{A}_2 \vdash P' = Q''$, so $\mathcal{A}_2 \vdash P' = \tau.Q'$, and by **A5** we infer that $\mathcal{A}_2 \vdash \alpha.P' = \alpha.Q'$. (This is the first time that **A5** has been used!) The third case is similar.

Thus, in each of the three cases, we have shown that from $\mathcal{A}_2$ each summand $\alpha.P'$ of P can be proved equal to a summand of Q. Similarly each summand $\beta.Q'$ of Q can be proved equal to a summand of P. Finally, by use of **A3** to eliminate duplicate summands, we conclude $\mathcal{A}_2 \vdash P = Q$.   ∎

So we can indeed claim that the τ laws tell us everything we need to know about Prefix, at least as far as finite agents are concerned.

7.5   Axioms for finite-state agents

If we were to look for a finite set of axioms and rules from which we could deduce all true equations between agents of any kind – or even limiting ourselves to those with finite Summation and finite sets of defining equations – we should certainly fail. This is a consequence of the fact that, as you may have discovered in doing Exercise 6.5, we can effectively build an agent TM$_i$ for the ith Turing machine such that

> TM$_i$ = $\tau.$**0** if and only if the ith Turing machine diverges when given a blank input tape.

But the set of such equations is not recursively enumerable, whereas the set of equations provable from a given finite set of axioms and rules is so.

The situation is different if we exclude the static combinators. In Definition 7 we defined an agent or expression to be *serial* if it is built without the static combinators. Then, if only finite Summation and finitely many defining equations are permitted, it is not hard to show that each serial agent is *finite-state*; that is, it has finitely many distinct derivatives. We shall now outline an argument that there is a finite set of axioms and rules which is complete for equality of finite-state serial agents.

To keep things simple, we confine ourselves to expressions E with the following syntax:

$$E ::= \quad X \quad | \quad \alpha.E \quad | \quad E + E \quad | \quad \textbf{fix}(X = E)$$

The restriction to single recursion equations loses no expressive power, since for example the double Recursion $\textbf{fix}(X = E, Y = F)$ can be also expressed as $\textbf{fix}(X = E\{\textbf{fix}(Y = F)/Y\})$. For formal studies such as proofs of completeness it is preferable not to admit Constants with defining equations, but to stick to the pure **fix** expressions introduced in Section 2.9 – even though they are not very pleasant to use in applications.

Now there are two very natural laws for Recursion, which capture the essence of Proposition 3.4 (or alternatively Props 4.14(1) and 7.11):

$$\textbf{R1} \quad \text{fix}(X = E) = E\{\text{fix}(X = E)/X\}$$
$$\textbf{R2} \quad \text{If } F = E\{F/X\} \text{ then } F = \text{fix}(X = E),$$
$$\text{provided that } X \text{ is guarded in } E$$

The question is: If we interpret P, Q, R in axioms $\mathcal{A}_2$ as serial agent expressions (i.e. allowing free variables), and add **R1** and **R2**, do we get enough power to prove all true equations between serial agents? (Actually, we would certainly need a law which allows us to change the bound variable X in $\text{fix}(X = E)$ to any other variable not free in E, but this law has no semantic significance.)

The answer is unfortunately: not quite enough. The reason has to do with unguarded Recursions. Take the simplest possible example; suppose we want to prove

$$\text{fix}(X = \tau.X) = \text{fix}(X = \tau.\tau.X)$$

If we set $F \equiv \text{fix}(X = \tau.X)$ then, by **R1**, we have $F = \tau.F$, so $F = \tau.\tau.F$; therefore $F = E\{F/X\}$ where $E \equiv \tau.\tau.X$, but we cannot use **R2** to deduce $F = \text{fix}(X = \tau.\tau.X)$ because X is not guarded in $\tau.\tau.X$.

However, if we only consider expressions in which all the Recursions are guarded – that is all Recursions are of form $\text{fix}(X = E)$ where X is guarded in E – then it turns out that $\mathcal{A}_2 \cup \{\textbf{R1}, \textbf{R2}\}$ is a system which is complete. The proof is rather long and detailed and we shall not give it, but the result is quite satisfying, because it shows us that the natural laws **R1** and **R2** for Recursion are sufficient when added to the simple laws for finite serial agents, in the case where all Recursions are guarded (which is the normal case in applications).

So how do we deal with *unguarded* Recursions? First, there are two elegant laws which remove the simplest unguarded occurrences of variables from a Recursion. They are:

$$\textbf{R3} \quad \text{fix}(X = X + E) = \text{fix}(X = E)$$
$$\textbf{R4} \quad \text{fix}(X = \tau.X + E) = \text{fix}(X = \tau.E)$$

The law **R3** is even valid for strong congruence. It is fairly intuitively clear; one can see that the extra X on the left allows no extra actions to be inferred by the transition rules. **R4** is more interesting semantically; it represents the fact that an extra τ-cycle does not disturb the meaning of an agent. **R4** may be depicted informally as follows:

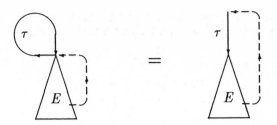

The dashed lines represent occurrences of X within E; they represent the possibility of other recursive activations of the agent from within itself. Notice that these two laws – considered as transformations from left to right – represent only the removal of 'tight' loops, i.e. loops which involve just a single node. (In fact the loop in **R3** is so tight that we cannot draw a good picture of it!)

And in fact these laws are not enough. Consider the equation $X = E$, where

$$E \equiv a.E_1 + \tau.(b.E_2 + \tau.X)$$

so that $\mathbf{fix}(X = E)$ may be depicted as follows:

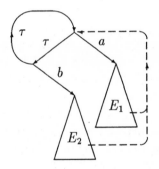

How can we eliminate the τ-cycle here? We have no way of converting this fixed-point expression into the form of the left-hand side of **R3** or **R4**. So what sort of rule can we add to do this conversion, so that **R3** and **R4** can be used to remove *all* τ-cycles? Well, an important insight is that, *because* of the τ-cycle in the diagram above, the order of the two branches beginning a and b really does not matter – since either may be entered at any time during the traversing of the τ-cycle. Thus the τ-cycle is a way of providing a choice, to be made by the environment, between the a-branch and the b-branch. This argument is only intuitive, but it turns out that the τ-cycle can indeed be excised to yield the equal transition graph:

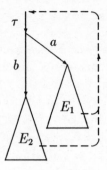

In other words, it can be shown that

$$\textbf{fix}(X = a.E_1 + \tau.(b.E_2 + \tau.X)) = \textbf{fix}(X = \tau.(a.E_1 + b.E_2)) \quad (*)$$

So what we want is a law which will 'reach down' into E to 'pull out' any unguarded X. It turns out, remarkably, that the following simple law is sufficient:

R5 $\textbf{fix}(X = \tau.(X + E) + F) = \textbf{fix}(X = \tau.X + E + F)$

Exercise 6   Use **R5**, together with **R4**, to prove $(*)$. The first step is to use a τ law to convert the left-hand side to

$$\textbf{fix}(X = a.E_1 + \tau.(X + b.E_2 + \tau.X)) \qquad \blacksquare$$

By repeated use of **R5** with **R3** and **R4**, it can be shown that any unguarded Recursion can be converted into a guarded Recursion; then the axioms $\mathcal{A}_2$ with **R1** and **R2** will (as we asserted above) be enough to prove any valid equation. Again, the rigorous proof is rather involved, and we omit it.

Exercise 7   It is, of course, vital to prove that rules **R3**–**R5** are sound! Do this by a bisimulation, in each case. Remember that you need only prove the laws valid in the case that there are no free variables, because two expressions are defined to be equal just when all their substitution instances are equal.

Hint: For **R4** you will need a bisimulation $\mathcal{S}$ which contains the pair

$$(\ G\{\textbf{fix}(X = \tau.X + E)/X\}\ ,\ G\{\textbf{fix}(X = \tau.E)/X\}\ )$$

for every G with at most one free variable X; but these are not quite all the pairs you need in $\mathcal{S}$. $\qquad \blacksquare$

One consequence of this completeness result is that equality of finite-state agents is semi-decidable. But a proof of full decidability exists, which does not depend on finding equational axioms; it rests upon the simple idea that, in searching for a bisimulation between two finite-state agents, one will either succeed or find an attribute of behaviour which distinguishes them, and that this will occur within a search time bounded by a simple function of the number of states. The importance of an axiomatisation is not so much that it may be used as a proof procedure, but rather that it provides a deep insight into the nature of the combinators, and of the kind of transformations of expressions which preserve equality.

Finally, we must emphasize that the limitation to finite-state agents still admits important applications. Although we have omitted the static combinators, it is very easy to show that if an agent expressed in such a way that the static combinators do not occur inside Recursion, then the static combinators can be eliminated from it. Many 'real-life' agents are defined in this way, and are essentially finite-state. One example is the Alternating-Bit protocol which we discussed in Chapter 6; other examples exist in profusion in digital hardware. A complete equational axiomatisation of such systems is a core ingredient of their theory, even though in many cases one will wish to verify properties which cannot be expressed easily as equations.

8

Defining a Programming Language

This chapter is devoted to the study of a simple but non-trivial parallel programming language. After a few preliminaries, the semantics of the language is defined quite simply by translation into the calculus. Then the problem is tackled of extending the language by adding procedures. The calculus is found to cope naturally with the difficulties involved in defining the behaviour of parallel activations of the same procedure.

8.1 Introduction

There are many ways in which parallel computation may be expressed in a programming language. They may be classified according to the ways in which communication or interaction is achieved between subprograms running in parallel. One way is by direct transmission of values; this way is exemplified by the rendezvous of Ada, or the input and output guards of CSP, and it corresponds closely to the hand-shake communication of our calculus. Another way, perhaps more natural to those familiar with sequential imperative programming languages like Pascal, is by common access to variables shared among two or many subprograms; this way is exemplified by concurrent versions of Pascal. Some languages combine both these styles.

There are also different methodologies for presenting the semantics of programming languages. The earliest way was by careful narrative; this was adopted for Algol60, and has the considerable advantage that it is accessible and intelligible (if carefully done, as in the case of Algol60) to a wide community. It has the disadvantage that even the most lucid narrative description is prone to omissions and ambiguities, and much recent work has been devoted to finding more rigorous mathematical methodologies which – though less accessible – are complete and unambiguous. One methodology is denotational semantics; in this approach

170

each program phrase is given a denotation, or meaning, as an object of some mathematical domain, and it is normally compositional in the sense that the meaning of each phrase is a function of the meanings of its subphrases. A second methodology is operational semantics; here, rules are given for the evaluation of each phrase, and the more modern version is also structured or compositional – which in this case means that the evaluation of each phrase is defined in terms of the evaluation of its subphrases. Indeed our calculus has been defined by the structured operational rules presented in Chapter 2.

A third semantic method is by translation. The lambda-calculus is a canonical, extremely parsimonious, language originally conceived by Alonzo Church as a basic means to express functions or sequential algorithms. (In fact it was the first language to be defined by the method of operational semantics; the general methodology of operational semantics stems from the few rules which define the lambda-calculus.) Therefore one may define the meaning of another sequential programming language by translating it, preferably in a way which respects its phrase structure, into the lambda-calculus. Peter Landin carried out just such a translation for a large part of Algol60, before denotational semantics was envisaged. Similarly, our calculus is a parsimonious and rigorously defined language which claims to express the basic concepts of parallelism in computation, and therefore it is a good test of its expressive power to contrive a natural translation of another language into it. The latter language is thereby given unambiguous meaning.

We shall choose a language $\mathcal{M}$ which extends a simple imperative language by allowing interaction via shared variables between concurrent subprograms; this form of interaction (the second of the two types described in the first paragraph) is different from our basic hand-shake, and is therefore a good test of the expressive power of the calculus. Since the translation will be phrase-by-phrase, it can actually be seen as defining the constructs of $\mathcal{M}$ as derived combinators of our calculus; this means that $\mathcal{M}$ is presented as just an extension-by-definitions of the calculus, requiring no new basic material. One important quality of the translation is the treatment of local declarations, which must feature in any reasonable programming language; it turns out that the Restriction combinator of the calculus renders the localisation of declarations in a most direct and lucid manner.

8.2   Some derived operators

The language $\mathcal{M}$ will contain program variables, to which values may be assigned, and the meaning of a program variable X will be a 'storage location'. We therefore begin by defining a storage register holding a value y as follows:

$$\text{put} \,\,\, \overset{\frown}{\underset{\smile}{\left(Reg(y)\right)}} \,\,\, \overline{\text{get}}$$

$$Reg(y) \overset{\text{def}}{=} \text{put}x.Reg(x) + \overline{\text{get}}y.Reg(y)$$

(We shall often write $\text{put}(x)$ as $\text{put}x$ etc.) Thus, via $\overline{\text{get}}$ the stored value y may be read from the register, and via put a new value x may be written to the register. For each program variable X – which must not be confused with a value variable x or agent variable X of our calculus – we introduce a register $Reg_X(y) \overset{\text{def}}{=} Reg(y)[f_X]$, where f_X is the relabelling function $(\text{put}_X/\text{put}, \text{get}_X/\text{get})$. Further, the initial storage location associated with X will be

$$Loc_X \overset{\text{def}}{=} \text{put}_X y.Reg_X(y)$$

ensuring that no value may be read until a value has been written.

This representation of registers – or program variables – as processes is fundamental to our translation; it indicates that resources like variables, as well as the programs which use them, can be thought of as processes, so that our calculus can get away with the single notion of process to represent different kinds of entity.

We can think of every declaration in $\mathcal{M}$ as providing – and naming – a resource for use within the scope of the declaration. Let $L_X = \{\text{put}_X, \overline{\text{get}}_X\}$, the sort of Loc_X. Then we define $ACC_X = \overline{L_X} = \{\overline{\text{put}}_X, \text{get}_X\}$, and we call it the *access sort* of the resource X; it is the means by which subprograms access the variable. In fact procedures, the other kind of resource which can be declared in $\mathcal{M}$, will also have an access sort – the means by which subprograms can call procedures and receive their returned results.

We now turn to sequencing. There is no basic notion of sequential composition of agents in our calculus, but we can define it. To do this, we introduce a convention that agents may indicate their termination by a distinguished label $\overline{\text{done}}$; the agents which arise from translating commands in $\mathcal{M}$ will always use this termination convention.

Definition 1 P is *well-terminating* if, for every derivative P' of P, $P' \xrightarrow{\overline{done}}$ is impossible and also if $P' \xrightarrow{\overline{done}}$ then $P' \sim \overline{done}.0$. ∎

Not that the definition does not demand that P should terminate, but only that whenever it performs $\overline{done}$ then it terminates. Note also the use of strong congruence, $\sim$, in this definition. A similar definition using $\approx$ would do, and might have wider application, but in fact our language $\mathcal{M}$ respects the stronger definition given here.

We would first like to know that well-termination is preserved both by derivation and by strong congruence:

Exercise 1 If P is well-terminating, prove:

(1) If $P \xrightarrow{\alpha} P'$ then P' is well-terminating.
(2) If $P \sim Q$ then Q is well-terminating. ∎

Now we shall define a combinator *Before* for sequential composition. We shall also define a combinator *Par* for parallel composition, which allows termination by $\overline{done}$ when and only when both component agents have terminated.

Definition 2

$$Done \stackrel{\text{def}}{=} \overline{done}.0$$

$$P \; Before \; Q \stackrel{def}{=} (P[b/done] \mid b.Q)\backslash b$$

$$P \; Par \; Q \stackrel{\text{def}}{=} (P[d_1/done] \mid Q[d_2/done] \mid$$
$$(d_1.d_2.Done + d_2.d_1.Done))\backslash\{d_1, d_2\}$$

where b, d_1, d_2 are new names. ∎

These definitions are made without any condition on P and Q, but *Before* and *Par* preserve well-termination:

Exercise 2 Prove that if P and Q are well-terminating, then so are $P \; Before \; Q$ and $P \; Par \; Q$.
Hint: Work by induction on the length of derivations of the form

$$P \; Before \; Q \xrightarrow{t} \xrightarrow{\overline{done}} R$$ ∎

In the definition of *Par*, the summand $d_2.d_1.Done$ could be omitted; but with it, it is rather easier to prove that *Par* has nice properties.

Exercise 3 Prove the following, by using the static laws only:

$$P \; Before \; (Q \; Before \; R) \;\; = \;\; (P \; Before \; Q) \; Before \; R$$
$$P \; Par \; Q \;\; = \;\; Q \; Par \; P$$
$$P \; Par \; (Q \; Par \; R) \;\; = \;\; (P \; Par \; Q) \; Par \; R$$

Also prove

$$Done \; Before \; P \;\; \approx \;\; P$$
$$Done \; Par \; P \;\; \approx \;\; P$$

These properties all hold without assuming well-termination of P, Q and R. But convince yourself that $P \; Before \; Done \approx P$ is false in general. (It holds if P is well-terminating, as we show later.)   ∎

Just as a *command* of $\mathcal{M}$ will be a well-terminating agent, so an *expression* of $\mathcal{M}$ will 'terminate' by yielding up its results via the label $\overline{\text{res}}$. If P represents such an expression, then we may wish another agent Q to refer to the result by using the value variable x. To this end, we define another combinator, *Into*:

Definition 3 $P \; Into(x) \; Q \stackrel{\text{def}}{=} (P \mid \text{res}(x).Q)\backslash\text{res}$ ∎

To be precise, Q here is not exactly an agent, but an agent expression in which the value variable x may occur free; *Into* then binds this variable. Also note that in using this combinator, we shall never have res or $\overline{\text{res}}$ in the sort of Q.

Armed with these combinators, we can now define and translate the language $\mathcal{M}$.

8.3   The language $\mathcal{M}_0$ and its translation

The language $\mathcal{M}_0$, a first approximation to $\mathcal{M}$, has *commands* C, *declarations* D and *expressions* E as its phrase classes. We assume a fixed set of *function symbols* F and *variables* X; F stands for a function f over values. We do not trouble to distinguish types of data value, but we assume that the truth values are among the values. Here is the syntax of the five syntactic classes:

$$X ::= \quad \text{X} \mid \text{Y} \mid \cdots \qquad\qquad \text{Variables}$$

$$F ::= \quad \text{+} \mid \text{-} \mid \cdots \mid \text{0} \mid \text{1} \mid \cdots \qquad \text{Function symbols}$$

$C ::=$	$X := E$	Assignment
	$C ; C'$	Sequential composition
	if E then C else C'	Conditional
	while E do C	Iteration
	begin D ; C end	Block
	C par C'	Parallel composition
	input X	Input
	output E	Output
	skip	No action
$D ::=$	var X	Variable declaration
$E ::=$	X	Variable
	$F (E_1 ,\ldots, E_n)$	Function application

Note that in a block construction begin D ; C end, C is the scope of the declaration D. Later we shall add procedure declarations and a command for procedure call, thus extending $\mathcal{M}_0$ to $\mathcal{M}$. Each function symbol F is assumed to have an *arity* (number of arguments) and we include constants as function symbols with zero arity, so that our syntax for expressions represents 'X+1' as '+(X,1())'.

The intended meaning of $\mathcal{M}_0$ is fairly clear, except for one point concerning the granularity of par. What should the following command mean?

```
X := 0 ;
X := X + 1 par X := X + 1
```

If the concurrent assignments can be overlapped in time then the resulting value in X could be 1 or 2; if not, then it must be 2. Our translation will take the former alternative; later we shall see how to get the latter.

Shortly we give the translation function $\mathcal{M}[\![-]\!]$ of phrases C, D and E into agents. First, we want to point out that the sorts of these translations will obey the following rules:

L1   If the command C contains non-local variables $X_1,\ldots,X_n$ then

$$\mathcal{L}(\mathcal{M}[\![C]\!]) \subseteq ACC_{X_1} \cup \cdots \cup ACC_{X_n} \cup \{\overline{\text{done}}, \text{in}, \overline{\text{out}}\}$$

(The labels in, $\overline{\text{out}}$ are used for input and output respectively, as will be seen.)

L2   If the declaration D is var X, then

$$\mathcal{L}(\mathcal{M}[\![D]\!]) = L_X = \{\text{put}_X, \overline{\text{get}_X}\}$$

L3   If the expression E contains variables $X_1, \ldots, X_n$ then

$$\mathcal{L}(\mathcal{M}[\![E]\!]) = \{\mathrm{get}_{X_1}, \ldots, \mathrm{get}_{X_n}, \overline{\mathrm{res}}\}$$

Of course we shall have to prove that these rules are obeyed! The proof will be a simple induction on the structure of phrases.

To permit the translation of expressions, we first give the translation of each function symbol F standing for function f. If F has arity n, then

$$\mathcal{M}[\![F]\!] = \mathrm{arg}_1 x_1. \cdots . \mathrm{arg}_n x_n. \overline{\mathrm{res}}(f(x_1, \ldots, x_n)).0$$

Then the translation of expressions is given by

$$
\begin{aligned}
\mathcal{M}[\![X]\!] &= \mathrm{get}_X x.\overline{\mathrm{res}}x.0 \\
\mathcal{M}[\![F(E_1, \ldots, E_n)]\!] &= (\mathcal{M}[\![E_1]\!][\mathrm{arg}_1/\mathrm{res}]\!|\cdots|\mathcal{M}[\![E_n]\!][\mathrm{arg}_n/\mathrm{res}]\,| \\
&\qquad \mathcal{M}[\![F]\!])\backslash\{\mathrm{arg}_1, \ldots, \mathrm{arg}_n\}
\end{aligned}
$$

Thus, for example, the translation of X-(Y+1) is shown by the following flow graph:

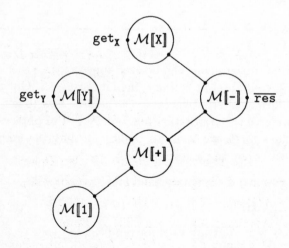

Exercise 4   Prove the property **L3**, about the sort of $\mathcal{M}[\![E]\!]$, by induction on the structure of E.   ∎

Notice that in translating an expression there will be an agent $\mathcal{M}[\![F]\!]$ for each *occurrence* of the function symbol F; $\mathcal{M}[\![F]\!]$ is capable of only one application of the function f. Another reasonable method would be to provide just one agent $\mathcal{M}[\![F]\!]$, capable of repeated applications:

$$\mathcal{M}[\![F]\!] \;=\; A_F, \text{ where}$$

$$A_F \;\stackrel{\text{def}}{=}\; \mathrm{arg}_{1F}x_1.\cdots.\mathrm{arg}_{nF}x_n.\overline{\mathrm{res}_F}(f(x_1,\ldots,x_n)).A_F$$

This amounts to providing $\mathcal{M}[\![F]\!]$ as a global resource to a program; the access sort ACC_F of this resource would be $\{\overline{\mathrm{arg}_{1F}},\ldots,\overline{\mathrm{arg}_{nF}},\mathrm{res}_F\}$. The advantage of this would be that, if we were to add function declarations to $\mathcal{M}$, then the basic function symbols F would be treated in the same way as function symbols declared by the programmer (this will become clearer when we see how procedure declarations are added to $\mathcal{M}_0$).

Exercise 5   Redefine the translation of expressions, assuming the alternative treatment of $\mathcal{M}[\![F]\!]$. If an expression E contains function symbols $F_1,\ldots,F_m$ as well as variables $X_1,\ldots,X_n$, what now is the sort $\mathcal{L}(\mathcal{M}[\![E]\!])$? (Compare property **L3**.)   ∎

Now, with the help of the auxiliary combinators introduced in the previous section, the translation of commands is quite succinct and straightforward:

$$
\begin{aligned}
\mathcal{M}[\![X := E]\!] \;&=\; \mathcal{M}[\![E]\!]\; Into(x)(\overline{\mathrm{put}_X}x.Done)\\
\mathcal{M}[\![C \, ; \, C']\!] \;&=\; \mathcal{M}[\![C]\!]\; Before\; \mathcal{M}[\![C']\!]\\
\mathcal{M}[\![\text{if } E \text{ then } C \text{ else } C']\!] \;&=\; \mathcal{M}[\![E]\!]\; Into(x)\\
&\qquad (\text{if } x \text{ then } \mathcal{M}[\![C]\!] \text{ else } \mathcal{M}[\![C']\!])\\
\mathcal{M}[\![\text{while } E \text{ do } C]\!] \;&=\; W, \text{ where } W \stackrel{\text{def}}{=} \mathcal{M}[\![E]\!]\; Into(x)\\
&\qquad (\text{if } x \text{ then } \mathcal{M}[\![C]\!]\; Before\; W \text{ else } Done)\\
\mathcal{M}[\![\text{begin } D \, ; \, C \text{ end}]\!] \;&=\; (\mathcal{M}[\![D]\!] \mid \mathcal{M}[\![C]\!])\backslash ACC_D\\
\mathcal{M}[\![C \text{ par } C']\!] \;&=\; \mathcal{M}[\![C]\!]\; Par\; \mathcal{M}[\![C']\!]\\
\mathcal{M}[\![\text{input } X]\!] \;&=\; \mathrm{in}x.\overline{\mathrm{put}_X}x.Done\\
\mathcal{M}[\![\text{output } E]\!] \;&=\; \mathcal{M}[\![E]\!]\; Into(x)(\overline{\mathrm{out}}\, x.Done)\\
\mathcal{M}[\![\text{skip}]\!] \;&=\; Done
\end{aligned}
$$

Of course, with the **fix** expressions introduced at the end of Chapter 2, we can write the meaning W of the `while` command directly as

$$\mathbf{fix}(X = \mathcal{M}[\![E]\!] \; Into(x) \; (\mathbf{if} \; x \; \mathbf{then} \; \mathcal{M}[\![C]\!] \; Before \; X \; \mathbf{else} \; Done))$$

Finally, for the only kind of declaration D in $\mathcal{M}_0$, we have

$$\mathcal{M}[\![\mathtt{var} \; X]\!] = Loc_X$$

with the access sort ACC_D given by ACC_X.

There are many things to discuss about this translation. Let us first look at the localisation provided by the Restriction $\backslash ACC_D$ in the translation of a block. Suppose that C has non-local variables X and Y; then (assuming property **L1** about sorts) the sort of the translation $\mathcal{M}[\![C]\!]$ satisfies

$$\mathcal{L}(\mathcal{M}[\![C]\!]) \subseteq ACC_X \cup ACC_Y \cup \{\mathtt{in}, \overline{\mathtt{out}}, \overline{\mathtt{done}}\}$$

and so $\mathcal{M}[\![C]\!]$ may be depicted by the flow graph

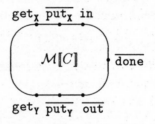

Now, in the (translated) block $\mathcal{M}[\![\mathtt{begin} \; \mathtt{var} \; X \; ; \; C \; \mathtt{end}]\!]$, the access sort of X is restricted, so the translated block has the flow graph

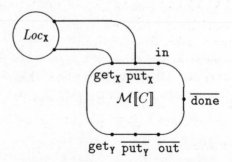

This indicates how the local variable X in the block is protected from confusion with any other variable X used elsewhere in a program. In fact, this is a special case of what will occur for any locally declared

resource. In this case, the resource is totally excluded from interaction with any other part of the program, and this is because the access sort ACC_X is *exactly* the complement of the sort of the resource Loc_X. In general, for example in the case of a procedure G which uses a variable Z not local to it, Restriction of the access sort ACC_G will still leave some ports of $\mathcal{M}[\![G]\!]$ unrestricted:

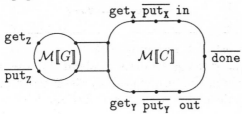

This is because $\overline{ACC_G} \neq \mathcal{L}(\mathcal{M}[\![G]\!])$. We are anticipating the later addition of procedures, just to see that localisation by restricting the access sort to a resource need not restrict all access to the resource.

Two essential properties of our translation are given as exercises:

Exercise 6   Prove by induction on the structure of commands C:

(1) Property **L1** about the sort $\mathcal{L}(\mathcal{M}[\![C]\!])$;

(2) $\mathcal{M}[\![C]\!]$ is well-terminating.

Hint: In (2), in the case of the while command with meaning W defined recursively, you will also need a subsidiary induction on the length of derivations of the form $W \xrightarrow{s} P' \xrightarrow{\overline{\text{done}}} P'$.   ∎

The vital question about our translation – or indeed about any semantic definition – is: how do we know that it is correct? We can never answer this question absolutely, because a formal semantic definition is a *definition*, supposed to capture an intuitive informal understanding. But what we can hope to do is to prove certain properties which are intended by the understanding. One such property is that C_1 par $(C_2$ par $C_3)$ should mean the same as $(C_1$ par $C_2)$ par C_3, and this is very easy to establish.

Exercise 7   Prove

$$\mathcal{M}[\![C_1 \text{ par } (C_2 \text{ par } C_3)]\!] \;=\; \mathcal{M}[\![(C_1 \text{ par } C_2) \text{ par } C_3]\!]$$
$$\mathcal{M}[\![\text{skip}\,;C]\!] \;\approx\; \mathcal{M}[\![C]\!]$$

by using Exercise 3.   ∎

We shall now list some other properties which we would expect. Just for now we take the liberty of abbreviating $\mathcal{M}[\![C]\!] \approx \mathcal{M}[\![C']\!]$ and $\mathcal{M}[\![C]\!] = \mathcal{M}[\![C']\!]$ respectively to $C \approx C'$ and $C = C'$:

(1) $C \,;\, \texttt{skip} \;\approx\; C$

(2) If X is not a non-local variable of C then

$$\texttt{begin var}\, X \,;\, C\, \texttt{end} \;=\; C$$
$$\texttt{begin var}\, X \,;\, C \,;\, C'\, \texttt{end} \;=\; C \,;\, \texttt{begin var}\, X \,;\, C'\, \texttt{end}$$
$$\texttt{begin var}\, X \,;\, C\, \texttt{par}\, C'\, \texttt{end} \;=\; C \,\texttt{par}\, \texttt{begin var}\, X \,;\, C'\, \texttt{end}$$

(3) If X is not in E then

$$\texttt{begin var}\, X \,;\, \texttt{if}\, E\, \texttt{then}\, C\, \texttt{else}\, C'\, \texttt{end} \;=$$
$$\texttt{if}\, E\, \texttt{then begin var}\, X \,;\, C\, \texttt{end else begin var}\, X \,;\, C'\, \texttt{end}$$

(4) $\texttt{while}\, E\, \texttt{do}\, C \;=\; \texttt{if}\, E\, \texttt{then}\, C \,;\, \texttt{while}\, E\, \texttt{do}\, C\, \texttt{else skip}$

Take (1) first. We know from Exercise 6 that $\mathcal{M}[\![C]\!]$ is well-terminating, so it will be enough to show that

$$\mathcal{S} = \{(P\ Before\ Done,\ P)\ :\ P\ \text{well-terminating}\} \cup \{(\mathbf{0},\mathbf{0})\}$$

is a bisimulation up to $\approx$. Now

$$P\ Before\ Done \;=\; (P[b/\texttt{done}] \mid b.Done)\backslash b$$

where b is new. Consider the actions of P:

- $P \xrightarrow{\overline{\texttt{done}}} P'$.   Then $P \sim Done$ and $P' \sim \mathbf{0}$ by well-termination; hence
$$P\ Before\ Done \sim (\overline{b}.\mathbf{0} \mid b.Done)\backslash b \sim \tau.Done$$
Hence $P\ Before\ Done \overset{\overline{\texttt{done}}}{\Longrightarrow} Q' \approx \mathbf{0}$ as required.

- $P \xrightarrow{\alpha} P'$, $\alpha \neq \overline{\texttt{done}}$.   Then, since $\alpha \neq b$ and $\alpha \neq \texttt{done}$, we also have
$$P\ Before\ Done \xrightarrow{\alpha} P'\ Before\ Done$$
as required.

We can also show that the derivatives of $P\ Before\ Done$ are matched in $\mathcal{S}$ by derivatives of P, up to $\approx$, and then the proof is complete.
Now consider the first equation of (2). We have

$$\mathcal{M}[\![\texttt{begin var}\, X \,;\, C\, \texttt{end}]\!] = (Loc_X \mid \mathcal{M}[\![C]\!])\backslash \mathcal{ACC}_X$$

But since X is not a non-local variable of C, by property **L1** we know that $\text{put}_X, \overline{\text{put}_X}, \text{get}_X, \overline{\text{get}_X}$ are not in $\mathcal{L}(\mathcal{M}[\![C]\!])$, so

$$
\begin{aligned}
(Loc_X \mid \mathcal{M}[\![C]\!]) \backslash \mathcal{ACC}_X &= (Loc_X \backslash \mathcal{ACC}_X) \mid \mathcal{M}[\![C]\!] \\
&= 0 \mid \mathcal{M}[\![C]\!] \\
&= \mathcal{M}[\![C]\!]
\end{aligned}
$$

This shows that our sort-classification of $\mathcal{L}(\mathcal{M}[\![C]\!])$ directly yields a property of local declarations which we would demand of our semantics.

Exercise 8   Use similar arguments about sort to establish the remainder of property (2) and property (3). Also prove (4).   ■

Now let us look at the question of granularity of **par**, which we raised at the beginning of this section.

Exercise 9   Show, by direct use of $\mathcal{M}[\![-]\!]$, that

$$\mathcal{M}[\![\text{X:=X+1}]\!] = \text{get}_X x.\overline{\text{put}_X}(x+1).Done \qquad ■$$

Now we can see that the command `X:=X+1 par X:=X+1` can interleave the two actions of both assignments, reading X twice, obtaining value v say, and then writing (twice) the value $v+1$ back into X. If we wished to make assignments to any variable X exclude each other, we could provide a semaphore

$$Sem_X \overset{\text{def}}{=} \text{up}_X.\text{down}_X.Sem_X$$

as part of the resource X; we would then redefine the semantics of a variable declaration as follows:

$$\mathcal{M}[\![\text{var } X]\!] = Loc_X \mid Sem_X$$

and the access sort as follows:

$$\mathcal{ACC}_X = \{\text{put}_X, \overline{\text{get}_X}, \overline{\text{up}_X}, \overline{\text{down}_X}\}$$

We would also redefine the semantics of the assignment command so that it acquires and releases the semaphore:

$$\mathcal{M}[\![X := E]\!] = \overline{\text{up}_X}.(\mathcal{M}[\![E]\!] \; Into(x)\,(\text{put}_X x.\overline{\text{down}_X}.Done))$$

Exercise 10   Consider the effect of this change on the parallel execution of assignments to *different* variables; for example `X:=Y par Y:=X+Y`.   ■

Before extending $\mathcal{M}_0$ to $\mathcal{M}$ let us look at a deeper property which we may like to establish. Consider the following two commands:

$$\text{begin var } X \text{ ; } C_1 \text{ ; } (C_2 \text{ par } C_3) \text{ end}$$
$$\text{begin var } X \text{ ; } (C_1 \text{ ; } C_2) \text{ par } C_3 \text{ end}$$

and suppose that X is the only non-local variable in C_1, that C_1 performs no input or output, and that C_3 does not refer to X at all. Under these conditions, it may seem that the two commands should have the same meaning, for they only differ in whether C_1 and C_3 can be concurrent, and the conditions seem to ensure that the presence or absence of this concurrency could make no discernible difference. But what if C_1 fails to terminate? Then there *is* a difference; in the first command C_3 will never be executed, while in the second it may be executed – and may perform input or output for example. We leave it open whether, under the assumption that C_1 terminates, the commands have equal meaning – and also, if so, how this should be proved in our calculus.

8.4   Adding concurrent procedures to $\mathcal{M}_0$

Let us now consider how to add procedures to $\mathcal{M}_0$, and especially how to allow different activations of the same procedure to run concurrently. For simplicity, we shall consider just procedures with one input parameter and one output parameter; so we extend the syntax of declarations thus:

$$D ::= \text{proc } G(\text{in } X, \text{out } Y) \text{ is } C \qquad\qquad (*)$$

where the command C is the body of procedure G (G is a procedure identifier). We also extend commands by

$$C ::= \text{call } G(E, Z) \qquad\qquad (**)$$

On a call, the value of E is to be the initial value of X, local to G, and on return the value of Y – also local to G – is to be transferred to the variable Z.

Now the sort L_G of G, i.e. the sort of $\mathcal{M}[\![D]\!]$ declared by $(*)$, will be

$$L_G = \{\text{call}_G, \overline{\text{return}_G}\} \cup \mathcal{L}(\mathcal{M}[\![C]\!]) - (ACC_X \cup ACC_Y)$$

and the access sort of the declaration will be

$$ACC_D = ACC_G = \{\overline{\text{call}_G}, \text{return}_G\} \ .$$

This means that the call is via call_G, the return via return_G, and G has as non-local variables all those of C except X, Y.

The translation of the procedure call (∗∗) seems easy:

$$\mathcal{M}[\![\texttt{call } G(E,Z)]\!] = \mathcal{M}[\![E]\!] \; Into(x)\,(\overline{\texttt{call}_G}x.\texttt{return}_G z.\overline{\texttt{put}_Z}z.Done)$$

This represents call by value; E is evaluated before transferring control to G. This form will be slightly modified later.

For the semantics of the declaration (∗) we give a first attempt, and we shall see that it is inadequate for three reasons:

$$\mathcal{M}[\![\texttt{proc } G(\texttt{in } X,\texttt{out } Y) \texttt{ is } C]\!] =$$
$$\texttt{call}_G x.(\; Loc_X \mid Loc_Y \mid$$
$$(\overline{\texttt{put}_X}x.\mathcal{M}[\![C]\!] \; Before \; \texttt{get}_Y y.\overline{\texttt{return}_G y}.0)$$
$$)\backslash L_X \backslash L_Y$$

This certainly gives the correct sort L_G, and correctly localises X and Y to the body C. Note also that if this declaration D is local to the block begin D ; C' end, then the other free identifiers of the body C will correctly refer to variables (or procedures) declared in the context of the block, rather than to variables in the context of any call.

But this meaning of G is not much use as a resource because it dies after one use! Just as *variable* resources are given indefinite life by the use of recursion, so should *procedure* resources be given indefinite life; that is, G should reinstate itself after executing its body. Let us try again:

$$\mathcal{M}[\![\texttt{proc } G(\texttt{in } X,\texttt{out } Y) \texttt{ is } C]\!] = W, \text{ where}$$
$$W \stackrel{\text{def}}{=} \texttt{call}_G x.(\; Loc_X \mid Loc_Y \mid$$
$$(\overline{\texttt{put}_X}x.\mathcal{M}[\![C]\!] \; Before \; \texttt{get}_Y y.\overline{\texttt{return}_G y}.W)$$
$$)\backslash L_X \backslash L_Y$$

The only difference here is the recursion on W (in place of **0**). Notice that the procedure, when reinstated after its first activation, will again have local variables X and Y, but these are – correctly – not the same as the local variables X and Y of the first activation, because Restriction keeps them separate.

There are two further deficiencies here. First, we must consider recursive calls of G from within C; at present, they are impossible. It is quite easy to solve this problem; we must provide C with another 'copy' of G restricted to its own use. Here is our next attempt at translation:

$$\mathcal{M}[\![\texttt{proc } G(\texttt{in } X,\texttt{out } Y) \texttt{ is } C]\!] = W, \text{ where}$$
$$W \stackrel{\text{def}}{=} \texttt{call}_G x.(\; Loc_X \mid Loc_Y \mid$$

$$(\overline{\text{put}_X}x.(\mathcal{M}[\![C]\!] \mid W)\backslash ACC_G \; \textit{Before } \text{get}_Y y.\overline{\text{return}_G}y.W)$$
$$)\backslash L_X\backslash L_Y$$

The second deficiency is to do with concurrency. Although there may be concurrent calls of G, for example

```
call G(6,Z) par call G(7,Z)
```

the resulting activations of G will not be concurrent; whichever call first performs $\overline{\text{call}_G}$ will gain priority, and the other call will wait until G restores itself after returning to the first call. To correct this, we would like to have G restore itself immediately after receiving its first call, rather than after executing its body:

$\mathcal{M}[\![\text{proc } G(\text{in } X, \text{out } Y) \text{ is } C]\!] = W$, where

$W \stackrel{\text{def}}{=} \text{call}_G x.((\; Loc_X \mid Loc_Y \mid$
$\quad (\overline{\text{put}_X}x.(\mathcal{M}[\![C]\!] \mid W)\backslash ACC_G \; \textit{Before } \text{get}_Y y.\overline{\text{return}_G}y.0)$
$\quad)\backslash L_X\backslash L_Y \mid W)$

But now, if a second activation of G occurs concurrently, the two activations may return – via their respective $\overline{\text{return}_G}$ actions – to the wrong callers! What is needed is some way for each call to be uniquely identified.

To this end, we now consider call_G and return_G to stand for indexed sets of names $\text{call}_{G,i}$ and $\text{return}_{G,i}$ $(i = 1, 2, \ldots)$. The first activation of G will be via $\text{call}_{G,1}$, and the reinstatement must ensure that the next activation is via $\text{call}_{G,2}$ and so on. So we define the relabelling function f_G as follows:

$$f_G = \{\text{call}_{G,i+1}/\text{call}_{G,i} \; , \; \text{return}_{G,i+1}/\text{return}_{G,i} \; : \; i \geq 1\}$$

and our final translation of the procedure is:

$\mathcal{M}[\![\text{proc } G(\text{in } X, \text{out } Y) \text{ is } C]\!] = W$, where
$W \stackrel{\text{def}}{=} \text{call}_{G,1}x.((\; Loc_X \mid Loc_Y \mid$
$\quad (\overline{\text{put}_X}x.(\mathcal{M}[\![C]\!] \mid W)\backslash ACC_G \; \textit{Before } \text{get}_Y y.\overline{\text{return}_{G,1}}y.0)$
$\quad)\backslash L_X\backslash L_Y \mid W[f_G])$

Finally, we must modify the semantics of the `call` command so that the caller can use whatever index i is currently available, ensuring that the same index is used both for call and return:

$$\mathcal{M}[\![\texttt{call } G(E,Z)]\!] \;=\; \mathcal{M}[\![E]\!] \; Into(x)$$
$$\sum_{i \geq 1}(\overline{\texttt{call}_{G,i}}x.\texttt{return}_{G,i}z.\overline{\texttt{put}_Z}z.Done)$$

This final translation is not easy to digest, though it is reasonably succinct. However, we should not *expect* it to be easy! We have described a semantics which gives to recursive procedures the fullest possible degree of concurrency, and since the procedures may also have side-effects (on non-local variables) it will be rather easy to write programs which are impossible to understand! The difficulty is partly to do with nondeterminism, arising from assignment to shared variables.

We do not propose to analyse the translation further, but we can offer a challenge. Intuitively, it appears that if we limit our use of C **par** C' to cases in which C assigns to no variable X which occurs non-locally in C', and conversely (with some analogous constraint on **input** and **output** commands), then all programs will be deterministic. The first part of the challenge is to prove this statement; it would be simpler to deal first with the language $\mathcal{M}_0$ without procedures. The second part of the challenge, which would go some way towards validating the translation of procedures, is to demonstrate that the fully concurrent translation which we have given for procedures is – under the limitation above – semantically equivalent to the earlier translation which only admits sequential procedure activation.

The discerning reader may note that we have modelled the parameter mechanism known as *call-by-value*, rather than *call-by-name*; that is, we have assumed that the value – not the address – of a parameter is passed to the procedure. Indeed, there is no easy way of modifying our translation to model call-by-name. The reason is that, to do it properly, we would wish to allow labels such as $\texttt{get}_X$ and $\texttt{put}_X$ to be sent and received as values, and the calculus has excluded this possibility. There is a subtle distinction between systems with *evolving structure*, which were explained in Chapter 6 and which can be represented in the present calculus, and systems with *dynamically varying linkage*, which are not directly representable. More is said on recent developments in this topic in Chapter 12.

The main purpose of this chapter has been to show that the calculus provides a powerful method of presenting the semantics of programming languages, and of demonstrating at least some properties of the languages.

9

Operators and Calculi

We have restricted attention so far in this book to a very basic calculus, with only a handful of combinators. There are at least two reasons for this. First, we wanted to show how powerful a single combinator for (concurrent) composition can be, with a few companions playing auxiliary roles. For example, we have seen in Chapter 8 that sequential composition is a special case, and is conveniently treated as such. Second, we wanted to set out some of the mathematical theory, and for that purpose fewer combinators means shorter proofs.

In this chapter we look at a variety of alternative operators, and at ways of defining them. There are two important ways; one can define them either by equations, as a generalisation of the way in which we already define agent Constants (which are the special case of operators with no parameters), or one can define them by transition rules just as we have defined our basic combinators. These two ways are treated in Sections 1 and 2. Section 3 then introduces a calculus which stands in its own right; we call it a *synchronous calculus*, because it takes as basic the idea that processes running concurrently proceed in lockstep (each performing one action at each time instant). However, we indicate how *asynchrony*, and in particular the main calculus of this book, can be defined in terms of the synchronous calculus. We also explain how the synchronous calculus has, at present, a stronger claim to completeness of expression than does the asynchronous calculus.

Finally, in Section 4 we briefly discuss some interesting equivalence relations which equate more agents than bisimilarity.

9.1 Definition by equations

Let us first look more closely at our definitional mechanism. We have allowed new Constants to be defined (possibly recursively) by equations like $A \stackrel{\text{def}}{=} P$, with the rule

$$\text{Con}\ \ \frac{P \xrightarrow{\alpha} P'}{A \xrightarrow{\alpha} P'}\ (A \overset{\text{def}}{=} P)$$

By the translation in Section 2.8 we were able to extend this to define agents with value parameters, with defining equations like $A(x) \overset{\text{def}}{=} E$ where x is a value variable occurring freely in E. But what about defining agents with *agent* parameters, or in other words defining *operators* upon agents? As for 'Constant', we shall henceforth begin 'Operator' with a capital letter when we mean an operator upon agents defined either (in this section) by equations, or (in the next section) by inference. The definition of an Operator is sometimes only a thin disguise for a family of agent-definitions, presented in convenient notation. Let us take an example which makes sense in terms of the well-terminating agents of Chapter 8:

$$Cycle(X) \overset{\text{def}}{=} \textsf{stop}.Done + \textsf{more}.(X\ Before\ Cycle(X))$$

Here X is an agent parameter, so *Cycle* is an Operator upon agents. Intuitively, $Cycle(P)$ (for any agent P) is a user-controlled repeater. Before each activation of P it will ask you if you want another activation; if you do you press the $\textsf{more}$ button, otherwise the $\textsf{stop}$ button.

Now the only occurrence of *Cycle* on the right-hand side carries the same parameter as on the left, namely the variable X. So the definition can be regarded as a schematic family of definitions of new Constants $Cycle_P$, one for each agent P:

$$Cycle_P \overset{\text{def}}{=} \textsf{stop}.Done + \textsf{more}.(P\ Before\ Cycle_P)$$

If we only need such schematic definitions, then we need no extension to our theory.

Some Operators take value parameters too, but still demand no extra theory. For example, consider a more automatic repeater, controlled by a pre-set integer parameter instead of by user intervention:

$$Iterate(n, X)\ \overset{\text{def}}{=}\ \text{if } n = 0 \text{ then } Done \text{ else } X\ Before\ Iterate(n-1, X)$$

Here, the Operator still takes the same *agent* parameter on the right-hand side as on the left. So we can again regard the definition as a schematic family of definitions, one for each P:

$$Iterate_P(n)\ \overset{\text{def}}{=}\ \text{if } n = 0 \text{ then } Done \text{ else } P\ Before\ Iterate_P(n-1)$$

and such definitions, taking only value parameters, are reduced to the pure calculus in Section 2.8.

Exercise 1 Prove that

$$Iterate(m, Iterate(n, X)) \approx Iterate(m \times n, X)$$

Hint: Recall from Chapter 8 that *Before* is associative. ∎

Exercise 2 Consider

$$Shuffle(X) \overset{\text{def}}{=} X \mid Shuffle(X)$$

For any P, $Shuffle(P)$ provides in effect unboundedly many copies of P in parallel. (Notice that *Shuffle* occurs unguarded on the right-hand side, so there may well be other Operators – besides the one defined – which satisfy the defining equation.) Prove that

$$Shuffle(Shuffle(X)) \sim Shuffle(X)$$

Hint: Prove that

$$S \overset{\text{def}}{=} \{(Shuffle(P) \mid Q, \; Shuffle(Shuffle(P)) \mid Q) \; : \; P, Q \in \mathcal{P}\}$$

is a strong bisimulation up to $\sim$. You may also need induction on the depth of inference of an action. ∎

In general, a recursive Operator definition may not be schematic in the straightforward sense of the examples given so far; that is, it may call itself recursively upon different agent parameters. Here is a possible case:

$$Triang(X) \overset{\text{def}}{=} Done + (X \; Before \; Triang(a.X))$$

In passing, you may like to get a feeling for *Triang* from the following:

Exercise 3 Prove (by any formal or informal means you think appropriate) that *Triang* represents the triangular numbers 0, 1, 3, 6, 10, 15, ..., in the sense that $Triang(Done) \overset{a^n \overline{done}}{\Longrightarrow}$ if and only if n is a triangular number. ∎

The point we wish to make is that it becomes a little cumbersome (though still possible) to treat such a definition as a schematic family of agent definitions, one for each P:

$$Triang_P \overset{\text{def}}{=} \cdots$$

(Things become even more cumbersome if recursive calls of the operator are nested inside one another.) Therefore it is reasonable to extend our calculus to treat Operator definitions directly.

Fortunately, the extension presents no difficulty. Indeed, we could have presented the more general calculus from the outset; the only reason we did not do so was to avoid considering too many things at once. But let us now see what is involved.

First, we assign an *arity* (number of agent parameters) to each new Operator A which we wish to define. Then we extend our set $\mathcal{E}$ of expressions to contain $A(E_1, \ldots, E_n)$ for all $E_1, \ldots, E_n$ already in $\mathcal{E}$ (where n is the arity of A). Next, we extend our defining equations to the form

$$A(\tilde{X}) \stackrel{\text{def}}{=} E$$

where $\tilde{X} = X_1, \ldots, X_n$ and $Vars(E) \subseteq \tilde{X}$. This must be accompanied by a generalisation of the **Con** rule to a form appropriate Operators, as follows:

$$\textbf{Opr} \quad \frac{E\{\tilde{F}/\tilde{X}\} \stackrel{\alpha}{\to} E'}{A(\tilde{F}) \stackrel{\alpha}{\to} E'} \; (A(\tilde{X}) \stackrel{\text{def}}{=} E)$$

Notice that this specialises to the original **Con** rule when A has arity 0.

The *sort* of an Operator A needs a little care, because A itself is not an agent. Originally we assigned to each Constant A a sort $\mathcal{L}(A)$, and we imposed the following condition:

$$\text{If } A \stackrel{\text{def}}{=} P \text{ then } \mathcal{L}(P) \subseteq \mathcal{L}(A)$$

Now, we shall assign to each Operator A (with arity n) not a *sort* but an n-ary *function over sorts*, denoted by $\mathcal{L}(A)$. We shall require this function to be monotonic; that is, if $K_1 \subseteq L_1, \ldots, K_n \subseteq L_n$, then we must have

$$\mathcal{L}(A)(K_1, \ldots, K_n) \subseteq \mathcal{L}(A)(L_1, \ldots, L_n)$$

There is nothing mysterious in this. Take as an example the Operator *Cycle* above, which is unary (has arity 1). Then we naturally define $\mathcal{L}(Cycle)$ by the following equation:

$$\mathcal{L}(Cycle)(L) \stackrel{\text{def}}{=} L \cup \{\texttt{stop}, \texttt{more}\}$$

because *Cycle* uses the ports `stop` and `more` besides those of its agent parameter. Clearly the function $\mathcal{L}(Cycle)$ is monotonic in its argument L.

Next we generalise the rule for assigning sorts to expressions in the following way:

$$\mathcal{L}(A(F_1, \ldots, F_n)) \stackrel{\text{def}}{=} \mathcal{L}(A)(\mathcal{L}(F_1), \ldots, \mathcal{L}(F_n))$$

Finally, we have to generalise the sort requirement placed upon a defining equation, since it now takes the form $A(\tilde{X}) \overset{\text{def}}{=} E$ in which $\tilde{X}$ are the formal parameters. The sort $\mathcal{L}(E)$ of E now depends, of course, upon the sorts ascribed to the variable $\tilde{X}$, since these variables may occur in E; we therefore require that

$$\mathcal{L}(E) \subseteq \mathcal{L}(A(\tilde{X}))$$

whatever sort $\mathcal{L}(X)$ is assigned to each variable X in $\tilde{X}$.

Having dealt with sorts, the remaining part of the theory generalises smoothly. We shall mention just a few important points. First, we have to add a sixth clause to Proposition 4.10 which asserts that $\sim$ is a congruence. The new clause says that if $P_1 \sim P_2$ then

$$(6) \quad A(\ldots, P_1, \ldots) \sim A(\ldots, P_2, \ldots)$$

and the proof is quite straightforward. Similar remarks apply to Proposition 7.7 which asserts that $=$ is a congruence.

There are also two propositions, Propositions 4.12 and 7.8, which assert that we can perform congruence-preserving transformations on the body of a recursive definition – i.e on the right-hand side of a defining equation – without altering the congruence class of the defined Constant; these propositions generalise to Operator definitions in the obvious way. Finally, Propositions 4.14 and 7.13 about the unique solution of equations generalise to the unique solutions of equations in Operators, provided that the notion of *sequentiality* is properly modified.

9.2   Definition by inference

We now turn to another kind of definition, which has greater power than the recursive definition method of the previous section, namely definition by *inference*. It is, in fact, exactly the method we used to define the basic combinators of the calculus; for a new Operator, we provide a finite set of new rules of action, each having a conclusion in which the new Operator occurs as the leading Operator of the left-hand side.

For some examples of new Operators, we can conveniently refer to Hoare's book *Communicating Sequential Processes*. Let us first consider the sequential composition

$$P; Q$$

where, informally speaking, Q begins when and only when P has finished. But what does 'P has finished' mean? Let us take it to mean that P performs a special action $\sqrt{}$, pronounced 'tick'. Then the following rules appear reasonable (though there are other possibilities):

$$\frac{E \xrightarrow{\alpha} E'}{E; F \xrightarrow{\alpha} E'; F} \ (\alpha \neq \sqrt{}) \qquad\qquad \frac{E \xrightarrow{\sqrt{}} E'}{E; F \xrightarrow{\tau} F}$$

The first rule is simple, but the second is more delicate. The intuition in the second rule is that if E 'finishes', in the context $E; F$, then this constitutes an internal action which discards E. Notice that the rule does not demand that E has *really* finished when it does the action $\sqrt{}$; E' may well have further actions, but the rule has the effect of prohibiting these actions, because E' does not occur on the right-hand side of the conclusion.

Exercise 4 Prove that $P; (Q; R) \sim (P; Q); R$.   ∎

There are further points to make about this definition. First, why did we not take sequential composition as a basic combinator, since it is so frequently used? One answer is in Chapter 8; we found there that we could define it directly in terms of $|$, and we called it *Before* (it used $\overline{\text{done}}$ in place of $\sqrt{}$). Strictly speaking, *Before* was not exactly like the present ';' because *Before* did not have the property of discarding the actions following $\sqrt{}$ in the first agent. But it was the same for well-terminating agents, since these were defined to have *no* actions after $\overline{\text{done}}$. Another reason for not taking ';' as basic is that it depends upon a distinguished action $\sqrt{}$, which would complicate our whole theory. But the main reason is that we wished to confine ourselves to a single combinator, namely $|$, to deal with *all* communications between agents, and the transfer of control from E to F via $\sqrt{}$ is indeed a kind of communication.

We can illustrate further points by considering some alternatives to the use of a special action $\sqrt{}$ in defining sequential composition. Let us say, instead, that 'P has finished' means that P has no possible actions. Then we may try the following definition of ';':

$$\frac{E \xrightarrow{\alpha} E'}{E; F \xrightarrow{\alpha} E'; F} \qquad\qquad \frac{F \xrightarrow{\alpha} F'}{\mathbf{0}; F \xrightarrow{\alpha} F'} \qquad (*)$$

This is seductively simple, but disastrous. The problem is that it will yield different behaviours for the two agents $\mathbf{0}; Q$ and $(\mathbf{0}; \mathbf{0}); Q$, which is certainly not what we want. To be precise, the former $\mathbf{0}; Q$ will have all the actions that Q has, and will be strongly congruent to Q, while the latter will have no actions at all! Why is this? Because the second rule can only be applied to yield an action for an agent which is *exactly* of the form $0; F$, and $(0; 0); Q$ is not of this form, even though $0; 0 \sim 0$.

Exercise 5 Prove also that, under the second definition of sequential composition, $P; (Q; R) \not\sim (P; Q); R$. This is in contrast with Exercise 4 above.   ∎

One attempt to mend the second definition would be to place a side-condition on the second rule:

$$\frac{E \xrightarrow{\alpha} E'}{E; F \xrightarrow{\alpha} E'; F} \qquad\qquad \frac{F \xrightarrow{\alpha} F'}{E; F \xrightarrow{\alpha} F'} \ (E = 0)$$

However, such a definition plays havoc with our theory, because of its circularity! For equality ($=$) was defined in terms of our transition system, and now we are trying to define our transition system in terms of equality. Even if we could somehow break out of this circularity, the complication would be a heavy burden. So we conclude that sequential composition must involve a special action representing termination.

Let us now justify our claim that definition by inference is more powerful than definition by equations. We know that every Operator *Op* defined by equations preserves equality; that is,

If $P_1 = Q_1, \ldots, P_n = Q_n$ then $Op(P_1, \ldots, P_n) = Op(Q_1, \ldots, Q_n)$

Indeed, this is the content of the extended form of Proposition 7.7, as we mentioned at the end of the previous section. But the (disastrous) form of sequential composition defined by our second pair of rules (∗) will *not* preserve equality, since it will satisfy $0; 0 = 0$ while in general – as we have seen – it will *not* satisfy $(0; 0); Q = 0; Q$. Therefore there are Operators definable by inference which are not definable by equations.

As a second example, let us take the elegant *interrupt* Operator, in Hoare's notation $P^\wedge Q$; we may pronounce it 'P interrupted by Q'. This is supposed to behave like P until Q does anything at all, and thereafter to behave like Q. It is like a too-hasty sequential composition which may not wait for P to finish. It is easy to define:

$$\frac{E \xrightarrow{\alpha} E'}{E^\wedge F \xrightarrow{\alpha} E'^\wedge F} \qquad\qquad \frac{F \xrightarrow{\alpha} F'}{E^\wedge F \xrightarrow{\alpha} F'}$$

Amusingly enough, it is exactly the same as our last attempt to redefine ';', except that the side-condition (which would cause such difficulty) is dropped. This Operator, or something very close to it, has been found important in practice; it is included in LOTOS, a language for formal description of communications protocols.

As Hoare shows, some remarkably powerful Operators can be defined using the interrupt Operator. A simple example is

$$Restart(X) \stackrel{\text{def}}{=} X^{\wedge}\mathbf{r}.Restart(X)$$

Restart(P) behaves like P, except that on $\mathbf{r}$ it begins all over again; it may be similarly restarted any number of times.

A more sophisticated version of *Restart* may be called *checkpointing*. Instead of going right back to the beginning on each $\mathbf{r}$, it will go back to the state in which the *checkpoint* action c was last performed. It is interesting that this Operator does not seem to be definable directly – i.e. by defining equations – in terms of the basic combinators and the interrupt Operator. Hoare gives a kind of conditional definition in his book; in our framework this is best presented as another definition by inference. We define a binary Operator *Check*, so that P *Check* Q means 'perform P, with Q as the current checkpoint':

$$\frac{P \stackrel{\alpha}{\to} P'}{P \ Check \ Q \stackrel{\alpha}{\to} P' \ Check \ Q} \ (\alpha \neq \mathbf{r}, \mathbf{c})$$

$$\overline{P \ Check \ Q \stackrel{\mathbf{r}}{\to} Q \ Check \ Q} \qquad\qquad \overline{P \ Check \ Q \stackrel{\mathbf{c}}{\to} P \ Check \ P}$$

Such definitions are quite easy to write down, but the properties of the Operators thus defined are often not easy to ascertain. They are sensitive to the finest detail of the definition. For example, note that we have imposed a side-condition ($\alpha \neq \mathbf{r}, \mathbf{c}$) upon the first rule. We need not have done perhaps, but notice the effect if we omit it. One effect is that an agent like (P *Check* Q) *Check* R can then nondeterministically choose whether to restart at Q or at R; that is, if the side-condition is lifted then both of the following are possible actions:

$$(P \ Check \ Q) \ Check \ R \stackrel{\mathbf{r}}{\to} (Q \ Check \ Q) \ Check \ R$$

$$(P \ Check \ Q) \ Check \ R \stackrel{\mathbf{r}}{\to} R \ Check \ R$$

Our side-condition, however, denies the first possibility. In fact, with the side-condition we can perhaps see, intuitively, that by superposing a second checkpoint agent R we override the first checkpoint agent Q completely. The following exercise makes this precise.

Exercise 6   Prove the following:

$$(P \ Check \ Q) \ Check \ R \sim P \ Check \ R$$

$$P \ Check \ (Q \ Check \ R) \sim P \ Check \ Q$$

Hint: You may need a larger bisimulation than you expect at first. ∎

As a final example, consider Hoare's combinator $P \parallel Q$, which we shall call *Conjunction*, and which is an alternative to the Composition $P \mid Q$ used in this book. Its meaning actually depends not only upon P and Q, but also upon explicitly supplied sorts K and L; Hoare calls these sorts *alphabets* and assumes that $P : K$ and $Q : L$. For a fixed choice of K and L we define Conjunction by three rules, whose side-conditions refer to K and L :

$$\frac{E \xrightarrow{\alpha} E'}{E \parallel F \xrightarrow{\alpha} E' \parallel F} \ (\alpha \notin L) \qquad\qquad \frac{F \xrightarrow{\alpha} F'}{E \parallel F \xrightarrow{\alpha} E \parallel F'} \ (\alpha \notin K)$$

$$\frac{E \xrightarrow{\ell} E' \qquad F \xrightarrow{\ell} F'}{E \parallel F \xrightarrow{\ell} E' \parallel F'} \ (\ell \in K \cap L)$$

The idea is that E and F must synchronise upon actions in $K \cap L$, but may perform actions outside this set independently. Note that the first two rules allow τ actions. The Conjunction combinator – which we should perhaps write $_K\|_L$ to make its sort parameters explicit – does not require the notion of complementary action ($\bar{\ell}$), and has two advantages over Composition. First, it permits multi-way synchronisation; if $P : K$, $Q : L$ and $R : M$ then $P \parallel Q \parallel R$ can perform a three-way synchronisation on any action in $K \cap L \cap M$. Second, it preserves determinacy (as we shall see in Chapter 11), provided that its arguments have the designated sorts; that is, if $P : K$ and $Q : L$ and both P and Q are determinate, then so is $P \ _K\|_L \ Q$. It is natural to accompany this Operator, as Hoare does, not with the Restriction combinator $\backslash L$ but with the Hiding combinator $/L$ introduced in Section 5.5, which may be directly defined as follows:

$$\frac{E \xrightarrow{\alpha} E'}{E/L \xrightarrow{\alpha} E'/L} \ (\alpha \notin L) \qquad\qquad \frac{E \xrightarrow{\ell} E'}{E/L \xrightarrow{\tau} E'/L} \ (\ell \in L)$$

(intuitively, $/L$ *permits* the actions in L to occur unobserved, while $\backslash L$ *prevents* them from occurring).

The advantage that $\parallel$ preserves determinacy, in contrast with $\mid$, is perhaps not as strong as it appears. Any system which is hard to analyse is likely to have at least some of its actions internalised, and this internalisation will be achieved by Restriction $\backslash L$ if $\mid$ is used for parallel composition, but by Hiding $/L$ if $\parallel$ is used. Now Restriction *does* preserve determinacy, while Hiding does *not*. It seems that whichever pair of Operators we choose, for parallel composition with some internalisation, determinacy cannot be guaranteed by their use; in each case, special arguments must be deployed to prove determinacy. Multi-way synchronisation is certainly useful, but ‖ achieves it at the expense of dependency upon sorts; it is in effect an infinite family of Operators. By contrast the definition of | does not depend upon sorts; this simplifies its treatment, which is why we chose it.

There is another way of formulating multi-way synchronisation. Instead of considering many agents participating in the same atomic action ℓ, we can consider an action – still indivisible in time – to be composed of many atomic actions occurring simultaneously. The representation of two-way communication as a pair of complementary actions is a special case of this, except that we have chosen to represent their simultaneous occurrence by the action τ in all cases. George Milne, in his calculus Circal for VLSI design, took a different course; he defined every action to be a *finite set* $\{\ell_1, \ell_2, \ldots\}$ of labels, and his combinators dictated exactly which sets could be synchronised, yielding an action consisting of their union.

Given this variety of possible disciplines, one is led to look for an underlying discipline in which they can all be modelled. In the next section we shall consider a very basic calculus in which all the combinators we have discussed, or their analogues, can be derived.

9.3   A synchronous calculus

There are some features of our calculus which appear arbitrary, especially after the discussion of the preceding two sections. In truth, there is nothing canonical about our choice of basic combinators, even though they were chosen with great attention to economy. What characterises our calculus is not the exact choice of combinators, but rather the choice of interpretation and of mathematical framework. Even in these aspects we claim only to present one aspect of a large subject.

We now wish to discuss a calculus which, though it adopts the same sort of interpretation and mathematical framework, also has a greater claim to completeness of expression – and hence a claim to be less arbitrary. It arose from the author's attempt to relate *asynchrony* to *synchrony*. The contrast between these terms may be understood in more than one way. Here, we mean the contrast between the assumption which we have hitherto made that concurrent agents proceed at indeterminate relative speeds (*asynchrony*), and the alternative assumption that they proceed in lockstep – i.e. that at every instant each agent performs a single action (*synchrony*). The latter assumption somewhat offends the popular relativistic view, since it suggests the idea of a global clock. But the synchronous view leads to a delightfully simple calculus, as we shall see shortly, and in fact asynchrony can be achieved within it just by introducing an explicit *waiting* action.

Let us first look a little more closely at Composition. Consider the Composition $A|B$, where $A \overset{\text{def}}{=} a.A'$ and $B \overset{\text{def}}{=} \tau.B$. Then certainly

$$A|B \overset{a}{\Rightarrow} A'|B$$

Moreover, this derivation may involve either *no* action by B, or a *silent* action by B (or indeed many silent actions). Why should we treat the *implicit* waiting by B, in the inference

$$\frac{A \overset{a}{\to} A'}{A|B \overset{a}{\to} A'|B}$$

differently from the *explicit* waiting by B in $B \overset{\tau}{\to} B$? Let us aim to identify these two kinds of waiting, by making them both explicit. Then we have to deny the above inference, which is one of the rules of Composition. What do we put in its place?

Our synchronous calculus rests upon two main ideas, and the rest falls into place around them:

(1) Instead of taking actions to be $Act \overset{\text{def}}{=} \mathcal{L} \cup \{\tau\}$, with complementation over $\mathcal{L}$, we take them to form a commutative group

$$(Act, 1, \times, \bar{\ })$$

in which the unit 1 is the silent (waiting) action, the commutative product $\times$ means simultaneous occurrence, and the inverse $(\bar{\ })$ as before means complementation. We assume that the group is generated by the set $\mathcal{A}$ of *particles*, or *particulate actions*. As before we shall use $a, b, \ldots$ to range over $\mathcal{A}$, and $\alpha, \beta, \ldots$ to range over Act. Thus every action $\alpha \in Act$ is (disregarding the order of factors) a unique product

$$\alpha = a_1^{z_1} \cdots a_n^{z_n}$$

of non-zero powers of distinct particles, where we take the usual liberty of omitting the multiplication sign. The z_i may be negative, so a^{-2} means $\bar{a}^2$). In the case $n = 0$ we have $\alpha = 1$. We shall write $a \in \alpha$ to mean that the particle a occurs with non-zero power in α.

We have chosen to call the members of $\mathcal{A}$ *particles* rather than *atoms* because we wish reserve 'atomic' to mean 'indivisible in time'. In this calculus an atomic action can have a complex particulate structure.

(2) In place of Composition as previously defined we define a *Product* of agents, also written '×', by just a single inference rule:

$$\frac{E \xrightarrow{\alpha} E' \qquad F \xrightarrow{\beta} F'}{E \times F \xrightarrow{\alpha\beta} E' \times F'}$$

Note that here the actions α and β may already be products of particles, representing simultaneous actions by components – or *factors*, as we may now call them – of E and of F respectively. Note also that, for example, we may have $\beta = 1$, and F' may be F; the action $F \xrightarrow{1} F$ means that F can wait, and the resulting action $E \times F \xrightarrow{\alpha} E' \times F$ corresponds to what we would derive from one of the other two rules of Composition, being an action due to E alone.

For Prefix we choose the new notation $\alpha : E$ (we shall shortly see why), and we keep Summation unchanged. We replace Restriction by a new form $E \upharpoonright S$ where S is now required to be a subgroup of Act; this is now intended to prevent all actions *except* those in S. We omit Relabelling, because we shall show that this combinator is definable from the others. Thus if we take for granted the previous rule for Constant definition, or for Recursion, we have just four basic combinators, each with a single rule:

$$\textbf{Act} \quad \frac{}{\alpha : E \xrightarrow{\alpha} E} \qquad\qquad \textbf{Sum}_j \quad \frac{E_j \xrightarrow{\alpha} E_j'}{\sum_{i \in I} E_i \xrightarrow{\alpha} E_j'} \ (j \in I)$$

$$\textbf{Prod} \quad \frac{E \xrightarrow{\alpha} E' \qquad F \xrightarrow{\beta} F'}{E \times F \xrightarrow{\alpha\beta} E' \times F'} \qquad \textbf{Res} \quad \frac{E \xrightarrow{\alpha} E'}{E \upharpoonright S \xrightarrow{\alpha} E' \upharpoonright S} \ (\alpha \in S)$$

Now this calculus, just as our original calculus, is a labelled transition system; it also has a distinguished action (or label) 1, which plays the role of τ. It is therefore amenable to just the same sort of theoretical development; strong and weak congruences can be set up analogously. In fact, the resulting algebraic theory is somewhat more elegant, and this can be traced to the simple definition of Product ×; the main gain is that Product distributes over Summation:

$$E \times (F + G) \sim E \times F + E \times G$$

(this property was not enjoyed by Composition). Of course a price has to be paid; it is the need to represent the *waiting* capacity of any agent, in a community of asynchronous agents running concurrently, by explicit 1 actions. We shall not develop the calculus fully here, but confine ourselves to discussing some of its salient characteristics.

Let us first look at how an asynchronous calculus can be derived. It turns out that the calculus of this book can in effect be derived fully from the synchronous calculus. The key step is to define a *delay* Operator, ∂, as follows:

$$\partial X \stackrel{\text{def}}{=} X + 1 : \partial X$$

Thus ∂P is the agent which behaves like P except that it can wait indefinitely before starting. That is, ∂P is idle according to the following definition:

Definition 1   An agent P in the synchronous calculus is *idle* if $P \stackrel{1}{\rightarrow} P'$, for some $P' \sim P$.   ∎

Notice that ∂P may still lack the capability to wait *between* its actions. We then define the asynchronous form of Prefix in the following way:

$$\alpha.X \stackrel{\text{def}}{=} \alpha : \partial X$$

(This, of course, explains why we chose a new notation with ':' in place of '.'.)   Again, notice that according to this definition $\alpha.P$ can wait after its first action, but not necessarily after later actions; for example $\alpha.\beta : \gamma.0$ can wait after α, and can (only) wait for ever after γ, but cannot wait between β and γ.

Exercise 7   How does $\gamma.0$ differ from $\gamma:0$? Consider for example the actions of the two agents $\alpha:\beta:P \times \gamma:0$ and $\alpha:\beta:P \times \gamma.0$.   ∎

Next, we can define a form of asynchronous composition as follows:

$$X \mid Y \stackrel{\text{def}}{=} X \times \partial Y + \partial X \times Y$$

We have seen that Restriction is essentially as before, and we shall show that Relabelling can be defined in terms of the new combinators. In fact what we now have, if we confine ourselves to using the (newly defined) asynchronous combinators '.' and | in place of the synchronous ones ':' and ×, is an asynchronous calculus very close to the one studied in this book. To underline this, let us make a simple definition:

Definition 2   An agent P in the synchronous calculus is said to be *asynchronous* if every proper derivative P' of P is idle. (A *proper* derivative P' of P is such that $P \xrightarrow{s} P'$ for some $s \neq \varepsilon$.)   ∎

(Note especially that P *itself* does not have to be idle, to be asynchronous; for example $\alpha.\beta.\mathbf{0}$ is asynchronous but not idle.) Now it can be shown that every agent definable in the new calculus, but from '.' and | in place of ':' and ×, is *indeed* asynchronous according to our definition. In fact, the only difference from the calculus of earlier chapters is that, due to the fact that the product of any two actions exists, the new calculus has the power of multi-way synchronisation. There is a theorem, tedious to prove, which states that if this new asynchronous calculus is further constrained to inhibit multi-way synchronisation then it becomes *isomorphic* to the old one.

Let us look now at some further definitions. First, we would like a form of Restriction $E \backslash L$, for $L \subseteq \mathcal{A}$, analogous to the familiar form; in the presence of composite actions, it should prevent any action which contains a particle of L. The definition is straightforward; if $K^{\times}$ means the subgroup of *Act* generated by $K \subseteq \mathcal{A}$, then we set

$$E \backslash L \stackrel{\text{def}}{=} E \restriction (\mathcal{A} - L)^{\times}$$

Next, observe that in the new calculus we have $P \times \mathbf{0} \sim \mathbf{0}$, in contrast with $P|\mathbf{0} \sim P$ in the old calculus. (This is, of course, consistent with our use of more conventional algebraic notation.) So we naturally look for an identity, $\mathbf{1}$, such that $P \times \mathbf{1} \sim P$. It indeed exists, and is given by

$$\mathbf{1} \stackrel{\text{def}}{=} \partial \mathbf{0}$$

This is the agent which can *only* delay; it is the quintessence of idleness. Poor $\mathbf{0}$ cannot even idle; it is a constant of our synchronous calculus which is far from reality, but which is undeniably useful in calculations, as can be seen in the example below (compare $\sqrt{-1}$).

With the help of $\mathbf{1}$ we can conveniently blur the distinction between actions and agents, by considering an action α to be the degenerate agent $\alpha : \mathbf{1}$ (or equivalently $\alpha.\mathbf{0}$) which can only do the single non-unit action α before idling. With careful abuse of notation, we can then write $\alpha \times P$, or just αP, as an abbreviation of $\alpha : \mathbf{1} \times P$. For example, with this convention, we have that

$$a(b : P + c : Q) \sim ab : P + ac : Q$$

Here, the left-hand side is short for $a : \mathbf{1} \times (b : P + c : Q)$, and should *not* be confused with $a : (b : P + c : Q)$. In the first case the action a *accompanies* the first action of $b : P + c : Q$, while in the second case it *precedes* it.

We shall shortly give two small examples of using the synchronous calculus; for this purpose let us collect together some algebraic laws which we shall need. We omit properties of Summation, which remain unchanged. For Product we have

$$E \times F \ \sim \ F \times E \qquad\qquad \alpha\!:\!E \times \beta\!:\!F \ \sim \ \alpha\beta\!:\!(E \times F)$$
$$E \times (F \times G) \ \sim \ (E \times F) \times G \qquad\qquad E \times 0 \ \sim \ 0$$
$$E \times (F + G) \ \sim \ E \times F + E \times G \qquad\qquad E \times 1 \ \sim \ E$$

and for Restriction

$$(\alpha\!:\!E) \backslash L \ \sim \ \begin{cases} \ 0 & \text{if } a \in L \text{ and } a \in \alpha \text{ for some } a; \\ \ \alpha\!:\!(E \backslash L) & \text{otherwise.} \end{cases}$$
$$(\partial E) \backslash L \ \sim \ \partial(E \backslash L)$$
$$(E + F) \backslash L \ \sim \ E \backslash L + F \backslash L$$

There are of course properties of weak bisimilarity or weak congruence also, but we shall not pursue them. We have all we need for our examples.

Example 1   We now substantiate our claim that Relabelling can be defined in the new calculus. We confine ourselves to a special case, but a general definition is possible. Assume that P may only perform actions which contain the particle a with power 1 or not at all; that is, every action of P and of its derivatives takes the form α or $a\alpha$, where $a \notin \alpha$. Then $A \stackrel{\text{def}}{=} \partial(\overline{a}b\!:\!A)$ is an agent which can always perform either 1 or $\overline{a}b$, and nothing else; so we may define the Relabelling $[b/a]$ (for $b \neq a$) as follows:

$$P[b/a] \stackrel{\text{def}}{=} (P|A) \backslash a$$

It is quite easy to show that this captures the intended effect.　　■

Exercise 8   Define similarly the Relabelling $[b_1/a_1, b_2/a_2]$. Can you also see how to define $[b/a]$ without the initial assumption that a only occurs with power 0 or 1 in actions?　　■

Example 2   We may call the following two agents M_1 and M_2 *biplexers*. When M_1 is connected to the $\overline{a}$ port of an agent to its left, the effect is to transform that port into two ports, labelled $\overline{b}$ and $\overline{c}$. M_2 is similar.

$$M_1 \stackrel{\text{def}}{=} \partial N_1 \qquad\qquad\qquad M_2 \stackrel{\text{def}}{=} \partial N_2$$
$$N_1 \stackrel{\text{def}}{=} a(\overline{b}\!:\!M_1 + \overline{c}\!:\!M_1) \qquad N_2 \stackrel{\text{def}}{=} b(\overline{d}\!:\!M_2 + \overline{e}\!:\!M_2)$$

(Note that in N_1, for example, a is synchronised with either $\overline{b}$ or $\overline{c}$, because $N_1 \sim a\overline{b}\colon M_1 + a\overline{c}\colon M_1$.) If we now compose M_1 and M_2, via b, then we should like to prove the result equivalent to a *triplexer*; that is, we should like to show $M \sim M_3$, where

$$M \overset{\text{def}}{=} (M_1 \times M_2)\backslash b$$
$$M_3 \overset{\text{def}}{=} \partial(a(\overline{c}\colon M_3 + \overline{d}\colon M_3 + \overline{e}\colon M_3))$$

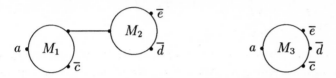

To prove that $M \sim M_3$, it will be enough to show that M satisfies the defining equation of M_3, i.e. that

$$M \sim \partial(a(\overline{c}\colon M + \overline{d}\colon M + \overline{e}\colon M))$$

since the synchronous calculus also enjoys a unique solution property. We shall now write out the steps without supplying the justifications; every step is justified by one of the equations or definitions appearing earlier in this section, or else by a known property of Summation, and it will be a good exercise for the reader to check this.

$$
\begin{aligned}
M \quad &\sim \quad (M_1 \times M_2)\backslash b \\
&\sim \quad ((N_1 + 1\colon M_1) \times (N_2 + 1\colon M_2))\backslash b \\
&\sim \quad (N_1 \times N_2)\backslash b + (1\colon M_1 \times N_2)\backslash b + (N_1 \times 1\colon M_2)\backslash b + 1\colon M
\end{aligned}
$$

Now computing the separate terms:

$$
\begin{aligned}
(N_1 \times N_2)\backslash b \quad &\sim \quad ((a\overline{b}\colon M_1 + a\overline{c}\colon M_1) \times (b\overline{d}\colon M_2 + b\overline{e}\colon M_2))\backslash b \\
&\sim \quad (a\overline{d}\colon(M_1 \times M_2) + a\overline{e}\colon(M_1 \times M_2) + \\
&\qquad a\overline{c}b\overline{d}\colon(M_1 \times M_2) + a\overline{c}b\overline{e}\colon(M_1 \times M_2))\backslash b \\
&\sim \quad a\overline{d}\colon M + a\overline{e}\colon M
\end{aligned}
$$

On the other hand

$$
\begin{aligned}
(1\colon M_1 \times N_2)\backslash b \quad &\sim \quad (1\colon M_1 \times (b\overline{d}\colon M_2 + b\overline{e}\colon M_2))\backslash b \\
&\sim \quad (b\overline{d}\colon(M_1 \times M_2) + b\overline{e}\colon(M_1 \times M_2))\backslash b
\end{aligned}
$$

$$\sim \ 0$$

and finally

$$(N_1 \times 1:M_2)\backslash b \ \sim \ (a\overline{b}:(M_1 \times M_2) + a\overline{c}:(M_1 \times M_2))\backslash b$$
$$\sim \ a\overline{c}:M$$

So adding all these up we get

$$M \sim a(\overline{c}:M + \overline{d}:M + \overline{e}:M) + 1:M$$

Thus, both M and $\partial(a(\overline{c}:M + \overline{d}:M + \overline{e}:M))$ satisfy the equation in X

$$X \sim a(\overline{c}:M + \overline{d}:M + \overline{e}:M) + 1:X$$

and it follows, by the usual unique solution property, that $M \sim M_3$. ∎

Exercise 9 Check all the steps of the above reasoning carefully. ∎

Exercise 10 In the main calculus of this book, the synchronisation of a with either $\overline{b}$ or $\overline{c}$ in M_1 above is not possible. This means that multiplexing must be directional – a must either precede or follow the other action. In fact, there are three reasonable alternatives:

$$M_1 \ \overset{\text{def}}{=} \ a.(\overline{b}.M_1 + \overline{c}.M_1)$$
$$M_1 \ \overset{\text{def}}{=} \ a.\overline{b}.M_1 + a.\overline{c}.M_1$$
$$M_1 \ \overset{\text{def}}{=} \ \overline{b}.a.M_1 + \overline{c}.a.M_1$$

with analogous alternatives for M_2 and M_3. Show that, even if $\sim$ is weakened to $\approx$, the equivalence proved in the example does not hold in any of the three cases. ∎

This example is quite small, and we shall not take the synchronous calculus further, but it shows that the algebra is quite elegant. The reader may indeed wonder, in view of its greater expressive power, why we did not adopt this calculus throughout. One strong reason is that if we formulate an expansion law for the synchronous calculus we find many more terms on the right-hand side than previously; for in an n-way Composition $P_1 \mid \cdots \mid P_n$, if multi-way synchronisation is possible, then any of the 2^n subsets of the P_i may engage in a single action. But with further experience with the synchronous calculus ways may be found to preserve its power without suffering excessive expansion.

Indeed, neither the synchronous calculus nor its asynchronous derivate has been used directly to a large extent in practice. But Gerard Berry's group have developed Meije, a calculus equipotent with the synchronous calculus, and have applied it with success – particularly in problems where real time is important. The reason for their success lies in their inspired choice of basic combinators; theirs are interderivable with those of our calculus (with one extension; see below), but lie comfortably 'under the hands' for application work.

We shall conclude this chapter by mentioning an important result from Berry's group, which gives a satisfying characterisation of the power both of Meije and of our synchronous calculus. First, we must admit that we have to add to our calculus an Operator which it possessed when first conceived, but which we have not yet mentioned. It is denoted by Δ, and is a companion to ∂. It may be called the *asynchroniser*; ΔP is just like P except that it can delay between any of its actions, so for example

$$\Delta(\alpha:\beta:0) \sim \alpha.\beta.0$$

Now Δ cannot apparently be defined by recursive equations, but it is easily given by a single rule of action, as follows:

$$\frac{E \xrightarrow{\alpha} E'}{\Delta E \xrightarrow{\alpha} \partial\Delta E'}$$

The addition of Δ brings the synchronous calculus in line with Meije in its expressive power.

To make this statement precise, we have to say what kind of expressiveness we mean. The simplest measure of expressiveness is the class of *processes* expressible; more precisely, it is the class of *derivation trees* expressible up to strong bisimilarity. In this sense, all calculi tend to be of equal power, since one only needs Prefix, Summation and Recursion to express all these (of course infinite branching requires infinite Summation). A more refined and interesting measure of expressiveness is the class of *Operators* expressible up to strong bisimilarity. With respect to this criterion, Robert de Simone has proved both Meije and our synchronous calculus to be *completely expressive* in the following sense: any Operator which can be defined by rules of action which obey certain natural conditions can also be defined directly in terms of the basic combinators of either calculus. This is a remarkable result, unique so far of its kind, and sets a standard to which other calculi may aspire. A result of this kind is of real importance in designing a calculus for practical use; it eliminates the danger of adding Operators one after another, as dictated by the needs of applications. Unfortunately we still await such an result for an asynchronous calculus.

9.4   Equivalence relations

We have seen that calculi can vary considerably in their choice of combinators, and usefully so. There is a quite different kind of variation among calculi, and that is in their choice of equivalence relations. Perhaps it would be more accurate to say that we have one all-embracing calculus, consisting of a few very basic combinators and some methods of defining new ones (as discussed earlier in this chapter), and that for any given purpose we may find a particular set of combinators and a particular equivalence relation more appropriate than others.

Hitherto we have studied two main equivalences: strong and weak bisimilarity. (Actually observation congruence is a third, but closely allied to weak bisimilarity.) In this section we shall look at two further equivalences. They both abstract from internal (τ) actions like weak bisimilarity, but they are both much more generous; they equate more agents.

Our first equivalence is perhaps the simplest of all: *trace equivalence*. It equates two agents if and only if they can perform exactly the same sequences of observable actions.

Definition 3 P and Q are (*weakly*) *trace equivalent*, written $P \approx_1 Q$, if for all $s \in \mathcal{L}^*$
$$P \overset{s}{\Rightarrow} \text{ if and only if } Q \overset{s}{\Rightarrow} \qquad\blacksquare$$

Proposition 1   If $P \approx Q$ then $P \approx_1 Q$.

Proof   Use the characterisation of $\approx$ given in Proposition 7.1. $\blacksquare$

The main disadvantage of trace equivalence is that it does not tell us anything about deadlock; for example, $a.0 + \tau.0 \approx_1 a.0$ even though the left-hand side can reach a state in which a and all other observable actions are impossible – i.e. a deadlock – while the right-hand side cannot avoid doing a. But if we are content with such a coarse equivalence then we can exploit several pleasant algebraic properties. First, $\approx_1$ is a congruence relation:

Proposition 2 $\approx_1$ is preserved by all the basic combinators. That is, if $P \approx_1 Q$ and $P_i \approx_1 Q_i$ then $\alpha.P \approx_1 \alpha.Q$, $\sum_i P_i \approx_1 \sum_i Q_i$, $P_0|P_1 \approx_1 Q_0|Q_1$, $P\backslash L \approx_1 Q\backslash L$ and $P[f] \approx_1 Q[f]$. $\blacksquare$

It can also be shown that $\approx_1$ is preserved by recursive definition, in the sense of Proposition 7.8. Thus, in contrast with $\approx$, we do not have to refine $\approx_1$ to obtain a congruence.

Second, there is a unique solution theorem for $\approx_1$, analogous to Propositions 3.4(2) and 7.13:

Proposition 3 Let the expressions E_i $(i \in I)$ contain at most the variables X_i $(i \in I)$ free, and let these variables be guarded and sequential in each E_i. Then

$$\text{If } \tilde{P} \approx_1 \tilde{E}\{\tilde{P}/\tilde{X}\} \text{ and } \tilde{Q} \approx_1 \tilde{E}\{\tilde{Q}/\tilde{X}\}, \text{ then } \tilde{P} \approx_1 \tilde{Q} \qquad \blacksquare$$

Third, there are three equational laws for $\approx_1$ which are false in general for $=$:

Proposition 4

(1) $\alpha.(P + Q) \approx_1 \alpha.P + \alpha.Q$
(2) $(P + Q) \mid R \approx_1 P\mid R + Q\mid R$
(3) $P \approx_1 \tau.P$ $\blacksquare$

The first two of these laws state that Prefix and Composition both distribute over Summation, up to $\approx_1$.

Example 3 Although we do not intend to spend much time on trace equivalence here, it may be instructive to see a proof of trace equivalence which uses the above properties to advantage. Define

$$A \stackrel{\text{def}}{=} a.A + c_1.c_2.A$$
$$B \stackrel{\text{def}}{=} \overline{c_1}.b.\overline{c_2}.B$$
$$D \stackrel{\text{def}}{=} a.D + b.D$$

where a, b, c_1, c_2 are distinct names. Now consider $(A|B)\backslash L$, where $L = \{c_1, c_2\}$; it is clearly not bisimilar with D, since it can reach a state in which the action a is impossible. But we can show $(A|B)\backslash L \approx_1 D$, by proving that $(A|B)\backslash L$ satisfies (up to $\approx_1$) the defining equation of D and then applying Proposition 3. In the argument below we use $\approx_1$ just in those places where $=$ would not hold. First, we distribute Composition and Restriction over Summation:

$$(A|B)\backslash L \approx_1 (a.A \mid B)\backslash L + (c_1.c_2.A \mid B)\backslash L$$

Now we compute for the two summands:

$$(a.A|B)\backslash L = a.(A|B)\backslash L$$
$$(c_1.c_2.A \mid B)\backslash L = \tau.(c_2.A \mid b.\overline{c_2}.B)\backslash L$$

$$\approx_1 \quad (c_2.A \mid b.\overline{c_2}.B)\backslash L$$
$$= \quad b.(A|B)\backslash L$$

So substituting for the summands we get

$$(A|B)\backslash L \approx_1 a.(A|B)\backslash L + b.(A|B)\backslash L$$

and the result follows by the unique solution property, Proposition 3. ∎

Exercise 11   Let $A' \stackrel{\text{def}}{=} c_1.a.c_2.A'$, $B' \stackrel{\text{def}}{=} c_1.b.c_2.A'$ and $C \stackrel{\text{def}}{=} \overline{c_1}.\overline{c_2}.C$. Find out whether $(A'|B'|C)\backslash L \approx (A|B)\backslash L$, or $(A'|B'|C)\backslash L \approx D$. Prove $(A'|B'|C)\backslash L \approx_1 D$.   ∎

Exercise 12   Prove the scheduler lemma in Section 5.5, but with $\approx_1$ in place of $\approx$. Avoid appealing to Corollary 3.3; instead, use more direct properties of $\approx_1$.   ∎

The fact that trace equivalence equates a deadlocking agent to one which does not deadlock indicates that it is too weak in general. In some cases, however, it will be adequate. In particular we shall see in Chapter 11 that, for agents which are known to be determinate, it agrees completely with bisimilarity.

An interesting equivalence which lies between trace equivalence and bisimilarity is Hoare's *failures equivalence*. It is important, because it appears to be the weakest equivalence which never equates a deadlocking agent with one which does not deadlock. We shall describe it briefly here; for a more detailed presentation the reader should consult Hoare's book. Matthew Hennessy, together with Rocco de Nicola, has given an elegant alternative characterisation of this equivalence called *testing equivalence*, in which two agents are equivalent just when they pass the same tests of a certain simple nature.

Definition 4   A *failure* is a pair (s, L), where $s \in \mathcal{L}^*$ is a trace and $L \subseteq \mathcal{L}$ is a set of labels. The failure (s, L) is said to belong to an agent P if there exists P' such that

- $P \stackrel{s}{\Rightarrow} P'$
- $P' \stackrel{\tau}{\not\rightarrow}$, i.e. P' is stable
- For all $\ell \in L$, $P' \stackrel{\ell}{\not\rightarrow}$ ∎

Thus, if (s, L) belongs to P it means that P can perform s and thereby reach a state in which no further action (not even τ) is possible if the environment will only permit actions in L. As a simple example, consider $A \stackrel{\text{def}}{=} a.(b.c.0 + b.d.0)$. Then A has the following failures:

- (ε, L) for all L such that $a \notin L$
- (a, L) for all L such that $b \notin L$
- (ab, L) for all L such that $\{c, d\} \not\subseteq L$
- (abc, L) and (abd, L) for all L

Most important here are the failures of the form (ab, L); if the environment wishes to *ensure* that A can continue after b then it must permit both c and d, since it cannot predict which will be chosen.

Definition 5   Two agents P and Q are said to be *failures-equivalent*, written $P \approx_f Q$, if they possess exactly the same failures.   ∎

It is easy to see that failures equivalence implies trace equivalence, since a trace is part of a failure. That they are not the same equivalence can be seen from the following exercise.

Exercise 13   Let $P \equiv a.(b.0 + c.0)$ and $Q \equiv a.b.0 + a.c.0$, where $b \neq c$. Show that $P \not\approx_f Q$, by working out the failures of each.   ∎

The contrast with bisimilarity can best be seen by considering the agent A defined above, together with $B \stackrel{\text{def}}{=} a.b.c.0 + a.b.d.0$:

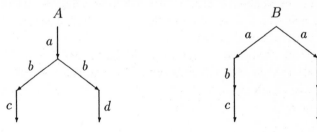

It turns out that A and B possess exactly the same failures, and therefore $A \approx_f B$; but it is easy to check that $A \not\approx B$. Intuitively, we may say that bisimilarity is more sensitive than failures equivalence to the branching structure of an agent. Indeed, this is emphasised by the following law for failures equivalence:

$$\alpha.(\beta.P + \beta.Q) \approx_f \alpha.\beta.P + \alpha.\beta.Q$$

which does not hold for bisimilarity. This is a constrained form of distributive law; it may be compared with the unconstrained distributive

law, Proposition 4(1), which holds for trace equivalence but not for
failures equivalence.

Failures equivalence has a pleasant algebra, and has also an associated partial ordering (based upon inclusion, rather than equality, of
the failure-sets of two agents) which makes it very useful as a means
of specification. Bisimilarity, on the other hand, benefits from the simple proof technique of finding bisimulations. Both have a good intuitive
character. As we have presented them, it is unfortunately not quite true
to say that $P \approx Q$ implies $P \approx_f Q$, because failures equivalence is more
discriminating with respect to divergent behaviour (infinite internal action). But it is possible to refine bisimilarity slightly in this respect, and
then the implication does indeed hold. Moreover, bisimilarity – or its
associated congruence – then appears to be the strongest equivalence
based upon observable actions that one can reasonably demand; it is
this characteristic which led us to give it primary place.

Exercise 14 This extended exercise explores yet another equivalence
relation, which may even have suggested itself to inquiring readers. It
has some intrinsic interest, in particular because it behaves a little more
simply than bisimilarity. But when you have answered the questions you
should see why bisimilarity is preferable.

(1) Let S be a binary relation over agents. S is said to be a *simulation*
if PSQ implies that, for all $\alpha \in Act$,

$$\text{If } P \xrightarrow{\alpha} P' \text{ then, for some } Q', Q \xrightarrow{\hat{\alpha}} Q' \text{ and } P'SQ'$$

Analogous to weak bisimulation we then define the largest simulation, $\prec$, to be the union of all simulations. Prove that $\prec$ is a
pre-order, i.e. transitive and reflexive. Prove also that $P \approx Q$
implies $P \prec Q$.

(2) Define the equivalence $\asymp \stackrel{\text{def}}{=} \prec \cap \succ$; that is, $P \asymp Q$ iff $P \prec Q$ and
$Q \prec P$. Prove that $P \approx Q$ implies $P \asymp Q$.

(3) Prove that $P \asymp Q$ implies $P + R \asymp Q + R$. This means that
Summation preserves $\asymp$, while we know that it does not preserve
$\approx$. In fact the proof that all other combinators preserve $\approx$ applies
easily to $\prec$, hence also to $\asymp$; thus $\asymp$ is a congruence.

(4) By considering $P \equiv a.b.0$ and $Q \equiv a.b.0 + a.0$, show that $P \asymp Q$
does not imply $P \approx Q$, and also that $\asymp$ does not respect the
capability of deadlock.

(5) Let $A \stackrel{\text{def}}{=} a.p.b.v.A$, $S \stackrel{\text{def}}{=} \bar{p}.\bar{v}.S$, and $A_i \stackrel{\text{def}}{=} A[a_i/a, b_i/b]$, $(i = 1, 2)$.

Define
$$Sys \overset{\text{def}}{=} (A_1|S|A_2)\backslash\{p, v\}$$

(Think of A_1 and A_2 sharing the semaphore S.) Further, let $B \overset{\text{def}}{=}$ $a.b.B$ and $B_i \overset{\text{def}}{=} B[a_i/a, b_i/b]$, $(i = 1, 2)$. Then is it true that $Sys \approx B_1|B_2$, or that $Sys \asymp B_1|B_2$?   ∎

10

Specifications and Logic

Throughout previous chapters we have emphasized the notions of equivalence and congruence among agents, and indeed our theory so far has been largely equational. But not entirely; we have sometimes been interested in a property which is definable directly in terms of the derivation trees of agents, and have been concerned to prove that a certain agent or class of agents possesses that property. We now wish to show that our calculus can be extended to admit properties of processes which are described formally in logic rather than in algebra.

In Section 1 we look informally at a few process descriptions and specifications, pertaining to examples in previous chapters, and we see how they can be naturally expressed in terms of action. This leads to a very simple *process logic*, $\mathcal{PL}$, based upon the notion of *possible action*; in Section 2 we define the logic and what it means for a process to satisfy a formula of $\mathcal{PL}$. We illustrate the use of $\mathcal{PL}$ as a formal specification language by means of further examples. In Section 3 we see how another logic – a Hoare logic for the parallel programming language $\mathcal{M}_0$ of Chapter 8 – can be derived from $\mathcal{PL}$ in a precise sense. Finally Sections 4 and 5, which will perhaps interest the more mathematical reader, show how $\mathcal{PL}$ provides an illuminating alternative account of bisimilarity.

10.1 Examples of specifications

There is no technical difference between the notion of 'specification' and the notion of 'property'; to say that a system or agent satisfies a certain specification is to say that it possesses a certain property. One can make the subjective distinction, of course, that only certain properties are specifications – namely those which are desirable! But in the absence of any firmer distinction it is best to treat the terms as synonymous. We now give some examples of properties which have arisen in earlier chapters.

First, let us take the notion of a *well-terminating* agent, Definition 8.1:

P is *well-terminating* if, for every derivative P' of P, $P' \overset{\mathbf{done}}{\Longrightarrow}$

is impossible and also if $P' \overset{\overline{\mathbf{done}}}{\Longrightarrow}$ then $P' \sim \overline{\mathbf{done}}.0$.

As presented, this definition depends upon strong congruence, but it is easy to rephrase it more directly in terms of derivation: we define P to be *well-terminating* if

(1) $P \overset{t}{\to} \overset{\mathbf{done}}{\to}$ is impossible, for any t.

(2) Whenever $P \overset{t}{\to} P' \overset{\overline{\mathbf{done}}}{\Longrightarrow}$ for some $t \in Act^*$ then, for every α and P'' such that $P' \overset{\alpha}{\to} P''$, $\alpha = \overline{\mathbf{done}}$ and P'' has no actions.

As another example, consider the way we informally specified the scheduler agent *Sched* in Section 5.4:

(1) The actions $a_1, \ldots, a_n$ are performed cyclically, starting with a_1.

(2) For each i, the actions a_i and b_i are performed alternately.

For clause (1), we note that it places no constraint on the occurrence of b_j actions either before or between the a_i. We can express clause (1) more precisely as follows:

- If $Sched \overset{t}{\to} \overset{a_i}{\to}$, and no a_k occurs in t, then $i = 1$.
- If $Sched \overset{t}{\to} \overset{a_i}{\to} \overset{t'}{\to} \overset{a_j}{\to}$, and no a_k occurs in t', then $j = i+1$ (modulo n).

Notice that this condition is a rather timid interpretation of the original clause; it does not imply that an a_i action is ever possible, but merely implies that those a_i actions which do occur must be in cyclic order.

Exercise 1   Express, equally timidly, the second clause in the specification of the scheduler.   ∎

Now a scheduler which performs no actions at all, i.e. $Sched \sim \mathbf{0}$, satisfies these timid conditions. We can ensure that *Sched* is more useful by demanding that, at least, it never deadlocks; that is, that it will allow *some* action whatever state it reaches. This condition can be expressed as follows:

If $Sched \overset{t}{\to} Sched'$ then for some i either $Sched' \overset{a_i}{\to}$ or $Sched' \overset{b_i}{\to}$.

Even with this addition, there are many schedulers which satisfy the conditions expressed so far; one such is the scheduler which can perform only the single infinite sequence $a_1 b_1 a_2 b_2 \cdots$. Extra conditions can be added, until we reach the point at which they determine the scheduler completely up to bisimilarity. If this is what is wanted then we may find – as we did in Section 5.4 – that the most convenient way of specifying the scheduler is not by a collection of conditions which it must satisfy, but by an abstract agent *Schedspec* to which it must be bisimilar. The same remark applies to the protocol system constructed in Chapter 6. But in many realistic situations we find partial specifications more appropriate, and in this chapter we wish to consider how they can be expressed formally.

As a third example, consider the vending machine W which you were asked to build in Exercise 1.6. One clause of the specification was

W cannot hold a credit of more than 4p

and it was also stipulated that W should be able to perform any action which does not violate this and the other clauses. Now recall that W's actions which affect credit are 2p, 1p which increase your credit with the machine, and big, little which decrease it (by 2p and 1p respectively). So if $t \in Act^*$ is any action sequence, let us define $\#(\alpha, t)$ to mean the number of occurrences of an action α in t, and define

$$Credit(t) \stackrel{\text{def}}{=} \#(\text{1p}, t) + 2\#(\text{2p}, t) - \#(\text{little}, t) - 2\#(\text{big}, t)$$

Then we can express the specification of W (in so far as credit controls its actions) by

(1) If $Credit(t) > 4$ then $W \stackrel{t}{\nrightarrow}$.

(2) If $Credit(t) \leq 3$ and $W \stackrel{t}{\rightarrow} W'$ then $W' \stackrel{\text{1p}}{\rightarrow}$.

(3) If $Credit(t) \leq 2$ and $W \stackrel{t}{\rightarrow} W'$ then $W' \stackrel{\text{2p}}{\rightarrow}$.

Notice that *Credit*, which we naturally think of as an attribute of the *state* of the vending machine, is conveniently expressed here as a function of the *action-sequence* which leads it into a state. (We wish to express all our specifications in terms of actions.)

Exercise 2 Continuing the vending machine example, define the property $Discharged(t)$ of sequences $t \in Act^*$ to mean that all previous purchases have been collected from the tray; it is clearly given (as a boolean value) as follows:

$$Discharged(t) \stackrel{\text{def}}{=} (\#(\text{big}, t) + \#(\text{little}, t) = \#(\text{collect}, t))$$

Now presumably our vague specification in Exercise 1.6 that 'W never makes a profit' means that you should be able to buy a big or a little chocolate (i.e. the `big` or `little` button should be unlocked) whenever the credit is large enough – provided that the previous purchase has been collected – and not otherwise. Express this (partial) specification precisely in the manner of the previous examples, using the functions *Credit* and *Discharged* appropriately. ∎

Many other systems have been considered in previous chapters, and probably in every case a partial understanding of the system can be given concisely in terms of conditions which it satisfies, expressed in the semi-formal style of the foregoing examples. This method of description is attractive because it is incremental; by adding further conditions one increases understanding of a system – or, if you like, one narrows the class of candidate systems which will meet the description. (The former remark is appropriate in describing a system which exists already; the latter in specifying a system to be built.)

But our conditions are so far only *semi*-formal. True, they have been expressed precisely enough that we can see fairly clearly how to check that they are satisfied. But the language in which they are expressed is not fully determined, so it is not yet clear which conditions are admissible and which are not.

Without further preamble we shall now define a logical language $\mathcal{PL}$ (process logic) in terms of which all the foregoing examples of conditions can be expressed. We shall define precisely what it means for an agent P to satisfy a formula $F \in \mathcal{PL}$, and shall then be able to answer many questions about the relationship between $\mathcal{PL}$ and our equivalence relations. Our aim, as with our agent calculus, is to base $\mathcal{PL}$ on as few primitive constructions as possible; we shall nevertheless find it to be remarkably powerful.

10.2   Logic for specifications

Recall that our calculus is a labelled transition system (LTS)

$$(\mathcal{P}, \; Act, \; \{\overset{\alpha}{\to} \, : \; \alpha \in Act\})$$

We shall define a simple logic $\mathcal{PL}$, whose formulae express conditions on the behaviour of members of $\mathcal{P}$, i.e. properties of derivation trees. In doing this we shall refer only to the relations $\overset{\alpha}{\to}$ over $\mathcal{P}$, not to the combinators; therefore our logic makes sense for any LTS whatever.

Definition 1 $\mathcal{PL}$ is the smallest class of *formulae* containing the following, where it is assumed that the formulae F and F_i are already in $\mathcal{PL}$:

(i) $\langle\alpha\rangle F$, a *possibility* $(\alpha \in Act)$
(ii) $\neg F$, a *negation*
(iii) $\bigwedge_{i \in I} F_i$, a *conjunction* $(I$ an indexing set$)$ ∎

Note that the first formula which demands a place in $\mathcal{PL}$, according to these rules, is the empty conjunction $\bigwedge_{i \in \emptyset} F_i$, which we write **true**. Thereafter we obtain formulae such as

$$\langle\alpha\rangle\mathbf{true} \qquad \langle\alpha\rangle(\langle\beta\rangle\mathbf{true} \wedge \neg\langle\gamma\rangle\mathbf{true})$$

and so on; here we use $\wedge$ (infixed) to mean binary conjunction.

   The possibility operator $\langle\alpha\rangle$ is an example of a *modal* operator; in fact $\mathcal{PL}$ is a *modal logic*, which means that its formulae make assertions about changing state. Informally $\langle\alpha\rangle G$, pronounced 'diamond–α G', asserts of an agent P that

It is possible for P to do α and thereby reach a state Q which satisfies G.

Further, if G is $\langle\beta\rangle\mathbf{true} \wedge \neg\langle\gamma\rangle\mathbf{true}$ then G asserts (of Q) that

It is possible for Q to do β (and thereby reach a state where **true** holds), but it is not possible for Q to do γ (and thereby reach a state where **true** holds),

or more briefly

Q can do β but not γ.

More formally, we now define a relation $\models$, pronounced '*satisfies*', between agents and formulae.

Definition 2   The *satisfaction* relation $\models$ between $\mathcal{P}$ and $\mathcal{PL}$ is defined as follows, by induction on the structure of formulae:

(i) $P \models \langle\alpha\rangle F$ if, for some P', $P \xrightarrow{\alpha} P'$ and $P' \models F$
(ii) $P \models \neg F$ if $P \not\models F$ (i.e. it is not the case that $P \models F$)
(iii) $P \models \bigwedge_{i \in I} F_i$ if, for all $i \in I$, $P \models F_i$ ∎

As another example, consider again the two agents of Section 4.1, $A' \stackrel{\text{def}}{=} a.(b.0 + c.0)$ and $B' \stackrel{\text{def}}{=} a.b.0 + a.c.0$, which we argued could be distinguished by a simple experiment:

Then we have $A' \models F$ and $B' \not\models F$, where

$$F \equiv \langle a \rangle (\langle b \rangle \mathbf{true} \wedge \langle c \rangle \mathbf{true})$$

Exercise 3 Find a formula G, not containing c, such that $A' \models G$ and $B' \not\models G$. ∎

Our basis language $\mathcal{PL}$ is, of course, *extremely* basic. We would find it hard to express useful descriptions or specifications in it; indeed, we might well be surprised that they can be expressed in it at all. Let us now introduce some derived forms for $\mathcal{PL}$, which will make its power more apparent. First, it is often more convenient to subscribe a conjunction by a condition Φ, in any suitable notation, instead of $i \in I$; for example $\bigwedge_{1 \leq i \leq 3}$ in place of $\bigwedge_{i \in \{1,2,3\}}$. Second, we define some more logical operators:

$$\mathbf{false} \overset{\text{def}}{=} \neg\mathbf{true}$$

$$F_0 \wedge F_1 \overset{\text{def}}{=} \bigwedge_{i \in \{0,1\}} F_i$$

$$\bigvee_{i \in I} F_i \overset{\text{def}}{=} \neg \bigwedge_{i \in I} \neg F_i$$

$$F_0 \vee F_1 \overset{\text{def}}{=} \bigvee_{i \in \{0,1\}} F_i$$

$$F \supset F' \overset{\text{def}}{=} \neg F \vee F'$$

Third, we enrich our repertoire of modal operators:

$$\langle \alpha_1 \cdots \alpha_n \rangle F \overset{\text{def}}{=} \langle \alpha_1 \rangle \cdots \langle \alpha_n \rangle F \qquad (n \geq 0)$$

$$[t]F \overset{\text{def}}{=} \neg \langle t \rangle \neg F \qquad (t \in Act^*)$$

We call $[t]F$ a *necessity*, and pronounce it 'box–t F'. From Definition 2 of satisfaction, we can see that $P \models [t]F$ means

> If P can perform the action-sequence t, it must thereby reach a state where F holds.

In particular, $[t]$**false** asserts that P cannot perform t.

Fourth, it is convenient to lift a condition Φ, which qualifies an index variable, to the same level as the modal formulae; for example we would like to write $\forall i.\,(i > 0 \supset \langle a_i \rangle F)$ in place of $\bigwedge_{i>0} \langle a_i \rangle F$. Here are some forms we shall use:

$$\forall i \in I.\,F_i \;\overset{\text{def}}{=}\; \bigwedge_{i \in I} F_i$$

$$\forall i.\,(\Phi \supset F_i) \;\overset{\text{def}}{=}\; \bigwedge_{\Phi} F_i$$

$$\exists i \in I.\,F_i \;\overset{\text{def}}{=}\; \bigvee_{i \in I} F_i$$

$$\exists i.\,(\Phi \wedge F_i) \;\overset{\text{def}}{=}\; \bigvee_{\Phi} F_i$$

$$F \supset \Phi \;\overset{\text{def}}{=}\; \neg\Phi \supset \neg F$$

So, for example, let us recall the first part of clause (1) of our scheduler specification:

If $Sched \overset{t}{\to} \overset{a_i}{\to}$, and no a_k is in t, then $i = 1$;

this will be expressed in the form

$$\forall t \in (Act - \{a_1, \ldots, a_n\})^*.\,\forall i.\,(\langle ta_i \rangle \textbf{true} \supset i = 1)$$

Now such a formula, though it is formal, is reasonably easy to understand; it is therefore quite natural for us to argue informally (though of course rigorously) when we wish to establish that a particular agent satisfies such a property. For example, let us prove that the scheduler specification $Schedspec(1, \emptyset)$ of Section 5.4 satisfies the above formula. The definition was as follows (where X is any subset of $\{1, \ldots, n\}$, and $i + 1, i - 1$ etc. are calculated modulo n):

$$(i \in X) \qquad Schedspec(i, X) \;\overset{\text{def}}{=}\; \sum_{j \in X} b_j.Schedspec(i, X - \{j\})$$

$$(i \notin X) \qquad Schedspec(i, X) \;\overset{\text{def}}{=}\; a_i.Schedspec(i + 1, X \cup \{i\})$$
$$+ \sum_{j \in X} b_j.Schedspec(i, X - \{j\})$$

In fact we shall show more generally that $Schedspec(1, X)$ satisfies the formula for any X. For if it performs an a_i immediately then we see from the second equation that i can only take the value 1. On the other hand if it performs any sequence of b_j for differing values of j then it can only reach states of the form $Schedspec(1, Y)$; the first parameter remains fixed at 1. Hence the first a_i action must be a_1.

We shall not deal here with any formalised proof system for the logic $\mathcal{PL}$; but in the next section we shall look at some formal rules of proof for a higher-level logic built from $\mathcal{PL}$.

Exercise 4   Express formally the second part of clause (1), and also clause (2) (see Section 5.4). Prove informally that $Schedspec(1, \emptyset)$ satisfies them both.   ∎

Exercise 5   Express formally the property of well-termination, and also the specification of the vending machine W which you wrote in Exercise 2.   ∎

As a final pair of derived forms, we may find it convenient to have weak versions of the possibility operator which ignore τ actions. We therefore introduce for each $s \in \mathcal{L}^*$ the derived modal operators $\langle\!\langle s \rangle\!\rangle$ and $[\![s]\!]$, which may be called *weak possibility* and *weak necessity*; they are defined as follows:

$$\langle\!\langle s \rangle\!\rangle F \; \overset{\mathrm{def}}{=} \; \exists t \in Act^*.\,(s = \hat{t} \wedge \langle t \rangle F)$$

$$[\![s]\!]F \; \overset{\mathrm{def}}{=} \; \forall t \in Act^*.\,(s = \hat{t} \supset [t]F)$$

Note particularly the case $s = \varepsilon$; by our earlier definition $\langle \varepsilon \rangle F$ and $[\varepsilon]F$ are both equivalent to F itself, but $\langle\!\langle \varepsilon \rangle\!\rangle F$ is more significant; it asserts that it is possible to reach a state satisfying F after a sequence of zero or more τ actions. We shall often omit ε in a modal operator, writing $\langle\rangle F$, $\langle\!\langle\rangle\!\rangle F$ etc.

Exercise 6   What does $[\![\,]\!]F$ assert?   ∎

Exercise 7   Find a formula of the form $\langle\!\langle\rangle\!\rangle F$ which is satisfied by $a.0 + \tau.b.0$ but not by $a.0 + b.0$. Would you be able to distinguish between these two agents using only $\langle\!\langle s \rangle\!\rangle$ operators such that $s \neq \varepsilon$ (i.e. $\langle\!\langle\rangle\!\rangle$ forbidden)?   ∎

Armed with these succinct derived forms in $\mathcal{PL}$, we shall now look at a more extensive example of its use.

10.3   Logic for imperative programs

As an illustration of the power of $\mathcal{PL}$, let us go back to the programming language $\mathcal{M}$ studied in Chapter 8. It is a conventional imperative language with parallelism added, in which communication between commands only occurs via shared variables; in the command

$$C_1 \text{ par } C_2$$

the sub-command C_1 can pass information to C_2 by writing values to a variable which C_2 reads. In fact it is precisely through such communication that programs in $\mathcal{M}$ can be nondeterministic, since the temporal order among C_1's writes and C_2's reads is not determined and can affect the computation.

A useful sub-language of $\mathcal{M}$ is gained by imposing a simple condition on all uses of $C_1 \text{ par } C_2$, namely that C_1 is not allowed to write to any variable which occurs free in C_2, and conversely. The sub-language still allows effective use of parallelism, because C_1 and C_2 can still *read* the same variables. It is also useful because it is easier to understand than the full language. This is just *because* it is deterministic – not in the sense that the order of all events is determined but in the sense that the effect of a program upon its variables is determined. (To be fully precise we should also impose some condition upon the use of input and output, but for the purpose of this chapter we shall assume that no input or output is used at all.)

Hoare initiated the use of a program logic, for a sequential language, which employs sentences of the form

$$P\{\!|C|\!\}Q$$

where C is a command, and P and Q are conventional formulae of logic, in which program variables may occur along with logical variables. The intended meaning of such a sentence is:

If C is executed in a state satisfying P, and if it terminates, then the terminating state will satisfy Q.

A natural inference rule in Hoare's logic is then

$$\frac{P\{\!|C_1|\!\}Q \qquad Q\{\!|C_2|\!\}R}{P\{\!|C_1;C_2|\!\}R}$$

In fact, this is the rule which represents the whole meaning of sequential composition. In contrast, it is not at all easy to get a sound inference rule representing the meaning of *parallel* composition, except under a constraint such as we have discussed above. But *with* the constraint there is, as Owicki and Gries showed, a very natural rule. We shall now examine it, and then see how it is related to $\mathcal{PL}$.

To formulate the rule, we shall first slightly refine Hoare sentences.

It will be convenient to decorate each sentence $P\{\!\{C\}\!\}Q$ with two disjoint sets $\tilde{X}$ and $\tilde{Y}$ of program variables; $\tilde{X}$ must contain all the variables which C reads but does not write, and $\tilde{Y}$ must contain all the variables which C writes. Further, we demand that all the program variables which occur in P or Q must be in $\tilde{X} \cup \tilde{Y}$. So we shall write the sentence as follows:

$$P\{\!\{C\}\!\}Q \mid_{\tilde{Y}}^{\tilde{X}}$$

and we shall only admit sentences which obey the above-stated conditions.

A Hoare logic for the language $\mathcal{M}$, with our constraint upon **par**, will include the following inference rules (we assume the normal interpretation of $\wedge$ (conjunction) and $\supset$ (implication) in the conventional logical formulae $P, Q, \ldots$):

Assignment

$$P\{E/X\}\{\!\{X := E\}\!\}P \mid_{\tilde{Y}}^{\tilde{X}}$$

Sequential

$$\frac{P\{\!\{C_1\}\!\}Q \mid_{\tilde{Y}_1}^{\tilde{X}_1} \qquad Q\{\!\{C_2\}\!\}R \mid_{\tilde{Y}_2}^{\tilde{X}_2}}{P\{\!\{C_1 ; C_2\}\!\}R \mid_{\tilde{Y}_1 \cup \tilde{Y}_2}^{(\tilde{X}_1 - \tilde{Y}_2) \cup (\tilde{X}_2 - \tilde{Y}_1)}}$$

Parallel (on condition that $\tilde{X}_1 \cap \tilde{Y}_2 = \tilde{Y}_1 \cap \tilde{X}_2 = \tilde{Y}_1 \cap \tilde{Y}_2 = \emptyset$)

$$\frac{P_1\{\!\{C_1\}\!\}Q_1 \mid_{\tilde{Y}_1}^{\tilde{X}_1} \qquad P_2\{\!\{C_2\}\!\}Q_2 \mid_{\tilde{Y}_2}^{\tilde{X}_2}}{P_1 \wedge P_2\{\!\{C_1 \text{ par } C_2\}\!\}Q_1 \wedge Q_2 \mid_{\tilde{Y}_1 \cup \tilde{Y}_2}^{\tilde{X}_1 \cup \tilde{X}_2}}$$

Weakening

$$\frac{P' \supset P \qquad P\{\!\{C\}\!\}Q \mid_{\tilde{Y}}^{\tilde{X}} \qquad Q \supset Q'}{P'\{\!\{C\}\!\}Q' \mid_{\tilde{Y}}^{\tilde{X}}}$$

In the **Parallel** rule, which is the most significant for our discussion, the side-condition enforces the constraint upon **par**. In general a Hoare logic will have one or more rules for each programming construct, but we shall be content here just to illustrate the idea with these few rules. The **Weakening** rule is of a different nature; it allows normal reasoning about formulae $P, Q, \ldots$ to be incorporated in proofs about programs.

For those unfamiliar with Hoare logics, we shall briefly digress to show how to use the above rules in proving a simple Hoare sentence, namely the sentence

$$\text{X} = 1 \wedge \text{Y} = 3 \ \{\!\{\text{Y:=Y+X par Z:=X+1}\}\!\} \ \text{Y} = 4 \wedge \text{Z} = 2 \mid_{\{\text{Y,Z}\}}^{\{\text{X}\}}$$

The proof proceeds as follows:

(1) $Y + X = 4$ $\{\!\| Y:=Y+X \|\!\}$ $Y = 4$ $|_{\{Y\}}^{\{X\}}$ by **Assignment**;

(2) $X = 1 \land Y = 3 \supset Y + X = 4$ by elementary arithmetic;

(3) $X = 1 \land Y = 3$ $\{\!\| Y:=Y+X \|\!\}$ $Y = 4$ $|_{\{Y\}}^{\{X\}}$ from (1) and (2)

by **Weakening**;

(4) $X + 1 = 2$ $\{\!\| Z:=X+1 \|\!\}$ $Z = 2$ $|_{\{Z\}}^{\{X\}}$ by **Assignment**;

(5) $X = 1 \supset X + 1 = 2$ by elementary arithmetic;

(6) $X = 1$ $\{\!\| Z:=X+1 \|\!\}$ $Z = 2$ $|_{\{Z\}}^{\{X\}}$ from (4) and (5) by **Weakening**;

(7) $X = 1 \land Y = 3 \land X = 1$ $\{\!\| Y:=Y+X$ par $Z:=X+1 \|\!\}$ $Y = 4 \land Z = 2$ $|_{\{Y,Z\}}^{\{X\}}$

from (3) and (6) by **Parallel**;

(8) $X = 1 \land Y = 3$ $\{\!\| Y:=Y+X$ par $Z:=X+1 \|\!\}$ $Y = 4 \land Z = 2$ $|_{\{Y,Z\}}^{\{X\}}$

from (7) and elementary logic by **Weakening**.

The point in the proof which is most relevant here is that step (7) is only possible because the side-condition of the **Parallel** rule is satisfied. In this constrained logic, nothing whatever can be proved about a command which violates our constraint on par; for example, we cannot even prove

$$X = 1 \land Y = 1 \ \{\!\| X:=Y \text{ par } Y:=X \|\!\} \ X = 1 \land Y = 1 \ |_{\{X,Y\}}^{\emptyset}$$

even though it is an admissible sentence and intuitively correct, because no instance of the **Parallel** rule can be found which has this conclusion and which also satisfies the side-condition.

We do not intend to go deeply into Hoare logics, despite their great interest (not the least of which is that they allow modular program verification). What we wish to do, though, is to show how such a logic for our language $\mathcal{M}$ can be proved sound, in terms of our more primitive logic $\mathcal{PL}$. To do this, we must first *interpret* a Hoare sentence $P\{\!\| C \|\!\}Q \ |_{\tilde{Y}}^{\tilde{X}}$ in terms of $\mathcal{PL}$. More precisely, we interpret it as a sentence of the form $C \models F$, where $F \in \mathcal{PL}$ is built in a uniform way from P, Q, $\tilde{X}$ and $\tilde{Y}$. Then we are able to show that every inference rule of our logic is valid according to our interpretation; in fact we shall outline the proof of validity just for the **Parallel** rule.

In the course of this endeavour, we shall see that sentences like $C \models F$ can also express things which Hoare sentences cannot. (This is partly in favour of the latter; their very strength is that, by confining ourselves to what they *can* express, we gain structured reasoning.) We shall also become more confident that $\mathcal{PL}$ is, in some sense, powerful enough.

First note that a formula F of $\mathcal{PL}$, asserted about C, is concerned with *all* possible behaviour of C, including its behaviour in the presence of other agents which may, concurrently with C, interfere with the variables which C uses; this is in contrast to the Hoare-sentence, which only makes its assertion on the assumption of no interference. For example if C is a command of the form $X:=X+X$ then one derivation for C is $C \xrightarrow{s} \overset{\overline{\text{done}}}{\Longrightarrow} 0$, where $s = \text{get}_X(5)\,\text{get}_X(6)\,\overline{\text{put}_X}(11)$. This represents reading X twice in succession, first with the value 5 and then with the value 6, which is clearly not possible in the absence of interference.

So the formula F, such that $C \models F$ carries the same meaning as $P\{\!|C|\!\}^{\tilde{X}}_{\tilde{Y}}Q$, must make an assertion which explicitly confines itself to derivations which do not exhibit the effect of interference. To achieve this, it is convenient to introduce the auxiliary notion of a *memory map* – a function from some subset of the program variables to values. We shall let m, m' stand for memory maps, and write $Dom(m)$ for the set of variables upon which m is defined. Next we define a property of an action-sequence $s \in \mathcal{L}^*$ in relation to two memory maps m and m'. We shall write it as $m\{\!|s|\!\}m'$, which may be pronounced 'm into s gives m''; informally, it will mean that some command could, in the absence of external interference, execute the action-sequence s starting from a memory with values given by m and ending with a memory with values given by m'. We define the triples which are in this relationship by induction on the length of s:

(1) $m\{\!|\varepsilon|\!\}m'$ iff $m = m'$;
(2) $m\{\!|s\,\overline{\text{put}_X}(v)|\!\}m'$ iff $m\{\!|s|\!\}m''$ for some m'' such that $m'(X) = v$ and, for all variables Y other than X, $m'(Y) = m''(Y)$ (where if one is defined then so is the other);
(3) $m\{\!|s\,\text{get}_X(v)|\!\}m'$ iff $m\{\!|s|\!\}m'$ and $m'(X) = v$.

We are now ready to give F, uniformly in terms of P, Q, $\tilde{X}$ and $\tilde{Y}$. Informally, F must assert the following about a command C: if P holds of m, and C has a terminating action-sequence s such that $m\{\!|s|\!\}m'$, then Q holds of m'. It will restrict attention to memory maps such that $Dom(m) = Dom(m') = \tilde{X} \cup \tilde{Y}$. Letting $\tilde{Z} \overset{\text{def}}{=} \tilde{X} \cup \tilde{Y}$, we express '$P$ holds of m' by the substitution $P\{m(\tilde{Z})/\tilde{Z}\}$, replacing each program variable in P by the value associated with it in m. Finally therefore, we claim that $C \models F$ exactly expresses $P\{\!|C|\!\}Q \mid^{\tilde{X}}_{\tilde{Y}}$ when we take as F the $\mathcal{PL}$ formula

$$\forall m, m', s. \ (\ Dom(m) = Dom(m') = \tilde{Z} \wedge m\{\!|s|\!\}m' \wedge P\{m(\tilde{Z})/\tilde{Z}\}\ )$$
$$\supset \ [\![s\,\overline{\text{done}}]\!]\,Q\{m'(\tilde{Z})/\tilde{Z}\}$$

It is worth remarking that if $m\{\!|s|\!\}m'$ and s is a possible action-sequence for C then m and m' must agree on $\tilde{X}$, since these variables are not written by C.

We now claim the following:

Proposition 1   The **Parallel** inference rule is valid, under the given interpretation.

Proof (in outline)   Let F_1, F_2 and F be the formulae of $\mathcal{PL}$ corresponding to the two hypotheses and the conclusion of the **Parallel** rule. Then we wish to show that $C_1 \operatorname{par} C_2 \models F$ follows from $C_1 \models F_1$ and $C_2 \models F_2$. The first step is to notice that F_1 can be rewritten in terms of $\langle\!\langle \ \rangle\!\rangle$ rather than $[\![\ ]\!]$ as follows, setting $\tilde{Z}_1 = \tilde{X}_1 \cup \tilde{Y}_1$:

$$\forall m, m', s. \quad (\ Dom(m) = Dom(m') = \tilde{Z}_1 \wedge m \{\!|s|\!\} m'$$
$$\wedge P_1\{m(\tilde{Z}_1)/\tilde{Z}_1\} \wedge \langle\!\langle s\ \overline{done}\rangle\!\rangle \mathbf{true}\ )$$
$$\supset Q_1\{m'(\tilde{Z}_1)/\tilde{Z}_1\}$$

Similarly F_2 may be rewritten as follows, setting $\tilde{Z}_1 = \tilde{X}_1 \cup \tilde{Y}_1$:

$$\forall m, m', s. \quad (\ Dom(m) = Dom(m') = \tilde{Z}_2 \wedge m \{\!|s|\!\} m'$$
$$\wedge P_2\{m(\tilde{Z}_2)/\tilde{Z}_2\} \wedge \langle\!\langle s\ \overline{done}\rangle\!\rangle \mathbf{true}\ )$$
$$\supset Q_2\{m'(\tilde{Z}_2)/\tilde{Z}_2\}$$

and finally F as follows, setting $\tilde{Z} = \tilde{Z}_1 \cup \tilde{Z}_2$:

$$\forall m, m', s. \quad (\ Dom(m) = Dom(m') = \tilde{Z} \wedge m \{\!|s|\!\} m'$$
$$\wedge (P_1 \wedge P_2)\{m(\tilde{Z})/\tilde{Z}\} \wedge \langle\!\langle s\ \overline{done}\rangle\!\rangle \mathbf{true}\ )$$
$$\supset (Q_1 \wedge Q_2)\{m'(\tilde{Z})/\tilde{Z}\}$$

Now assume the hypotheses $C_1 \models F_1$ and $C_2 \models F_2$. To show $C_1 \operatorname{par} C_2 \models F$, we first assume that the antecedent formulae of F hold for some m, m' and s; in particular, that $C_1 \operatorname{par} C_2 \models \langle\!\langle s\ \overline{done}\rangle\!\rangle \mathbf{true}$. From this it follows that $C_1 \models \langle\!\langle s_1\ \overline{done}\rangle\!\rangle \mathbf{true}$ and $C_2 \models \langle\!\langle s_2\ \overline{done}\rangle\!\rangle \mathbf{true}$ for some s_1 and s_2 which may be interleaved to form the sequence s. Now let us define m_1, m_1' to be the restrictions of m, m' to the domain $\tilde{Z}_1$. The crucial part of the proof is that from the side-condition of the **Parallel** rule, which asserts the disjointness of certain sets and thereby ensures non-interference between s_1 and s_2, we can deduce $m_1 \{\!|s_1|\!\} m_1'$. We then find that the antecedent formulae of F_1 are satisfied for the values m_1, m_1' and s_1, and so deduce the conclusion of F_1 for these values since we are given that $C_1 \models F_1$.

By a similar argument, defining m_2, m_2' to be the restrictions of m, m' to the domain $\tilde{Z}_2$, we deduce that the conclusion of F_2 holds for the values m_2, m_2' and s_2. Finally, putting these two conclusions together yields the conclusion of F, and we have therefore shown $C_1 \operatorname{par} C_2 \models F$ as required.   ∎

So, in the limited case of non-interfering parallelism, we are able to explain the Hoare-style rules of inference, which are often called the *axiomatic semantics* of our programming language, in terms of the operational semantics of our calculus.

To relax the non-interference constraint, interesting logics have been proposed for this type of imperative language, by Cliff Jones and Colin Stirling among others. Are we entitled to expect that these could all be reduced to $\mathcal{PL}$? Unfortunately, no. The reason is that some such logics – even for the restricted language – are logics of so-called *total correctness*, rather than (as in our discussion so far) of *partial correctness*; they can assert not only that certain properties will hold *if* a program terminates, but also that the program *does indeed* terminate. $\mathcal{PL}$, however, is a logic which only expresses *safety* (= partial correctness) properties, not *liveness* (= total correctness) properties. On the other hand, it is hard to think of any reasonable safety property which $\mathcal{PL}$ fails to express.

10.4   Stratification of bisimilarity

Let us digress from logic for a while, and look at strong bisimulation in a new light. We shall here find it convenient to describe it slightly differently from its original Definition 4.1, namely in terms of the multiple transition relations $\xrightarrow{t}$ ($t \in Act^*$) in place of the single transition relations $\xrightarrow{\alpha}$. The following proposition tells us that this does not change the concept:

Proposition 2 $\mathcal{S}$ is a strong bisimulation iff, for all $(P,Q) \in \mathcal{S}$ and $t \in Act^*$:

(i) Whenever $P \xrightarrow{t} P'$ then, for some Q', $Q \xrightarrow{t} Q'$ and $(P',Q') \in \mathcal{S}$

(ii) Whenever $Q \xrightarrow{t} Q'$ then, for some P', $P \xrightarrow{t} P'$ and $(P',Q') \in \mathcal{S}$ ∎

Exercise 8   Prove this from Definition 4.1.
Hint: Look at Proposition 7.1, which similarly describes weak bisimulation in terms of the relations $\xRightarrow{s}$, $s \in \mathcal{L}^*$.   ∎

Now strong bisimilarity, $\sim$, is the *largest* strong bisimulation; to put it another way, we arrive at $\sim$ from below by taking the union of all strong bisimulations. As we have seen, there are some very small strong bisimulations. The empty relation is one, and a simple one containing only four pairs was given in Section 4.2; the identity relation $Id_{\mathcal{P}}$ is one, too.

There is another way of reaching $\sim$; not from *below*, as the limit of an increasing collection of smaller relations (the strong bisimulations), but instead from *above* as the limit of a decreasing sequence of relations (none of which is itself a strong bisimulation). In fact $\sim$ was originally defined in this way, beginning naturally from the largest relation of all, the universal relation $\mathcal{P} \times \mathcal{P}$. A sequence of relations $\sim_0, \sim_1, \ldots, \sim_\kappa, \ldots$ is defined, one for each ordinal number κ, and the relations decrease (as we shall see) as κ increases.

In what follows, we shall need to consider ordinal numbers beyond just the finite ones, the natural numbers. The first infinite ordinal is ω, and the sequence goes

$$0, \; 1, \; 2, \; \ldots, \; \omega, \; \omega+1, \; \omega+2, \; \ldots, \; \omega+\omega, \; \ldots$$

We shall only need to know the following elementary facts about $\mathcal{O}$, the class of all ordinals:

(1) Every ordinal κ has a *successor* $\kappa + 1$, whose *predecessor* is κ.

(2) Each ordinal is either a successor, or it is a *limit* ordinal which consists of the collection of all previous ordinals (and it has no unique predecessor). Here we regard 0 – which of course has no predecessor – as the limit ordinal $\emptyset$, because no ordinals precede it. The next limit ordinal is ω, and the next thereafter is $\omega + \omega$.

(3) If we wish to show that a certain property Φ_κ holds for every ordinal κ, then we may use the principle of *ordinal induction* which states that the following is sufficient:

> Show that, for each ordinal λ, Φ_λ follows from the assumption that Φ_κ holds for all $\kappa < \lambda$.

For 0, this amounts to proving Φ_0 outright (as in mathematical induction) since there is no κ for which $\kappa < 0$; for a successor ordinal $\lambda = \kappa + 1$ one often shows (as in mathematical induction) that $\Phi_{\kappa+1}$ follows from Φ_κ alone.

Some readers may feel uneasy about ordinals bigger than ω. Even so, they may still follow the main points below by thinking of κ and λ as standing for a natural number or ω, and thinking just of ω when a limit ordinal is mentioned.

We are now able to define the equivalence relations which, we claim, approximate $\sim$ from above:

Definition 3

- $P \sim_0 Q$ holds for all P and Q; that is, $\sim_0 = \mathcal{P} \times \mathcal{P}$;
- $P \sim_{\kappa+1} Q$ holds iff, for all $t \in Act^*$,

  (i) Whenever $P \xrightarrow{t} P'$ then, for some Q', $Q \xrightarrow{t} Q'$ and $P' \sim_\kappa Q'$;

  (ii) Whenever $Q \xrightarrow{t} Q'$ then, for some P', $P \xrightarrow{t} P'$ and $P' \sim_\kappa Q'$;

- For each limit ordinal λ, $P \sim_\lambda Q$ iff, for all $\kappa < \lambda$, $P \sim_\kappa Q$; that is, $\sim_\lambda = \bigcap_{\kappa < \lambda} \sim_\kappa$. ∎

Notice what $P \sim_1 Q$ means. Put $\kappa = 0$ in the second clause, and observe that $P' \sim_0 Q'$ holds vacuously; so $P \sim_1 Q$ means simply

For all $t \in Act^*$, $P \xrightarrow{t}$ iff $Q \xrightarrow{t}$

In other words, P and Q have exactly the same action-sequences. We call this *strong trace equivalence*; the corresponding notion for weak bisimilarity is called (*weak*) *trace equivalence*, which we studied in Section 9.4.

We may now justify our use of the multiple action relations $\xrightarrow{t}$ in Definition 3, rather than just the single action relations $\xrightarrow{\alpha}$, $\alpha \in Act$. If we had used the latter, then $P \sim_1 Q$ would hold whenever P and Q have the same initial actions, and this is not a very interesting equivalence relation. With our present definition, by contrast, we see that relations $\sim_i$ distinguish finer aspects of the *branching* in derivation trees as i increases.

Now the following is not hard to show, though we omit the proof:

Proposition 3   If $\lambda > \kappa$ then $\sim_\lambda \subseteq \sim_\kappa$. ∎

In other words, the relations $\sim_\kappa$ decrease non-strictly as κ increases. Moreover, by standard mathematical arguments – concerning fixed-point theory, which we touched upon briefly in Section 4.6 – it can be shown that the limit of this decreasing chain is indeed the largest strong bisimulation:

Proposition 4 $\sim \; = \; \bigcap_{\kappa \in \mathcal{O}} \sim_\kappa$. ∎

Our remaining concern in this chapter is first to get a feeling for what these decreasing relations are, and then to demonstrate how their decreasing size – or increasing strength – is beautifully captured by $\mathcal{PL}$.

Proposition 5 The relations $\sim_0, \sim_1, \ldots, \sim_\omega$ form a strictly decreasing sequence.

Proof We exhibit a sequence of pairs (P_i, Q_i), for $i < \omega$, with the property that $P_i \sim_i Q_i$ but $P_i \not\sim_{i+1} Q_i$. The definitions are

$$P_0 \stackrel{\text{def}}{=} b.0 \qquad\qquad Q_0 \stackrel{\text{def}}{=} c.0$$
$$P_{i+1} \stackrel{\text{def}}{=} a.(P_i + Q_i) \quad Q_{i+1} \stackrel{\text{def}}{=} a.P_i + a.Q_i$$

where we assume a, b, c to be distinct. The transition graphs are as follows:

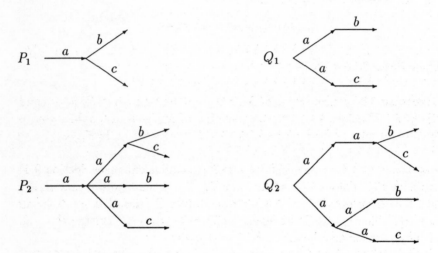

In fact, one has to prove the following, each by induction on i:

(1) $P_i \sim_i Q_i \sim_i P_i + Q_i$, but
(2) $P_i \not\sim_{i+1} Q_i \not\sim_{i+1} P_i + Q_i \not\sim P_i$.

We shall omit most of the details, but let us look at the part of the induction step which proves $P_i \not\sim_{i+1} Q_i$ for $i > 0$. We have on the one hand

$$P_i \stackrel{a}{\rightarrow} P_{i-1} + Q_{i-1}$$

while on the other hand the only a-derivatives of Q_i are P_{i-1} and Q_{i-1}, and we know by induction that $P_{i-1} \not\sim_i P_{i-1} + Q_{i-1}$ and $Q_{i-1} \not\sim_i P_{i-1} + Q_{i-1}$. ∎

Exercise 9 Complete the details of this proof. In (1) take care to consider action-sequences t of any length. ∎

You may be pardoned for thinking that our chain of relations ought at least to settle down at ω – i.e. you may expect that $\sim_\omega = \sim_{\omega+1} = \sim_{\omega+2} = \cdots$. In fact this is true if we only consider finitely branching agents, but not in general. But we shall not concern ourselves with the details.

More importantly, our construction in Proposition 4 gives us a hint that whenever two agents P and Q are not strongly bisimilar – that is, $P \not\sim_i Q$ for some i – then there is some formula of $\mathcal{PL}$ satisfied by P but not by Q (or vice versa, which amounts to the same because of negation); moreover, the smaller i the simpler the formula. We have already seen in Section 10.2 that if F_1 is

$$\langle a \rangle (\langle b \rangle \mathbf{true} \wedge \langle c \rangle \mathbf{true})$$

then $P_1 \models F_1$ and $Q_1 \not\models F_1$; you can now easily see that if F_2 is $[a]F_1$ then $P_2 \models F_2$ and $Q_2 \not\models F_2$.

Exercise 10   Draw P_3 and Q_3, and find F_3 such that $P_3 \models F_3$ and $Q_3 \not\models F_3$. Can you see a general pattern emerging which enables you to define, for all i, a formula F_i such that $P_i \models F_i$ and $Q_i \not\models F_i$?   ■

Exercise 11   The strong form of failures equivalence (see Section 9.4) is defined as follows. If $t \in Act^*$ and $M \subseteq Act$ then we say that (t, M) is a *strong failure* of P if P has a t-derivative P' such that $P' \not\xrightarrow{\alpha}$ for all $\alpha \in M$. Then P and Q are *strongly failures-equivalent*, written $P \sim_f Q$, if they possess exactly the same strong failures.

Use the two agents A and B of Section 9.4 to show that $P \sim_f Q$ does not imply $P \sim_2 Q$; also find the simplest formula F which distinguishes between A and B.

Prove that $P \sim_2 Q$ implies $P \sim_f Q$. The conclusion is that $\sim_f$ lies strictly between $\sim_1$ and $\sim_2$.   ■

You may now begin to expect that the formulae of $\mathcal{PL}$ have an intimate structural link with the degree of non-bisimilarity between two agents; this is precisely what we set out to show in the next section.

10.5   Stratification of process logic

In this section we establish the single important result that the degree of dissimilarity between P and Q, i.e. the least κ such that $P \not\sim_\kappa Q$, is exactly the depth of nesting of modal operators needed in a $\mathcal{PL}$ formula which distinguishes P from Q. As a consequence, we learn that P and Q are bisimilar if and only if *no* $\mathcal{PL}$ formula distinguishes between them. Thus in $\mathcal{PL}$ we have found an alternative way of characterising the concept of bisimilarity.

In keeping with our use of multiple transitions $\xrightarrow{t}$ in the previous section, to define the sequence of relations $\sim_i$, we shall here assume that the derived modal operators $\langle t \rangle$ are primitive in $\mathcal{PL}$. This is because we are interested in distinguishing the depth of nesting of modal operators in a formula like $\langle a \rangle [b] \langle c \rangle \mathbf{true}$, which cannot be reduced using the derived operators, from that in a formula like $\langle abc \rangle \mathbf{true}$. We shall henceforth write $\mathcal{PL}^{\sim}$ for the logic in which the operators $\langle t \rangle$ are taken as primitive.

Definition 4 The *depth*, $depth(F)$, of a formula $F \in \mathcal{PL}^{\sim}$ is an ordinal number defined inductively as follows:

   (i) $depth(\langle t \rangle F) = depth(F) + 1$
   (ii) $depth(\neg F) = depth(F)$
   (iii) $depth(\bigwedge_{i \in I} F_i) = sup_{i \in I}(depth(F_i))$

where 'sup' stands for the least upper bound of a set of ordinals.   ■

We now use depth to stratify $\mathcal{PL}^{\sim}$, regarding it as the union of a collection of languages $\mathcal{PL}^{\sim}_{\kappa}$, each containing only those formulae of depth no greater than κ:

Definition 5   For each ordinal κ, $\mathcal{PL}^{\sim}_{\kappa} \overset{\mathrm{def}}{=} \{F \ : \ depth(F) \leq \kappa\}$.   ■

The main result of this section now follows. We show that two agents are strongly congruent if and only if there is no formula of $\mathcal{PL}^{\sim}$ which distinguishes between them. In order to prove this we need to use ordinal induction to prove a finer result about our stratified language, which is also important in its own right: that two agents are in the relation $\sim_{\kappa}$ if and only if there is no formula of $\mathcal{PL}^{\sim}_{\kappa}$ which distinguishes between them.

Proposition 6

   (1) For each $\kappa \in \mathcal{O}$, $P \sim_{\kappa} Q$ iff for every $F \in \mathcal{PL}^{\sim}_{\kappa}$

$$P \models F \Longleftrightarrow Q \models F$$

   (2) $P \sim Q$ iff for every $F \in \mathcal{PL}^{\sim}$

$$P \models F \Longleftrightarrow Q \models F$$

Proof   First, (2) may be deduced easily from (1) since $\sim = \bigcap_{\kappa \in \mathcal{O}} \sim_\kappa$ and $\mathcal{PL}^\sim = \bigcup_{\kappa \in \mathcal{O}} \mathcal{PL}_\kappa^\sim$. We prove (1) by induction on κ. So assume that (1) holds for all $\lambda < \kappa$.

In one direction, assume that $P \sim_\kappa Q$, and that $P \models F$ where $depth(F) \leq \kappa$. We wish to show that $Q \models F$. It is rather easy to see that the critical case is when F takes the form $\langle t \rangle F'$, where $depth(F') = \lambda < \kappa$, and we shall treat only this case. Then $P \xrightarrow{t} P'$, for some P' such that $P' \models F'$. Also, since $P \sim_\kappa Q$ by assumption, and $\lambda + 1 \leq \kappa$, we have $P \sim_{\lambda+1} Q$ from Proposition 3. So $Q \xrightarrow{t} Q'$, for some Q' such that $P' \sim_\lambda Q'$. Hence from the induction hypothesis at λ we have $Q' \models F'$; from this it directly follows that $Q \models \langle t \rangle F'$, i.e. $Q \models F$ as required.

In the other direction, assume that $P \not\sim_\kappa Q$. We look for a formula $F \in \mathcal{PL}_\kappa^\sim$ such that $P \models F$ and $Q \not\models F$.

Consider first the case that $\kappa = \lambda + 1$. Then without loss of generality we can assume that for some t and P' we have $P \xrightarrow{t} P'$ and, for every Q', if $Q \xrightarrow{t} Q'$ then $P' \not\sim_\lambda Q'$. Now let $\{Q_i \; : \; i \in I\}$ be the set of all t-derivatives of Q. Then for each $i \in I$, since $P' \not\sim_\lambda Q_i$, there is by induction a formula $F_i \in \mathcal{PL}_\lambda^\sim$ for which $P' \models F_i$ and $Q \not\models F_i$. Now define F to be the formula $\langle t \rangle \bigwedge_{i \in I} F_i$. Since $P \xrightarrow{t} P'$ we have $P \models F$. On the other hand no t-derivative of Q satisfies $\bigwedge_{i \in I} F_i$, so $Q \not\models F$. But by construction $depth(F) \leq \kappa$, so we are done.

Now consider the case that κ is a limit ordinal. Then, by Definition 3, $P \not\sim_\lambda Q$ for some $\lambda < \kappa$. Hence by induction there is a formula $F \in \mathcal{PL}_\lambda^\sim$ such that $P \models F$ and $Q \not\models F$, and we are done since $F \in \mathcal{PL}_\kappa^\sim$ also.   ∎

Now the satisfaction relation $\models$ for $\mathcal{PL}^\sim$ depends only upon the transition relations $\xrightarrow{t}$; more precisely, it depends only upon the fact that

For all $t \in Act^*$, $P \models \langle t \rangle F$ iff $P \xrightarrow{t} P' \models F$ for some P'.

It is therefore clear that Proposition 6, although stated for this particular transition system, can be regarded as a general result relating the bisimulation equivalence relation over any transition system and the logic interpreted over that system. In particular, we may introduce approximants $\approx_\kappa$ to weak bisimilarity, in the same way as we introduced approximants $\sim_\kappa$ to strong bisimilarity in Definition 3. We may also define $\mathcal{PL}^\approx$ to be the logic $\mathcal{PL}$ but with the derived operators $\langle\!\langle s \rangle\!\rangle$ $(s \in \mathcal{L}^*)$ taken as primitive and the operators $\langle t \rangle$ removed. This removal weakens the logic in just one sense: the operator $\langle \tau \rangle$ is no longer expressible, so silent actions cannot be specified in a formula. Again we have

For all $s \in \mathcal{L}^*$, $P \models \langle\!\langle s \rangle\!\rangle F$ iff $P \overset{s}{\Rightarrow} P' \models F$ for some P'.

Then, with notion of depth adjusted in the obvious way (replacing $\langle t \rangle$ by $\langle\!\langle s \rangle\!\rangle$) we obtain the version of Proposition 6 appropriate for weak bisimilarity, or observation equivalence, as follows:

Proposition 7

(1) For each $\kappa \in \mathcal{O}$, $P \approx_\kappa Q$ iff for every $F \in \mathcal{PL}^{\approx}_\kappa$

$$P \models F \Longleftrightarrow Q \models F$$

(2) $P \approx Q$ iff for every $F \in \mathcal{PL}^{\approx}$

$$P \models F \Longleftrightarrow Q \models F \qquad \blacksquare$$

In conclusion therefore, we can claim to have found a logic of just the right power, if what we wish to do is to specify agents up to weak bisimilarity. We also saw in the earlier sections of this chapter that it is possible to dress up the logical operators in clothes which make them practically useful in specification.

11

Determinacy and Confluence

Determinacy has been mentioned earlier in this book, for example in Chapter 10 when we considered syntactic restrictions on a concurrent programming language to ensure non-interference between concurrent parts of a program. But it has not been defined precisely, and indeed it can be defined in a variety of ways. This chapter begins by settling upon a precise notion of determinacy, and then looks in some depth at the problem of ensuring that the compound agents which we construct are determinate.

In Section 1 we look first at two notions of determinacy, and settle upon the one which respects observation equivalence. Our choice is guided by the wish that a property of an agent should, where possible, be a property of its *meaning*, i.e. of the bisimilarity class or congruence class to which it belongs. In Section 2 we tackle the question of which combinators preserve determinacy, because system-designers would often prefer to confine themselves to combinators which are guaranteed to produce determinate systems, provided that the elementary components are determinate. We find, however, that the combination of Composition and Restriction, or equally Hoare's Conjunction and Hiding, cannot be relied upon to preserve determinacy.

In Section 3 we introduce a special kind of determinacy, called *confluence*, and we develop some of its properties. Section 4 demonstrates the point of this new notion; the point is that it is preserved by a reasonably broad class of Restricted Compositions. It is shown also that our scheduler system, first studied in Chapter 5, is built using only such confluence-preserving combinators, so there is hope that a reasonable class of useful systems will be constructable in this way. A key result of the chapter is Proposition 5 in Section 1, which states that trace equivalence coincides with observation equivalence for determinate systems; this considerably eases the task of verifying confluent systems.

11.1   Determinacy

First let us see why determinacy is important. Whatever its precise definition, it certainly must have a lot to do with predictability; if we perform the same experiment twice on a determinate system – starting each time in its initial state – then we expect to get the same result, or behaviour, each time. Furthermore, predictability is something we often demand from engineered systems. Thus, if we choose to specify such a system S by giving an abstract agent *Spec* to which S should be equivalent (in one of our senses of equivalence), then *Spec* will often be determinate. Indeed this is the case in most, if not all, of the systems analysed in earlier chapters; examples are the specification *Schedspec* for the scheduler system in Chapter 5, and the specification *Buff* for the communications protocol in Chapter 6.

It is instructive to look more closely at these two examples, because there is an important difference between them which provides a good cue for the work of the present chapter. In the first case, our scheduler *Sched* was constructed from several copies of a simple agent A, which will turn out to be determinate according to our definition below. By contrast, in the second case the protocol system AB was constructed from components some of which are obviously *not* determinate; indeed, it is hardly an exaggeration to say that the main challenge in designing such a system is to attain determinacy in the presence of components – in this case the communication lines – which may fail unpredictably.

Now it is unlikely that we could find general design rules which would ensure that from indeterminate components we must arrive at a determinate system. But it is more reasonable to hope that there *are* design rules, not too restrictive, which ensure that from *determinate* components we must arrive at a determinate system. This is what we demonstrate below. It is important to realise that by no means every system built from determinate components is determinate, and we shall soon see examples; so some design rules are necessary. When we have defined a set of rules, we shall also see that our construction of the scheduler *Sched* does indeed obey them; this shows that the rules do admit the construction of non-trivial systems.

We shall be concerned in this chapter with various subclasses of the class $\mathcal{P}$ of agents, and we shall find the following definition helpful:

Definition 1   A subclass $\mathcal{Q}$ of $\mathcal{P}$ is *derivation-closed* or *closed under derivation* if, whenever $P \in \mathcal{Q}$ and $P \xrightarrow{\alpha} P'$, then $P' \in \mathcal{Q}$.   ∎

Now let us define a form of determinacy which combines well with strong bisimilarity:

Definition 2 P is *strongly determinate* if, for every derivative Q of P and for all $\alpha \in Act$, whenever $Q \xrightarrow{\alpha} Q'$ and $Q \xrightarrow{\alpha} Q''$ then $Q' \sim Q''$. ∎

For example, $a.(b.0 + c.0)$ is strongly determinate, but $a.b.0 + a.c.0$ is not because it has two different a-derivatives. This definition is one obvious way of making precise the informal requirement that the same experiment should always yield the same result. Also, this notion of determinacy is quite well-behaved, as the following two easy propositions show.

Proposition 1   Strong determinacy is closed under derivation; that is to say, if P is strongly determinate and $P \xrightarrow{t} P'$ then P' is strongly determinate.   ∎

Proposition 2   Strong determinacy is preserved by strong bisimilarity; that is, if P is strongly determinate and $P \sim Q$ then Q is strongly determinate.   ∎

When we look more closely, however, we find that strong determinacy is not a very satisfactory notion. In fact, it seems not strong enough. (We have called it *strong* determinacy only because it is the natural companion to strong bisimilarity.) Consider for example $A \overset{\mathrm{def}}{=} a.0 + \tau.0$; A is strongly determinate (because in Definition 2 τ is treated like any other action), but one would hardly call it predictable because it can preclude its a action by doing a τ. In fact the notion of *experiment* seems to be better represented by the transition relations $\xrightarrow{s}$ ($s \in \mathcal{L}^*$) than by $\xrightarrow{\alpha}$ ($\alpha \in Act$), because an experimenter cannot inhibit τ actions. We also prefer $\xrightarrow{s}$ to $\xrightarrow{\ell}$ ($\ell \in \mathcal{L}$) because the former admits the case $s = \varepsilon$, which represents an experiment with no visible content.

    We therefore introduce the following as a natural companion to *weak* bisimilarity:

Definition 3 P is *(weakly) determinate* if, for every derivative Q of P and for all $s \in \mathcal{L}^*$, whenever $Q \xRightarrow{s} Q'$ and $Q \xRightarrow{s} Q''$ then $Q' \approx Q''$. ∎

Thus A as defined above, though strongly determinate, is not weakly determinate since $A \Rightarrow A$ and $A \Rightarrow 0$. By contrast, $B \overset{\mathrm{def}}{=} a.0 + a.\tau.0$

is weakly determinate but not strongly determinate, since $B \xrightarrow{a} \mathbf{0}$ and $B \xrightarrow{a} \tau.\mathbf{0}$, and $\mathbf{0} \approx \tau.\mathbf{0}$ but $\mathbf{0} \not\sim \tau.\mathbf{0}$. So weak and strong determinacy are incomparable – neither implies the other. However, the weak version is what mainly interests us, so the term 'determinacy' will henceforth refer to weak determinacy.

Exercise 1   There is an asymmetry between our two definitions; in Definition 2 we used a single action α, while in Definition 3 we used a sequence s of observable actions. Show that, because of this, the following simpler definition is equivalent to Definition 3:

- P is (*weakly*) *determinate* if, for all $s \in \mathcal{L}^*$, whenever $P \xRightarrow{s} P'$ and $P \xRightarrow{s} P''$ then $P' \approx P''$.

All that you need to do, clearly, is to show that with this simpler definition determinacy is derivation-closed.   ∎

We now record the fact that weak determinacy also behaves well:

Proposition 3   Determinacy is closed under derivation.   ∎

Proposition 4   Determinacy is preserved by weak bisimilarity; that is, if P is determinate and $P \approx Q$ then Q is determinate.   ∎

Exercise 2   Show that strong determinacy is not preserved by weak bisimilarity.   ∎

Let us now recall our discussion of trace equivalence, in Section 9.4. We saw there that trace equivalence is too weak a relation in general, since it does not respect deadlock. But if we know by some means or other that both P and Q are determinate, perhaps because we have built them from determinate components using certain design rules, then the following proposition shows that to establish $P \approx Q$ it is enough to establish $P \approx_1 Q$; thus knowledge of determinacy can free us to use a wider repertoire of equational laws. (Recall also that $P \approx Q$ further implies $P = Q$ when both are stable.)

Proposition 5   If P and Q are determinate, then $P \approx Q$ iff $P \approx_1 Q$.

Proof   The implication from left to right is Proposition 9.1. In the other direction, it is enough to show that

$$\mathcal{S} \stackrel{\text{def}}{=} \{(P, Q) \ : \ P \approx_1 Q \text{ and } P, Q \text{ determinate}\}$$

is a bisimulation up to $\approx$. The details are not hard.   ∎

11.2   Preserving determinacy

We must now tackle the question: which of our combinators preserve determinacy? It turns out that every basic combinator preserves it, under some constraint.

Proposition 6   If P and P_i are determinate, then so also are the following:

(1) $\mathbf{0}$, $\alpha.P$ and $P\backslash L$ always.
(2) $\sum_i \ell_i.P_i$, provided that the ℓ_i are all distinct.
(3) $P_1|P_2$, provided that $\mathcal{L}(P_1) \cap \mathcal{L}(P_2) = \emptyset$ and $\overline{\mathcal{L}(P_1)} \cap \mathcal{L}(P_2) = \emptyset$.
(4) $P[f]$, provided that $f \upharpoonright \mathcal{L}(P)$ is one-to-one.

Proof   Routine.   ∎

Let us see why, in (3), we have to impose such a strong side-condition. First, we can see that P_1 and P_2 must have disjoint sorts – i.e. $\mathcal{L}(P_1) \cap \mathcal{L}(P_2) = \emptyset$ – by considering $P_1 \equiv a.b.\mathbf{0}$ and $P_2 \equiv a.\mathbf{0}$; for in this case we have two inequivalent a-derivatives

$$P_1|P_2 \xrightarrow{a} b.\mathbf{0} \mid a.\mathbf{0} \qquad\qquad P_1|P_2 \xrightarrow{a} a.b.\mathbf{0} \mid \mathbf{0}$$

But unfortunately disjointness of sorts is still not enough. We can introduce indeterminacy via communication between P_1 and P_2; for example, if $P_1 \equiv a.\mathbf{0}$ and $P_2 \equiv \overline{a}.\mathbf{0}$ then we have two distinct ε-descendants:

$$P_1|P_2 \Rightarrow a.\mathbf{0} \mid \overline{a}.\mathbf{0} \qquad\qquad P_1|P_2 \Rightarrow \mathbf{0}|\mathbf{0}$$

The side-condition rules out this possibility, but at the price of forbidding all communication. We shall later see how to pay a smaller price.

It is instructive to see in more detail why indeterminacy has arisen here. If we look at the flow graph of $P_1|P_2$

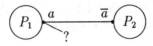

then we can see that we have allowed the possibility that a third agent – not yet part of the system – may compete with P_2 for communication with P_1, via the label a. (The same applies with P_1 and P_2 exchanged, of course.) Having seen this, we may therefore expect that determinacy will be preserved if we always accompany a Composition by a Restriction of those labels which may be a vehicle for communication; that is, we may expect that if P_1 and P_2 are determinate then so is $(P_1|P_2)\backslash L$ provided that

$$\mathcal{L}(P_1) \cap \overline{\mathcal{L}(P_2)} \subseteq L \cup \overline{L}$$

Indeed, we can see that the flow graph of a system built only with such restricted Compositions will never have two arcs sharing a port, and we may think that this removes all forms of competition which can lead to indeterminacy.

But unfortunately there is another form of competition. Consider $P_1 \equiv a.0 + b.0$, $P_2 \equiv \overline{a}.0$. Both are determinate, and yet the restricted Composition $(P_1|P_2)\backslash a$ is strongly congruent to $\tau.0 + b.0$, which is indeterminate since it may unpredictably preclude the b action.

The competition here is for access to P_1 through two *different* ports. In the presence of this kind of competition, then, it seems that there could be no constrained form of Composition which both preserves determinacy and is useful (i.e. allows some communication). However, we shall find that there is a more refined form of determinacy, which we shall call *confluence*, which is indeed preserved by the above type of restricted Composition.

Let us finish this section by looking at how Hoare's alternative combinators, Conjunction and Hiding, behave with respect to determinacy (see Section 9.2 for their definitions). For Conjunction there is little difficulty:

Proposition 7 If P and Q are determinate then so is the Conjunction $P_K \|_L Q$, provided that $P : K$ and $Q : L$.   ∎

Intuitively, the reason for this is simple. If an action of P or Q belongs to $K \cap L$ then it *must* be a synchronization, and otherwise it *must* occur unsynchronized; there is no ambiguity. Moreover, no τ actions are manufactured by the Conjunction combinator, as they are by Composition.

In fact the difficulty now arises with the Hiding combinator $/L$; it is easy to see that Hiding does *not* preserve determinacy by considering $(a.0 + b.0)/a \sim \tau.0 + b.0$. Apparently, whichever way we choose (i.e. either by Composition or by Hiding) to convert observable actions into τ actions, we run the risk of losing determinacy.

However, we can already see that confluence, which we have yet to define, *will* be preserved by Hiding; for this is a special case of our promise that a certain kind of restricted Composition will preserve confluence. For example,

$$P/a \stackrel{\text{def}}{=} (P \mid Ever(a))\backslash a$$

and *Ever(a)* (see Section 5.5) will itself be confluent.

Now that we have some motivation to improve upon determinacy, we shall proceed to study confluence.

Exercise 3   Show that Proposition 7 is false in general, without the condition that $P : K$ and $Q : L$.   ∎

11.3   Confluence

The notion of confluence arises in different forms and with different motivations in various parts of computation theory. In our case, the motivation is to strengthen determinacy in such a way that it will be preserved by restricted Composition. So let us look again at our example $P_1 \equiv a.0 + b.0$ and $P_2 \equiv \overline{a}.0$, where we found that $(P_1|P_2)\backslash a$ – strongly congruent to $\tau.0 + b.0$ – is not determinate. We said that this was due to competition for access to P_1 through different ports. But more precisely, it arises because the winning action, say a, precludes the other action b from occurring. The situation is quite different if, instead, $P_1 \equiv a.b.0 + b.a.0$; for in this case the winning action merely delays rather than precludes the other. In fact we find that

$$(P_1|P_2)\backslash a \sim \tau.b.0 + b.\tau.0 = \tau.b.0$$

which is perfectly determinate.

This is the essence of confluence; of any two possible actions, the occurrence of one will never preclude the other. For a precise definition, let us first suppose that we do not wish to give the τ action any special status. In that case, we would be content with the following definition:

Definition 4 P is *strongly confluent* if it is strongly determinate, and also for every derivative Q of P, whenever $Q \stackrel{\alpha}{\to} Q_1$ and $Q \stackrel{\beta}{\to} Q_2$ with $\alpha \neq \beta$, then agents Q'_1 and Q'_2 can be found to complete the following diagram:

$$
\begin{array}{ccc}
Q & \stackrel{\alpha}{\longrightarrow} & Q_1 \\
{\scriptstyle \beta}\downarrow & & \downarrow{\scriptstyle \beta} \\
Q_2 & \stackrel{\alpha}{\longrightarrow} Q'_2 \sim & Q'_1
\end{array}
$$

∎

Note that strong confluence is derivation-closed, since we demand a property not only of P but of all its derivatives. Note also that we do not require Q_2' to be identical with Q_1', but only strongly bisimilar; this is to ensure that strong bisimilarity preserves strong confluence. Let us record these facts:

Proposition 8 Strong confluence is derivation-closed, and is preserved by strong bisimilarity.

Proof We discussed the first part briefly above; let us look at the second part. It clearly reduces to showing that if $Q \sim R$, and if the diagram in Definition 4 can be closed for Q, then a similar diagram can also be closed for R. This can be done by routine use of the definition of strong bisimilarity. ∎

We shall often avoid mentioning Q_1' and Q_2' in diagrams like that in Definition 4, representing them perhaps by a dot; thus we shall simply say that P is strongly confluent if for every derivative Q of P the diagram

$$
\begin{array}{ccc}
Q & \xrightarrow{\alpha} & Q_1 \\
{\scriptstyle\beta}\downarrow & & \downarrow{\scriptstyle\beta} \\
Q_2 & \xrightarrow{\alpha}\sim & \cdot
\end{array}
$$

can be completed when $\alpha \neq \beta$, by which we imply that this must hold for every Q_1 and Q_2 such that the upper and left derivations exist.

It may help the reader to see an example. The following is the transition graph of a strongly confluent agent:

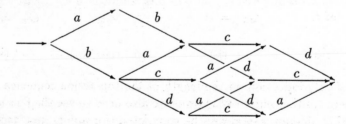

In fact this agent can be expressed as $a.0 \mid b.(c.0|d.0)$. We shall later see that the absence of Summation, and use of Composition with only a constrained form of communication (none at all in this case), ensures confluence.

We shall not dwell on strong confluence, because we wish to take account of τ actions. These require careful handling, just as they did in the definition of (weak) bisimulation. Let us recall that we had two characterisations of bisimulation; one (Definition 5.5) used a single derivation $\xrightarrow{\alpha}$, and the other (Proposition 7.1) used a compound derivation $\xRightarrow{s}$ where $s \in \mathcal{L}^*$. We shall also have two characterisations of confluence. The first shows how a single (possibly silent) action α commutes with other actions:

Definition 5 P is (*weakly*) *confluent* if for every derivative Q of P the following diagrams can be completed:

$$
\begin{array}{ccc}
Q & \xrightarrow{\tau} & Q_1 \\
\Downarrow & & \Downarrow \\
Q_2 & \Rightarrow \approx & \cdot
\end{array}
\qquad
\begin{array}{ccc}
Q & \xrightarrow{\tau} & Q_1 \\
\ell \Downarrow & & \Downarrow \ell \\
Q_2 & \Rightarrow \approx & \cdot
\end{array}
\qquad
\begin{array}{ccc}
Q & \xrightarrow{\ell_1} & Q_1 \\
\ell_2 \Downarrow & & \Downarrow \ell_2 \\
Q_2 & \xRightarrow{\ell_1} \approx & \cdot
\end{array}
\qquad
\begin{array}{ccc}
Q & \xrightarrow{\ell} & Q_1 \\
\ell \Downarrow & & \Downarrow \\
Q_2 & \Rightarrow \approx & \cdot
\end{array}
$$

$$
\text{(i)} \qquad\qquad \text{(ii)} \qquad\qquad \text{(iii) } (\ell_1 \neq \ell_2) \qquad\qquad \text{(iv)}
$$
∎

There are several points to note here. First, the top line of each diagram is a single action; this formulation is convenient for the purpose of the proof that certain combinators preserve confluence. But it is easy to derive the more general property which is symmetric in the two derivations leading to Q_1 and Q_2 respectively:

Proposition 9 P is confluent if and only if, for every derivative Q of P, the following diagrams can be completed:

$$
\begin{array}{ccc}
Q & \Longrightarrow & Q_1 \\
\Downarrow & & \Downarrow \\
Q_2 & \Rightarrow \approx & \cdot
\end{array}
\qquad
\begin{array}{ccc}
Q & \Longrightarrow & Q_1 \\
\ell \Downarrow & & \Downarrow \ell \\
Q_2 & \Rightarrow \approx & \cdot
\end{array}
\qquad
\begin{array}{ccc}
Q & \xRightarrow{\ell_1} & Q_1 \\
\ell_2 \Downarrow & & \Downarrow \ell_2 \\
Q_2 & \xRightarrow{\ell_1} \approx & \cdot
\end{array}
\qquad
\begin{array}{ccc}
Q & \xRightarrow{\ell} & Q_1 \\
\ell \Downarrow & & \Downarrow \\
Q_2 & \Rightarrow \approx & \cdot
\end{array}
$$

$$
\text{(i)} \qquad\qquad \text{(ii)} \qquad\qquad \text{(iii) } (\ell_1 \neq \ell_2) \qquad\qquad \text{(iv)}
$$

Proof   By induction on the length of the top action sequence in each diagram. In the course of the proof we also need to use the fact that the following diagram can always be completed (for *any* Q, not necessarily confluent):

$$
\begin{array}{ccc}
Q & \approx & Q_1 \\
s \Downarrow & & \Downarrow s \\
Q_2 & \approx & \cdot
\end{array}
$$

This holds, of course, for any bisimulation in place of $\approx$, and is a restatement of Proposition 7.1.
∎

Second, the definition does imply determinacy, but only indirectly. The fourth diagram would represent determinacy if we could show that it must be the case that $Q_1 \approx Q_2$ in this diagram, and indeed this will follow shortly.

Third, it is clear that the third and fourth diagrams of Proposition 9 can be stuck together to yield composite diagrams, yielding a pair of action sequences which may have some actions in common. For example, we can deduce that if P is confluent then the following diagram can be completed:

$$
\begin{array}{ccc}
P & \overset{aba}{\Longrightarrow} & P_1 \\
{\scriptstyle ca}\big\Downarrow & & \big\Downarrow {\scriptstyle c} \\
P_2 & \overset{ba}{\Longrightarrow} \approx & \cdot
\end{array}
$$

This asserts that each one of the action sequences aba and ca can be extended by a further sequence, containing the extra actions present in the other one, to reach a common state (up to $\approx$).

To obtain the general form of this assertion let us first define, for two sequences $r, s \in \mathcal{L}^*$, the *excess* of r over s, which we shall write r/s. Intuitively, we obtain r/s by working through r from left to right deleting any label which occurs in s, but taking account of the multiplicity of occurrence. For the sequences in the diagram, for example, we have $aba/ca = ba$, and $ca/aba = c$. More precisely:

Definition 6   The *excess of r over s*, written r/s, is defined recursively upon r as follows:

$$
\varepsilon/s \overset{\text{def}}{=} \varepsilon
$$

$$
(\ell r)/s \overset{\text{def}}{=}
\begin{cases}
\ell\,(r/s) & \text{if } \ell \notin s \\
r/(s/\ell) & \text{if } \ell \in s
\end{cases}
\qquad\blacksquare
$$

This binary operation on sequences has several nice properties; at present we shall just record a few which we shall need for the proof of Proposition 11 below. If the reader is ready to accept that this proposition does give an alternative characterisation of confluence, then he can ignore the lemma and read on after Proposition 11.

Lemma 10   For all $r, s, t \in \mathcal{L}^*$

(1) $rs/rt = s/t$

(2) $r/st = (r/s)/t$

(3) $rs/t = (r/t)(s/(t/r))$

Proof By induction on r in each case.   ■

Now we can establish our alternative characterisation of confluence, which is very succinct:

Proposition 11 P is confluent iff, for all $r, s \in \mathcal{L}^*$, the following diagram can be completed:

$$
\begin{array}{ccc}
P & \stackrel{r}{\Longrightarrow} & P_1 \\
s\Downarrow & & \Downarrow s/r \\
P_2 & \stackrel{r/s}{\Longrightarrow} \approx & \cdot
\end{array}
$$

Proof   Let us say that P has property (∗) if the above diagram can be completed for all P_1, P_2 and for all $r, s \in \mathcal{L}^*$.

Assume that P has property (∗). First we show that every derivative Q of P also has property (∗). Let $P \stackrel{t}{\Rightarrow} Q$, $t \in \mathcal{L}^*$, and let

$$
\begin{array}{ccc}
Q & \stackrel{r}{\Longrightarrow} & Q_1 \\
s\Downarrow & & \\
Q_2 & &
\end{array}
$$

Then also

$$
\begin{array}{ccc}
P & \stackrel{tr}{\Longrightarrow} & Q_1 \\
ts\Downarrow & & \\
Q_2 & &
\end{array}
\qquad , \text{ whence} \qquad
\begin{array}{ccc}
& & Q_1 \\
& & \Downarrow ts/tr \\
Q_2 & \stackrel{tr/ts}{\Longrightarrow} \approx & \cdot
\end{array}
$$

since P has property (∗). So from Lemma 10 we deduce

$$
\begin{array}{ccc}
& & Q_1 \\
& & \Downarrow s/r \\
Q_2 & \stackrel{r/s}{\Longrightarrow} \approx & \cdot
\end{array}
$$

which shows that Q has property (∗). From this it follows directly that P is confluent, since each of the four diagrams in Definition 5 is a special case of property (∗) for Q.

Now, in the opposite direction, assume that P is confluent. Starting from Proposition 9, we first prove that the following diagrams can be completed for every derivative Q of P (including P itself), and for every $\ell \in \mathcal{L}$ and $r \in \mathcal{L}^*$:

$$
\begin{array}{ccc}
Q & \stackrel{r}{\Longrightarrow} & Q_1 \\
\Downarrow & & \Downarrow \\
Q_2 & \stackrel{r}{\Rightarrow} \approx & \cdot
\end{array}
\qquad
\begin{array}{ccc}
Q & \stackrel{r}{\Longrightarrow} & Q_1 \\
\ell\Downarrow & & \Downarrow \ell/r \\
Q_2 & \stackrel{r/\ell}{\Rightarrow} \approx & \cdot
\end{array}
$$

The proof is by induction on r. We then prove property $(*)$ for P by induction on s. In both these proofs we appeal to Lemma 10.   ∎

The reader may feel that we should have *defined* confluence by the property in Proposition 11, since it is briefer and more memorable than Definition 5. However this may be, the important point is that there are two characterisations, and both serve a good purpose. (In fact, Definition 5 is more useful in many proofs.)

The next proposition establishes that confluence is a property of bisimilarity classes, so it is a semantic property.

Proposition 12 If $P \approx Q$ and P is confluent, then so is Q.

Proof An easy exercise in sticking diagrams together.   ∎

The next two propositions establish confluence as a refinement of determinacy.

Proposition 13 If $P \Rightarrow Q$ and P is confluent, then $P \approx Q$.

Proof It suffices to show that

$$\mathcal{S} \overset{\text{def}}{=} \{(P,Q) \ : \ P \text{ is confluent and } P \Rightarrow Q\}$$

is a bisimulation up to $\approx$.   ∎

Exercise 4 Complete this proof. Be sure that you see why 'up to $\approx$' is needed here.   ∎

Proposition 13 is conceptually important. It shows that silent actions cannot change the state of a confluent agent, up to $\approx$, so they cannot preclude actions which were previously possible.

Proposition 14 If P is confluent then it is determinate.

Proof Let P be confluent, let Q be any derivative of P, and let

$$\begin{array}{ccc} Q & \overset{s}{\Longrightarrow} & Q_1 \\ {\scriptstyle s}\Downarrow & & \\ Q_2 & & \end{array}$$

Then from Proposition 9 we deduce that there exist Q_1', Q_2' such that $Q_1 \Rightarrow Q_1'$, $Q_2 \Rightarrow Q_2'$ and $Q_1' \approx Q_2'$. Now by Proposition 13 we deduce $Q_1 \approx Q_2$, which is the condition required by Definition 3 for determinacy of Q.   ∎

11.4   Preserving confluence

Our main interest in confluence is that it will turn out to be preserved by a form of restricted Composition, which we saw was not the case for determinacy. Let us first record some simpler facts:

Proposition 15   If P, P_1 and P_2 are confluent, then so also are the following:

(1) $\mathbf{0}$, $\alpha.P$ and $P\backslash L$.
(2) $P[f]$, provided that $f \restriction \mathcal{L}(P)$ is injective.

Proof   Routine.   ■

By comparison with Proposition 6, Summation and Composition are missing here. Let us first look at Summation, and recall that although $a.\mathbf{0} + b.\mathbf{0}$ is not confluent, $a.b.\mathbf{0} + b.a.\mathbf{0}$ is so. This suggests that we define a composite form of Prefix, as follows:

Definition 7   For $\alpha_1, \ldots, \alpha_n \in Act$, $n \geq 0$, the *Confluent Sum* $(\alpha_1 | \cdots | \alpha_n).P$ is defined recursively as follows:

$$().P \stackrel{\text{def}}{=} P$$
$$(\alpha_1 | \cdots | \alpha_n).P \stackrel{\text{def}}{=} \sum_{1 \leq i \leq n} \alpha_i.(\alpha_1 | \cdots | \alpha_{i-1} | \alpha_{i+1} | \cdots | \alpha_n).P \qquad (n > 0)$$
                                                                       ■

Thus, for example,

$$\begin{aligned} (a|b|c).P \;\equiv\; & a.(b.c.P + c.b.P) + \\ & b.(a.c.P + c.a.P) + \\ & c.(a.b.P + b.a.P) \end{aligned}$$

Richer forms can be defined, replacing the α_i by action-sequences, but this form will suffice for our present purposes. The following is easy to prove:

Proposition 16   If P is confluent, then so is $(\alpha_1 | \cdots | \alpha_n).P$.   ■

An example of Confluent Sum is the cell A from which we built the scheduler in Section 5.5; it may now be written as

$$A \stackrel{\text{def}}{=} a.c.(b|d).A$$

In fact, recursive definition can be shown to preserve confluence, so the cell A is confluent. We shall now see also that the restricted Composition which was used in building the scheduler $Sched$ is of the kind which preserves confluence, from which we can conclude immediately – without any specific analysis of its behaviour – that $Sched$ itself is confluent.

Definition 8   For $L \subset \mathcal{L}$ we define the *Restricted Composition*

$$P_1 \mid_L P_2 \overset{\text{def}}{=} (P_1 \mid P_2) \backslash L$$

and we call it a *Confluent Composition* if $\mathcal{L}(P_1) \cap \mathcal{L}(P_2) = \emptyset$ and $\overline{\mathcal{L}(P_1)} \cap \mathcal{L}(P_2) \subseteq L \cup \overline{L}$.   ∎

Thus the sorts in a Confluent Composition must be disjoint; the earlier example $a.b.0 \mid a.0$ shows the need for this, because it is indeterminate even though its components are not only determinate but even confluent. But – in contrast to Proposition 6(3) – we now allow the components P_1 and P_2 to communicate provided that all communication labels are restricted. Indeed, we now claim:

Proposition 17   Let P_1 and P_2 be confluent. Then if $P_1 \mid_L P_2$ is a Confluent Composition it is also confluent.

Proof   We shall not give the whole proof, since it is quite a long case-analysis, but we shall deal with one case in some detail. We work with the original definition of confluence, Definition 5. We first observe that every derivative of $P_1 \mid_L P_2$ will take the form $Q_1 \mid_L Q_2$, and will be a Confluent Composition of confluent agents; therefore we need only ensure that the four diagrams of Definition 5 can be completed for any Confluent Composition of confluent agents.

We shall consider the proof for one diagram, and leave the rest to the reader. We wish to show that the diagram

$$
\begin{array}{ccc}
Q_1 \mid_L Q_2 & \overset{\ell}{\longrightarrow} & Q_1' \mid_L Q_2' \\
\ell \Downarrow & & \Downarrow \\
Q_1'' \mid_L Q_2'' & \Rightarrow \approx &
\end{array}
$$

can be completed, and we consider the particular case in which the upper action is due to Q_1; that is, we assume that $Q_1 \overset{\ell}{\rightarrow} Q_1'$ and that $Q_2 \equiv Q_2'$. Now the condition of disjoint sorts ensures that $\ell \notin \mathcal{L}(Q_2)$, so the ℓ in the left (vertical) derivation must also be performed by Q_1, or more exactly by a τ-descendant of Q_1. In fact the derivation $Q_1 \mid_L Q_2 \overset{\ell}{\Rightarrow} Q_1'' \mid_L Q_2''$ may contain τ actions arising from communications, so in general we

have
$$Q_1 \overset{r\ell s}{\Longrightarrow} Q_1'' \quad \text{and} \quad Q_2 \overset{\overline{rs}}{\Longrightarrow} Q_2''$$

where $r, s \in (\mathcal{L} \cup \overline{\mathcal{L}})^*$. Hence ℓ does not appear in any of $r, s, \overline{r}, \overline{s}$; this follows from the second condition on Confluent Composition. Thus $r\ell s/\ell = rs$, $\ell/r\ell s = \varepsilon$, and so we have (because Q_1 is confluent) that

$$
\begin{array}{ccc}
Q_1 & \overset{\ell}{\longrightarrow} & Q_1' \\
r\ell s \big\Downarrow & & \big\Downarrow rs \\
Q_1'' & \Rightarrow \approx & \cdot
\end{array}
$$

can be completed. Now recalling that $Q_2 \equiv Q_2'$, we have $Q_2' \overset{\overline{rs}}{\Longrightarrow} Q_2''$, and we are now able to complete the diagram for $Q_1 \mid_L Q_2$ as required.

The other diagrams raise no extra difficulties. The case treated above needs both of the conditions of Confluent Composition. ∎

Exercise 5 Complete this proof.   ∎

The situation with respect to Hoare's alternative combinators, Conjunction and Hiding, is rather simpler; in our next proposition we state without proof the result that they both preserve confluence, as they are normally used. More precisely, we have to constrain the Conjunction $P_K \|_L Q$ by the condition that $P : K$ and $Q : L$, and we shall call this constrained form Confluent Conjunction. We have chosen to give the proof for the somewhat more complex case of Confluent Composition, since it can also be adapted to analyse the preservation of confluence by other parallel combinators which Hoare and others have considered, but which we shall not treat here.

Proposition 18   Let P and Q be confluent. Then the Hiding P/L is confluent; also, if $P_K \|_L Q$ is a Confluent Conjunction then it is confluent. ∎

Now we have a repertoire of confluence-preserving combinators which can indeed be used to build non-trivial systems. We state the following without proof; we have laid the groundwork for its proof, but a little extra care is needed in dealing with recursively defined agents.

Proposition 19   Let P, and all Constants upon which it depends, be defined using only **0**, one-to-one Relabelling, Confluent Sum, Restriction, Confluent Composition, Hiding, Confluent Conjunction and Constants. Then P is confluent. ∎

As an example, we return to the scheduler of Section 5.5. We have already seen that the cell $A \stackrel{\text{def}}{=} a.c.(b|d).A$ is confluent. Also the relabelling functions

$$f_i = a_i/a, b_i/b, c_i/c, \overline{c_{i+1}}/d$$

are one-to-one on the sort $\{a, b, c, d\}$, i.e. they do not identify any of these labels, and therefore $A_i \stackrel{\text{def}}{=} A[f_i]$ is confluent for each i. Finally, the scheduler *Sched* can be reformulated as

$$Sched \stackrel{\text{def}}{=} (\cdots (A_1 \mid_{c_1} A_2) \mid_{c_2} \cdots \mid_{\{c_{n-1}, c_n\}} A_n)$$

using Confluent Composition $n-1$ times. Furthermore the specification *Schedspec* can be shown to be even strongly confluent, directly from Definition 4; this is easy to show because it performs no silent actions. It therefore follows from Proposition 5 that to prove $Sched \approx Schedspec$ it suffices to prove $Sched \approx_1 Schedspec$. In Exercise 9.12 we suggested doing part of this proof; it turns out to be somewhat easier than the proof of $Sched \approx Schedspec$ given in Section 5.5.

For large systems, the effort saved in proving only trace equivalence, rather than observation equivalence, may be considerable. Just as importantly, the use of a repertoire of combinators which preserve confluence will be a valuable insurance against design errors, such as introducing unintended deadlocks.

Confluence is but one example of a system property which can be guaranteed to hold simply by confining one's use of combinators in building the system. The world of communicating systems is so vast and baffling that we shall only extend our understanding of it appreciably if we can discover other, preferably benign, properties which can also be guaranteed by using only certain constructions. In other words, we are looking for a classificatory theory of communicating systems, allowing us to characterise each one to a certain extent by its structure alone.

This book has only begun a classification, but has tried to provide a framework in which it can be carried forward.

12

Sources and Related Work

The important influences and stages in the growth of the calculus are cited here. So also are some important related developments. No attempt has been made to be complete in citing related work; there is now so much literature on concurrent systems that the task would be daunting. We mention each item under the chapter to which it is most relevant.

Preface: The author's first work on concurrent processes [26] modelled processes as functions of a particular kind, and presented the important combinators – such as parallel composition – as functions of higher type. This work was done in ignorance of earlier work by Hans Bekić [4]. The two approaches were quite similar, particularly in their emphasis on atomic actions; one difference was that Bekić was somewhat more concerned with actions upon a state, while the author was more concerned with communications. Both, however, were motivated by the wish to extend current semantic methods to embrace parallelism in programming languages.

It began to appear that a more fundamental approach was needed; a new calculus rather than an application of existing mathematical abstractions. An important stage in the development of this calculus was in joint work with George Milne [25]. Then, in finally introducing transitional semantics as basic, the author was led to *A Calculus of Communicating Systems* [27]. The present book is a development and refinement of that monograph. (This is no longer available from the publishers, but it can be obtained in the form of an internal report [28] from the Computer Science Department at Edinburgh University.)

Meanwhile, and independently, similar ideas about communication were incorporated in the programming language CSP by Tony Hoare [17]. With two colleagues he developed a theory [8] which complements the one in this book. Hoare has published an introductory textbook based upon this theory [18].

The basic notations of this book are almost identical with those in the earlier monograph, but the theory is improved; the main technical advance is David Park's notion of bisimulation [36]. Peter Aczel's recent book [1] explains the close parallel between process theory and the theory of non-well-founded sets.

An early report by Petri on Net theory is in [39]. An accessible modern introduction to Net theory is by Wolfgang Reisig [42].

Chapter 2: The foundation of the calculus, containing essentially all the combinators defined in this chapter, was laid by the author in [29]. The notion of *sort* was also introduced there. The method of transitional semantics is a development of the method of structured operational semantics given by Gordon Plotkin [40], which in turn is a development of the evaluation rules for the lambda-calculus. The reduction of the full calculus to the basic calculus (Section 2.8) was first done in Milner [30]. The principle of transition induction is a special case of induction upon the depth of an inference tree, or proof tree, which is familiar in mathematical logic. In the semantics of computation an early example of such reasoning is by Gordon [11], concerned with the operational semantics of Lisp.

Chapter 3: The dynamic laws and the expansion law were put forward and shown to be sound in Milner [27]. The static laws were given earlier, by Milne and Milner in [25], and shown to be sound in a different interpretation. In a companion paper (Milner [31]) they were also shown to be complete – that is, to entail all true equations – for the algebra of flow graphs. The unique solution of equations was originally treated in [27], and the conditions under which it exists uniquely were broadened by Michael Sanderson [43]; the treatment in terms of bisimulation first appears in Milner [30].

Chapter 4: The notion of strong equivalence or strong bisimilarity is essentially the strong congruence defined in Chapter 5 of [27]. But the notion of bisimulation, introduced by Park [36], gives both a more revealing conceptual view of the congruence and an important proof technique: the technique of exhibiting a bisimulation containing a given pair of agents. It was developed in the context of a calculus by Milner [30]; in particular, the idea of bisimulation *up to* equivalence was defined there.

Chapter 5: The observation equivalence introduced in this chapter, based upon a weak version of Park's bisimulation, is almost but not exactly the same as in [27]. The difference, which is explained by Sanderson [43] based on an example by the author, is important theoretically since the version based upon bisimulation is clearly more satisfactory, and could not easily be handled without the bisimulation idea. Sanderson [43] also gave the first proof of the correctness of the Jobshop system, of which an improved version appears in this chapter. **Chapter 6:** The alternating-bit protocol was first presented by Bartlett *et al.* [3], and is a classic example for verification. The verification of this protocol is also given by Larsen and Milner [22] as an example of proof by *relativised* bisimulation, which is a development of the bisimulation technique to handle proofs about complex systems in a modular way. For an example of a proof of a more complex protocol in the calculus, see [38].

The question of equivalence relations which respect the possibility of divergence of agents, which is briefly discussed at the end of the chapter, is strongly related to the notion of *fairness* in modelling concurrency. In his PhD thesis [37] Joachim Parrow treats this question at length, particularly in the context of modelling communications protocols in process calculus. Fairness is a difficult topic; a good survey of the state of understanding (up to 1986) is given in Nissim Francez's book [10].

Chapter 7: The notion of equality or observation congruence, which is the main topic of this chapter, was first put forward in [27], though in relation to the original definition of observation equivalence treated there. After Park's introduction of bisimulation, the theory needed some reworking, and this appears in [30, 32]. The demonstration that the monoid laws and the τ laws together form a complete axiomatic system for equality of finite agents was presented by Hennessy and Milner [13], and the corresponding result for finite-state agents by Milner [33].

The programming language semantics given in this chapter is a slight modification of what was done in [27].

At the end of the chapter it is mentioned that the parameter mechanism known as *call-by-name* cannot easily be modelled in the present calculus, since the natural method would be to admit labels ℓ among the values which can be sent and received in communications. The author discussed this at length with Mogens Nielsen at Aarhus in 1979, reaching the conclusion that it was better at first to omit this possibility from the calculus, because the theory – in particular the algebraic treatment – appeared to be difficult. It is important to note that several authors [2, 15, 21, 46] have designed notations – or languages – which allow this label-passing, thus achieving the ability to *express* dynamically varying linkage; but it is much harder problem to provide an adequate algebraic theory. However, Nielsen and his student Uffe Engberg have made a crucial step in this direction [9]; they have given a transitional semantics and derived from it a good set of laws. Their work is still hard to follow, but the author believes that their path, with some simplifying ideas, will turn out to be the right one.

Chapter 9: The work of Hoare on communicating sequential processes [18] is important at many points in this chapter. As far as operators are concerned, the interrupt and checkpoint operators are essentially his idea; more fundamental is his alternative operator for combining agents in parallel (which we call Conjunction), accompanied by his Hiding operator which is alternative to our Restriction. All these can be found in his book [18]. Starting from Hoare's ideas, Prasad [41] has studied fault-tolerant systems in the calculus; in particular he studies combinators (such as the checkpoint operator) which are suitable for modular construction of restartable systems.

The LOTOS language, for formal description of communications protocols, is largely the work of Ed Brinksma [7], and is a Draft International Standard. Its semantic description was based upon that of the present calculus; Hoare's work has also strongly influenced its design.

The synchronous calculus of Section 9.3 was devised by the author [30] mainly as a substratum for process algebras, in the recognition that they (e.g. the present calculus and Hoare's) are not always easily interderivable; this applies in particular to Hoare's calculus and the present one. The Meije language of Gérard Berry and his group at Sophia-Antipolis, reported by Gérard Boudol [6], was designed with real-time applications in mind, and is very close to the synchronous calculus. Robert De Simone [44] has proved that both calculi are in a natural sense complete in their expressive power. This means, for example, that the present calculus is expressible in the synchronous calculus. Also expressible are Hoare's parallel combinator which we have called Conjunction, and the form of parallel composition adopted by Goerge Milne in Circal [24], a calculus for VLSI design.

The failures equivalence of Hoare and his group [8], discussed in Section 9.4, was the first equivalence relation to be discovered which lies strictly between observation equivalence and trace equivalence and has conceptual and practical significance. Matthew Hennessy and Rocco de Nicola [34], later but independently, defined testing equivalence; this is a different characterization of failures equivalence, and this fact lends strength to the notion. Hennessy's recent book [12] gives a theoretical account of it.

In the Mathematical Centre at Amsterdam, the group led by Jan Bergstra and Jan Willem Klop has made an extensive study of process algebra, both in its theory and its applications. This work [5] has refined the theory (e.g. with respect to abstraction), and has been applied to the analysis of many non-trivial systems.

Chapter 10: Since Hoare's pioneering paper [16] presenting a logic for programs, it has become widely accepted that logic must play a part in reasoning about programs and that a program specification can conveniently be formalised as a logical formula. Susan Owicki and David Gries [35] extended Hoare's approach to encompass parallel programs under certain restrictions. More recently Cliff Jones [20] introduced the idea of *rely* and *guarantee* conditions, in addition to the conventional *pre-* and *post*-conditions of Hoare logic, as a means of reasoning about processes which may affect each other's variables. Colin Stirling [45] has placed such ideas in a logical setting.

There is also a strong trend to use non-classical logics in concurrency, and of these temporal logic has been the most common; Zohar Manna and Amir Pnueli ([23] for example) were early advocates of this approach, and the recent literature on temporal logic is large. The logic $\mathcal{PL}$ in this chapter is not a temporal logic but a *modal* logic; it was put forward by Hennessy and Milner [13], where it was proved to provide a characterisation of observation equivalence. In $\mathcal{PL}$ as given here it is not possible to express the property of a process that a certain action will *eventually* occur. This is in contrast with temporal logic; however, Hennessy and Stirling [14] have shown how to extend the modal logic with this power.

Chapter 11: The notions of confluence and determinacy in process calculus were studied in [27], but the treatment here is much improved by the presence of bisimulation. For a basic treatment of confluence, see Gérard Huet [19]. The treatment in this chapter differs from Huet's because we are concerned with *labelled* transitions, whereas Huet is concerned with rewriting systems which are an example of unlabelled transition systems; however, the basic ideas have much in common.

Bibliography

[1] Aczel, P., **Non-well-founded Sets**, CSLI Lecture Notes no. 14, Stanford University, 1988.

[2] Astesiano, E. and Zucca, E., *Parametric Channels in CCS and their Applications*, Proc. 2nd Conference on Foundations of Software Technology and Theoretical Computer Science, Bangalore, 1982.

[3] Bartlett, K., Scantlebury, R. and Wilkinson, W., *A Note on Reliable Full-duplex Transmission over Half-duplex links*, Communications of ACM, Vol 12, No. 5, pp260–261, 1969.

[4] Bekić, H., *Towards a Mathematical Theory of Processes*, Technical Report TR 25.125, IBM Laboratory Vienna, 1971. Published in *Programming Languages and their Definition*, selected papers of H.Bekić, ed. C.Jones, Lecture Notes in Computer Science, Vol 177, Springer-Verlag, pp168–206, 1984.

[5] Bergstra, J.A. and Klop, J.W., *Algebra for Communicating Processes with Abstraction*, Journal of Theoretical Computer Science, Vol 37, pp77–121, 1985.

[6] Boudol, G., *Notes on Algebraic Calculi of Processes*, Logics and Models of Concurrent Systems, NATO ASI Series f13, ed. K.Apt, 1985.

[7] Brinksma, E., *Information Processing Systems – Open Systems Interconnection – LOTOS – A Formal Description Technique based upon the Temporal Ordering of Observational Behaviour*, Draft International Standard ISO8807, 1988.

[8] Brookes, S.D., Hoare, C.A.R. and Roscoe, A.W., *A Theory of Communicating Sequential Processes*, Journal of ACM, Vol 31, pp560–599, 1984.

[9] Engberg, U. and Nielsen, M., *A Calculus of Communicating Systems with Label Passing*, Research Report DAIMI PB–208, Computer Science Department, University of Aarhus, 1986.

[10] Francez, N., **Fairness**, Springer-Verlag, 1986.

[11] Gordon, M.J.C., *Operational Reasoning and Denotational Semantics*, Proc. Conference on Proving and Improving Programs, Arcet-Senans, France, 1975.

[12] Hennessy, M.C., **Algebraic Theory of Processes**, MIT Press, 1988.

[13] Hennessy, M.C. and Milner, A.J.R.G., *Algebraic Laws for Nondeterminism and Concurrency*, Journal of ACM, Vol 32, No. 1, pp137–161, 1985.

[14] Hennessy, M.C. and Stirling, C.P., *The Power of the Future Perfect in Program Logics*, Information and Control, Vol 67, pp23–52, 1985.

[15] Hewitt, C., Bishop, P. and Steiger, R., *A Universal Modular Actor Formalism for Artificial Intelligence*, Proc. International Joint Conference on Artificial Intelligence, pp235–245, 1973.

[16] Hoare, C.A.R., *An Axiomatic Basis for Computer Programming*, Communications of ACM, Vol 12, pp576–580, 583, 1969.

[17] Hoare, C.A.R., *Communicating Sequential Processes*, Communications of ACM, Vol 21, pp666–677, 1978.

[18] Hoare, C.A.R., **Communicating Sequential Processes**, Prentice Hall, 1985.

[19] Huet, G., *Confluent Reductions: Abstract Properties and Applications to Term-rewriting Systems*, 18th Annual Symposium on Foundations of Computer Science, pp30–45, 1977.

[20] Jones, C.B., *Specification and Design of (Parallel) Programs*, Proc. IFIP 9th World Computer Congress, North Holland, pp321–332, 1983.

[21] Kennaway, R. and Sleep, R., *Syntax and Informal Semantics of DyNe, a Parallel Language*, Lecture Notes in Computer Science, Vol 207, Springer-Verlag, pp222–230, 1980.

[22] Larsen, K.G. and Milner, A.J.R.G., *A Complete Protocol Verification using Relativised Bisimulation*, Journal of Information and Computation, (to appear).

[23] Manna, Z. and Pnueli, A., *How to Cook a Temporal Proof System for your Pet Language*, Proc. 10th Annual ACM Symposium on Principles of Programming Languages, Austin, Texas, 1983.

[24] Milne, G.J., *Circal and the Representation of Communication, Concurrency and Time*, ACM Transactions on Programming Languages and Systems, Vol 7, pp270–298, 1985.

[25] Milne, G.J. and Milner, A.J.R.G., *Concurrent Processes and their Syntax*, Journal of ACM, Vol 26, No. 2, pp302–321, 1979.

[26] Milner, A.J.R.G., *Processes: a Mathematical Model of Computing Agents*, Proc. Logic Colloquium '73, ed. Rose and Shepherdson,

North Holland, pp157–174, 1973.

[27] Milner, A.J.R.G., **A Calculus of Communicating Systems**, Lecture Notes in Computer Science, Vol 92, Springer-Verlag, 1980.

[28] Milner, A.J.R.G., **A Calculus of Communicating Systems**, Report ECS-LFCS-86-7, Computer Science Department, University of Edinburgh, 1986.

[29] Milner, A.J.R.G., *Synthesis of Communicating Behaviour*, Proc 7th Symposium on Mathematical Foundations of Computer Science, Lecture Notes in Computer Science, Vol 64, Springer-Verlag, 1978.

[30] Milner, A.J.R.G., *Calculi for Synchrony and Asynchrony*, Journal of Theoretical Computer Science, Vol 25, pp267–310, 1983.

[31] Milner, A.J.R.G., *Flow Graphs and Flow Algebras*, Journal of ACM, Vol 26, No. 4, , pp794–818, 1979.

[32] Milner, A.J.R.G., *Lectures on a Calculus for Communicating Systems*, in **Control Flow and Data Flow** (ed. M.Broy), Proc. International Summer School at Marktoberdorf, pp205–228, Springer-Verlag, 1985.

[33] Milner, A.J.R.G., *A Complete Axiomatization for Observation Congruence of Finite-state Behaviours*, Journal of Information and Computation, (to appear).

[34] de Nicola, R. and Hennessy, M.C., *Testing Equivalence for Processes*, Journal of Theoretical Computer Science, Vol 34, pp83–133, 1983.

[35] Owicki, S. and Gries, D., *An Axiomatic Proof Technique for Parallel Programs I*, Acta Informatica, Vol 14, pp319–340, 1976.

[36] Park, D.M.R., *Concurrency and Automata on Infinite Sequences*, Lecture Notes in Computer Science, Vol 104, Springer-Verlag, 1980.

[37] Parrow, J.G., *Fairness Properties in Process Algebra*, PhD Thesis, DoCS 85/03, Department of Computer Systems, Uppsala University, Sweden, 1985.

[38] Parrow, J.G., *Verifying a CSMA/CD-Protocol with CCS*, Report ECS-LFCS-87-18, Computer Science Department, University of Edinburgh, 1987.

[39] Petri, C.A., *Kommunikation mit Automaten*, Bonn: Institut für Instrumentelle Mathematik, Schriften des IIM No. 2, 1962. Also in English translation: Technical Report RADC-TR-65-377, Vol 1, Suppl 1, Applied Data Research, Princeton, NJ, Contract AF 30 (602)-3324, 1966.

[40] Plotkin, G.D., **A Structural Approach to Operational Semantics**, Report DAIMI-FN-19, Computer Science Dept, Århus University, Denmark, 1981.

[41] Prasad, K.V.S., *Combinators and Bisimulation Proofs for Restartable Systems*, PhD Thesis, Computer Science Department, University of Edinburgh, 1987.

[42] Reisig, W., **Petri Nets: an Introduction**, EATCS Monographs on Theoretical Computer Science, Springer-Verlag, 1985.

[43] Sanderson, M.T., *Proof Techniques for CCS*, PhD Thesis CST-19-82, Computer Science Dept, University of Edinburgh, 1982.

[44] de Simone, R., *Higher-level Synchronising Devices in Meije–SCCS*, Journal of Theoretical Computer Science, Vol 37, pp245–267, 1985.

[45] Stirling, C.P., *A Generalisation of Owicki–Gries' Hoare Logic for a Concurrent While Language*, Journal of Theoretical Computer Science, Vol 58, pp 347–360, 1988.

[46] Strom, R.E. and Yemini, S., *The NIL Distributed Systems Programming Language: a Status Report*, Lecture Notes in Computer Science, Vol 197, pp512–523, Springer-Verlag, 1980.

Index